AWAKE

A Moslem Woman's Rare Memoir of Her Life and
Partnership with the Editor of *Molla Nasreddin*,
the Most Influential Satirical Journal of the
Caucasus and Iran, 1907–1931

HAMIDEH KHANUM JAVANSHIR

TRANSLATED FROM THE AZERI BY

HASAN JAVADI & WILLEM FLOOR

MAGE PUBLISHERS
WASHINGTON DC

Library of Congress Cataloging-in-Publication Data
Available in detail at the Library of Congress

ISBN
1-933823-87-9
978-1-933823-87-4

Printed and Manufactured in the United States

MAGE PUBLISHERS
WASHINGTON DC

202-342-1642 • as@mage.com
Visit Mage Publishers online at
www.mage.com

CONTENTS

ILLUSTRATIONS

PREFACE

These are the memoirs of a courageous Moslem woman, Hamideh Khanum, who had grown up in the traditional Azerbaijani society that relegated women to a self-effacing and submissive role with no identity of their own and no function in society outside the home and family.

Hamideh Khanum lived in a cultural milieu that had changed and continued to change significantly before and during her lifetime. Qarabagh, her homeland (like much of the Caucasus), which had been part of Iran, had been ceded to Russia after two wars (1813, 1826-28). She was a member of a family that had ruled Qarabagh since about 1750, but after the Russian takeover the Javanshir family became just another aristocratic family. Like the elites all over the Caucasus the Javanshirs became Russified and most male members became Russian officers. This was also the case of Hamideh Khanum's father, who was an Azeri poet, and also a translator of Russian literature into Azeri. Her father, who was a major influence in Hamideh's life, schooled her and taught her about farming, he also taught her how to think for herself.

Due to increased Russification of all ethnic and religious groups, Tiflis, the capital of the Caucasus became a cultural melting pot, where Russians, Armenians, Georgians, Azeris and other Caucasian groups lived and worked together; they also befriended each other. In particular, among the intelligentsia the cultural and religious differences became less consequential than what you knew and what you contributed. Being raised in this nurturing environment formed Hamideh Khanum's character and world view.

This hopeful co-existence was undermined (and finally vanished) by the growing social and political unrest in the Caucasus. The resistance to Russia's oppressive rule, reinforced by revolutionary ideas

from within Russia itself, acquired both socio-political and religious overtones. These revolutionary ideas aimed to change Russian society and unite members from all classes; ethnicity and religion played no role. The latter emphasized what separated people through religion, and used the age-old enmities and cleavages to mobilize support. For a few centuries prior to the Russian conquest, the main concentration of Armenians in Azerbaijan was in Nogorno-Karabagh, but their presence in other parts of Azerbaijan rose dramatically in the first half of the nineteenth century. Immigration into Azerbaijan was primarily from Turkey and Iran following the Turkmanchay (1828) and Adrianapole (1829) treaties. The resulting economic disparities between Armenians, who generally occupied better positions, and Moslems as well as the depression in the oil industry were part of the backdrop for eruptions of ethnic violence on a mass scale from 1905 to 1907. Despite the cosmopolitanism of Baku, the build up of tensions exploded in 1905 and led to violence. Ironically, in that same year a revolt broke out in Russia with people demanding more freedom, which, unlike the Baku events, was a movement for more inclusivism.

The revolt in Russia also had its impact on the countries south of its border, where socio-economic and political conditions had reached a boiling point. As a result, in Iran the constitutional movement broke out in 1906 leading to the establishment of a parliamentary government. Likewise, in Ottoman Turkey in 1908, the Young Turks took power to establish a modernizing and more secular state. In Turkestan, demands were also made to give the people more freedom.

In the aftermath of these political changes the Russian government allowed a larger degree of freedom in political expression. Many intellectuals and politicos used this window of opportunity to air their views. Hamideh Khanum's second husband, Mirza Jalil Mamadqulizadeh, launched *Molla Nasreddin*, an Azeri-language satirical weekly criticizing hypocrisy, superstition, and bigotry. It was read by, and influenced people in the Caucasus, Iran, Turkey and Turkistan.

Hamideh Khanum was part of this new wave of hope, and she rode it by co-creating a Moslem Charitable Society for Women, by trying to share her experience as a farm manager with the attendees of an all-male conference in Baku, where she was rebuffed for being a woman. However, a few years later her persistence won out and she was allowed to present a paper at a similar conference. In spite of being an Azeri-speaking Moslem woman, Hamideh Khanum had many non-Moslem friends, she wrote in Russian, and socialized with Armenians.

Other more divisive forces, however, were also at work. Moslem, Armenian and Georgian nationalism grew, while socialist ideas also made inroads among the populace, leading to strikes and other political activities. All this might have evolved in a peaceful manner were it not for World War I. The war meant shortages and censorship, which accentuated the existing political, ethnic and religious cleavages. The build up of these tensions exploded after the 1917 October Revolution. The Caucasus fell apart in warring national/ethnic/religious groups, though on the local level there were people of goodwill. The year 1918 was another period of mass violence, marked by the Armenian massacre of the Azeris in March, and the Azeri revenge in September. Hamideh Khanum and her friends tried to maintain a peaceful co-existence between Armenian Christians and Moslems. However, the forces of evil were stronger and soon civil war broke out, which forced many to flee. Among them were Mirza Jalil and Hamideh Khanum, who in June 1920 fled across the Aras River to Iran, where they hoped to be able to publish *Molla Nasreddin*

in a more democratic environment created by the *Azadistan* movement in Tabriz. Their journey was not an easy one; there was the constant threat of being attacked and even in Iran they almost got embroiled in the fights between the local Kurdish Khans. However, they made it safely to Tabriz, where only two days after their arrival the governor-general of Azerbaijan killed Mohammad Khiyabani, the leader of the *Azadistan* movement and imposed martial rule. Despite this setback, Mirza Jalil was allowed to publish his journal, which resulted in 8 memorable and influential issues. Hamideh Khanum's support was essential at that time as she was a natural diplomat and was able to establish good relations with Tabriz society and officials. It was also here that one of Mirza Jalil's plays (*The Dead*) was performed.

However, the call of Baku and Qarabagh was stronger than that of Iran. When the victorious Bolshevik government in Baku invited them to come back to help rebuild the country and society, they heeded the call. Despite the red carpet treatment on their return it soon became clear that Bolshevik rule was as repressive as Tsarist rule (and it became even more repressive over time). Hamideh Khanum continued trying to improve farming and living conditions in her village of Kahrizli, but immediately ran into opposition from local Communist bosses. Although she got a reprieve, she finally had to give up, because her absences from Baku had a heavy toll on Mirza Jalil's well-being. In Baku, the two raised their family, helped friends, and published the journal, which increasingly was ordered to toe the Communist party line, so much so that Mirza Jalil finally resigned, one year prior to his death.

Hamideh Khanum in old age

In 1954, a tall woman, whose hair was snow-white, came to the Azerbaijani Writers Association. In spite of being more than 80 years old she had not lost her deportment and beauty. The beauty and attraction that once conquered the heart of a great writer and a great man had not completely lost its luster. The harshness of old age had neither broken her spirit nor muffled her love for life. She still wanted to help and be useful to people around her; she was still working and wanted to be engaged in benevolent activities of life. In literary gatherings we were sitting with her, talking with her and after the meeting, either by tram or sometimes on foot we, members of the Writers Association, accompanied her to her house. We would listen and be fascinated by the witty conversation of this lady who was a living witness of a period gone by. We would read the history of the past from her bright face. Who was this lady loved by everyone? She was the life-long companion and close colleague of Jalil Mamadqulizadeh, Hamideh Khanum.

Thus, Abbas Zamanov starts his Introduction to his translation of Hamideh Khanum's Memoirs.[1] Hamideh Khanum Javanshir was born on 6 January 1873 in the village of Kahrizli in the Qarabagh district of Aghjabadi. She was the great-granddaughter of Memed Bey (1756-97), the brother's son of Ibrahim Khan, once the governor of Qarabagh. Hamideh Khanum did not go to school, but was home-schooled by her father Ahmad Bey Javanshir (1828-1903), a gentleman-farmer. Like many intellectuals of Qarabagh, apart from writing poetry and prose, he translated Russian poetry. His poems and translations were published in Tiflis in 1906 under the title "The works of Ahmad Bey."

Being an avid reader Hamideh Khanum became one of the important intellectuals of her time.

Towards the end of 1880's she married a certain Ibrahim Bey Davatdarov (1851-1902), who was born in the village of Arablar in the district of Barda`. He was also a member of the nobility. They had two children: Mina (1890-1923) and Muzaffar (1900-59). Losing her husband in 1902 and one year later her father, Hamideh Khanum devoted her life raising her children and managing her family farm and the village of Kahrizli.

In 1905, in Tiflis, in the course of publishing her father's poetry, she became acquainted with Mirza Jalil Mamadqulizadeh in Tiflis, and they were married in 1907. The marriage of Hamideh, the daughter of the leading noble family of Qarabagh to the rebellious and almost "kafir" editor of the journal *Molla Nasreddin* created an incredible wave of resentment in the reactionary circles of Qarabagh. They wrote diatribes against him and there were even death threats against Mamadqulizadeh. In one instance Hamideh's relative Ibish Bey provided an armed escort to ensure that a planned attack would fail. But she faced all these slanderous attacks and threats with unbelievable courage and throughout their 25 years of married life she remained a pillar of strength and an

---

1. Mămmădguluzadă, Hămidă. *Moi vospominaniia o Dzhalile Memedqulizade. Podgotovka teksta, predislovie i kommentarii Abbasa Zamanova.* Baku: ELM, 1970. Translated from Russian into Azeri as *Mirză Jălil haggynda khatirălărim* by Abbas Zamanov. Baku: Ganjlik, 1981. This Azeri edition was transliterated into Persian script as *Mirza Jalil Haqindah Khaterlarim* by Karim Mashrutehchi, with an Introduction by Abbas Zamanov. Tehran: Negah-e Sabz, 1385/2006.

intellectual partner for him. They loved, respected and supported each other.

Apart from helping with the publication of *Molla Nasreddin*, Hamideh Khanum's social activities were unusual for Middle Eastern women of her time. She tirelessly worked for "The Women's Charitable Society" and with the help of Mamadqulizadeh she opened a school for boys and girls in Kahrizli. She was instrumental in establishing an Azeri language program for the school for girls in Tiflis and she studied medical books to help her villagers with health problems. For instance, she learned inoculation against smallpox and introduced it to Kahrizli and nearby villages. In spite of many problems she successfully managed her farm, her grain mill and a small weaving factory that she established (1918-20) for poor women in Kahrizli. At every step the opposition from the reactionaries was great. For instance, she was not allowed to address a conference which was held in Baku to find ways to stop the famine of 1907, because she was unveiled. But she never gave up and when in 1912 she was allowed to address the conference of cotton producers in the Caucasus she gave a well researched presentation about the ways to prevent locust attacks which destroyed the harvest (see Annex 1). From the press reports of that time it appears that the fact that an Azerbaijani woman gave a public talk left an important impression.

Hamideh Khanum was very much interested in the writings of Mirza Jalil and his friends and she tried to help him in any way she could. For example, Mirza Jalil often would give his draft writings to her for criticism. She also encouraged him in his literary endeavors, in particular in writing his plays and stories. Hamideh also supported Mirza Jalil and the journal in other ways, such as assisting members of the journal's staff who were in need of help. In 1911, the poet and major contributor to the journal, Ali Akbar Saber (1862-1911), who was sick at the time, wrote to his friend Abbas Sehat: "I am

very grateful to Mirza Jalil and Hamideh Khanum. You don't know how much they respect and care for me. All this while they have been looking after me and paying my bills. They would not allow me to stay in a hotel or hospital and took me to their own house. In short, I don't know how to thank them."[2] Furthermore, Hamideh arranged domestic living conditions in such a manner that the noise-sensitive Mirza Jalil did not suffer over much from botheration. She also contributed to the journal by not opposing that part of their house in Baku was used as the journal's office, while she and her family suffered from lack of space.

Twenty-five years of married life of Hamideh Khanum and Mirza Jalil coincided with many eventful years. The author came face to face with many big political events and with courage faced many difficulties. We see that during these hard days she always was a steadfast friend and supporter of her husband. For example, she tried to dissuade Mirza Jalil from burning his unpublished works, when in 1931 their house was cold and without heating. Since 1934, Hamideh Khanum became a member of the Writers Association. She translated 'The Mailbox, The Russian Girl, Yan Tutagi' by Mamadqulizadeh into Russian as well as a novel by Mir Jalal, but her great literary contribution is a journal that she kept in Russian, which starts from the time of their marriage until the death of Mamadqulizadeh, which gives a vivid picture of the life, works, friends and foes of Mamadqulizadeh and the society in which they lived.

In the manuscript, which is kept at the national archives of Azerbaijan in Baku, she writes: "After the death of Mirza Jalil Mamadqulizadeh on 4 January 1932 and five months later on 4 June when my son Midhat died, I was so dejected and depressed that I was bedridden. Only two years later I became myself again and at the recommendation of the SSSR Academy of Sciences, Azerbaijan

---

2. See Appendix 3, page TK

independent branch I began to write my Memoirs about Mirza Jalil Mamadqulizadeh."[3]

This invitation came from the very top of the Communist Party and it happened as follows, as related by Mehriban Vezir, the other translator of Hamideh Khanum's Memoirs. In 1932 the author Mirza Ibrahimov sent an official car[4] to Hamideh Khanum and invited her to the Writers Association. This was a special honor. He told her with great respect that Comrade Bagirov[5] "would like you to write your Memoirs as well as the incidents that happened in Qarabagh and the revolutionary movements and what you know about the great Bolshevik figures." Hamideh Khanum accepted this task with great interest. She had already written a Memoir about her father at the request of Ali Azhdar Sayyedzadeh, who had published "The poetry of Ahmad Bey Javanshir." Bagirov's request aimed to expand on this Memoir and include later years as well. After accepting, she became in the same year a member of the Writers Association. She was given 2 to 3 years' time to write the Memoirs. During these years they paid her a high salary, gave her a service car, and many other privileges. She finished the Memoirs after four years in 1938. When the time to deliver had come she took what she had written and in the car went to the Writers Association. They were expecting her and Comrade Ibrahimov had to give an account to Comrade Bagirov. She gave the Memoirs, written in Russian, consisting of 59 note-books, each of which contains 20 pages, to the head of the Writers Association. The only thing left was to publish the book. It was promised that it would be published in a large number and she would receive a substantial remuneration and it would become a book to be used at schools. She very much wanted the future generation to be informed about the situation of those days in Qarabagh, and the exemplary life of a great intellectual Ahmad Bey Javanshir, and her husband Jalil Mamadqulizadeh and how *Molla Nasreddin* had become her own struggle, her life in Tabriz as well as the lives of the great personalities that she had met. One month later Hamideh Khanum was invited to the Writers Association.

> Hamideh Khanum, Comrade Bagirov wants you to write about him in this work of yours; about that fiery Qarabagh revolutionary and the Bolshevik activities in great length. Only you can make the future generations aware of all these great events and what you have seen with your own eyes of Comrade Bagirov's personality and his greatness. This is very important for our ideological work. Mir Jafar Bagirov has done such great works for our nation that these should not be forgotten and they should be an example for future generations and the Communist youth.

Hamideh Khanum looked stupefied at Ibrahimov and after a long silence with dignity and poise said: "I cannot write what I have not seen."

The deed Bagirov referred to happened at the end of WW I, which were terrible years. The Tsar's government was tired of war. The authority of local government had broken down and bandits were in league with government officials, and were becoming increasingly bolder. In Qarabagh it was not possible to go from one village to another one. The bandits were robbing people in broad day light. Bandit bands were coming from Iran and took from people whatever they could get. Meanwhile, fights were breaking out among the various bandit groups. Hamideh Khanum writes that in Kahrizli

---

3. This is a summary of Zamanov's Introduction to his translation of *My Memoirs*.

4. The GAZ M1 (Emka) was an iconic passenger car produced by the Soviet Russian GAZ company between 1936 and 1943 at their plant in Gorki.

5. Mir Jafar Bagirov was the communist leader of Azerbaijan SSR from 1932 till 1953.

the big door of her yard opened to the main road. Many people who were going to Shusha, Khankandi and Aghdam would stay with them. At one time, government officials were guests there. At that time, somebody came and insisted to see the lady or man of the household. She could not lodge these people as she had guests from the viceroy. After some consultation she sent them with Abdal Gulabli to one of her relatives, Jamal Bey Mirzayev. In this manner Mir Jafar Bagirov and his six comrades, who were hungry and wounded bandits as well as full of lice and fleeing from the law, were taken by Abdal via secret roads to her relative and thus they were saved. According to Hamideh Khanum, Mir Jafar stayed one month with Jamal Bey where he got well. At the end they gave him some money and provisions and sent him via secret paths to Baku and this was Mir Jafar's claim to "revolutionary activities" and being "the Bolshevik hero" in Qarabagh. The Mirzayev family benefited from this event and was spared many mishaps. The son of Jamal Bey, Shirin Mirzayev, even was a high judge during Bagirov's rule. Many years later this bandit became the ruler of Azerbaijan and in this way wanted to whitewash his unsavory past. During his rule thousands of people were jailed and killed.

Not complying with Bagirov's request had many consequences for Hamideh Khanum. All her privileges were taken away. Her son Muzaffar, who was the sole breadwinner of the family, was fired and subjected to all kinds of harassment. But not even her motherly anxiety would induce her to write lies. Moreover, Hamideh Khanum's Memoirs became the target of Bagirov's wrath. For many years it was lying unpublished in a corner of an office. One month after Abbas Zamanov's last meeting with Hamideh Khanum she died on 6 February 1955. The following day she was buried next to her husband in the cemetery in Fakhri Avenue.[6]

In 1970, Abbas Zamanov published Hamideh Khanum's "Memoirs of Jalil Mamadqulizadeh," but he did not include her "Memoirs" about her father Ahmad Javanshir. In short, 30 years passed before 'My Memoirs' was published. In 2012, a new translation of the Memoirs (*Hamideh Khanum Javanshir: Khatərəlarin*) was published in Baku by Mehriban Vəzir. This new translation includes Hamideh Khanum's Memoirs about her father as well as those about Mirza Jalil Mamadqulizadeh. Here, for the first time, the entire text in English about Mirza Jalil is made available. However, like Zamanov, we have not included Hamideh Khanum's Memoirs about her father, because these do not deal with the subject of this publication, viz. the life and works of Mirza Jalil Mamadqulizadeh.

Mirza Jalil Mamadqulizadeh himself also wrote his own Memoirs, which are unfinished and have been published as part of his *Collected Works*. The printed text comprises 49 pages of which the first 30 pages or so deal with his youth trauma, to wit: his exposure, or should we say suffering, due to religious 'education'. Among other things Mirza Jalil mentions that he could not stand the call to prayer, because it would wake him up every time and he resented that. The remaining parts of his memoirs discuss the beginning of his literary career, in particular the publication of his first story "The Postbox," which was published in 1904 in the journal *Sharq-e Rus*. Furthermore, it discusses the beginnings of the vicissitudes of the journal *Molla Nasreddin*.

This book has three objectives. One is to inform people about an important periodical (*Molla Nasreddin*) and its editor (Mirza Jalil Mamadqulizadeh), both of whom had a major influence, not only in Azerbaijan, but also in Iran, Turkey and Central Asia. The second is to provide those who are somewhat familiar with the literary and political events discussed here, with the most comprehensive information in English about Mirza Jalil Mamadqulizadeh, his family, his children, his

---

6. In this cemetery famous Azerbaijanis are buried.

youth and details of his personal life, his friends, his views about different people and other aspects of literary life and personality. The third is to inform the reader about the exceptional personality of Hamideh Khanum, who, although having been raised in the traditional Moslem society of Qarabagh in the late nineteenth century, nevertheless became a model for change and perseverance in the fight for equality for other Moslem women in the Caucasus. Because the first two objectives are discussed in detail in the appendices, here we focus on Hamideh Khanum's role.

You may wonder, why publish an English translation of these memoirs? Although only home-schooled she became one of the leading intellectuals of Azerbaijan, and was active in the movement to change the role of women in society. For example, she helped create a Women's Charitable Society in Tiflis and attended conferences unveiled, which resulted in her being barred from such a conference in 1905. She also was a reformer in the field of rural development. She was the manager of her estate, of a grain mill and of a weaving manufactory and she also founded a co-ed school in her village, where she introduced inoculation and other medical innovations. As such she blazed a trail that either evoked strong opposition or admiration. Under the early Soviet regime, when all private estates were confiscated, she had to fight to keep her farm, mill, and manufactory, to be able to continue helping her workers as well as the population of Kahrizli. The Soviet regime recognized the importance and effectiveness of her developmental activities in Qarabagh and allowed her to continue managing these properties.

Finally, it is our pleasure to express our gratitude to Mehrban Vazir, who has allowed us to use her Azeri translation of the *Memoirs* and who has supplied us with many of the photographs in this book. Also, we wish to thank Keith Openshaw for his diligent and careful reading of the draft text.

Hamideh Khanum Javanshir with Mirza Jalil Mamadqulizadeh and their family in Shusha, 1918

In his passport Mirza Jalil's birthdate is given as 1869.[1] In the 1840's Mirza Jalil's grandfather, Ustad Hoseynquli came from the Iranian city of Khoy to Nakhchivan. At that time, his father Mashhadi Mamadqulizadeh was only a child and accompanied his parents. Mashhadi Mamadqulizadeh had a small shop in Nakhchivan where he sold salt. About 1860 he married Sara Babayev from that city. The famous lease-holders of the salt works of Nakhchivan, then the Jan Puladov Brothers, gave Mashhadi Mamadqulizadeh a salt contract during the war of 1877[2]. As a result, his financial situation improved a little. Mashhadi Mamadqulizadeh had three sons and one daughter with Sara. The oldest son, Mirza Yusef was a watch maker and it is said that he had a very good knowledge of Persian, but he died young. The second son was Mirza Jalil, and the third one Mirza Ali Akbar, who participated in the Iranian revolution.[3] The fourth son was Khalil who died in childhood. Mashhadi Mamadqulizadeh had a very good knowledge of Azeri.

Mirza Jalil's parents were very religious. They prayed every day and fasted the whole month of Ramadan and made their children observe these practices. When Mirza Jalil was little he listened to them, but when he grew up he did not care for such practices. When he was about seven years old he first went to the *maktab* of Haji Mulla Baqer and later to that of Mulla Ali. Mirza Jalil in his

Memoirs writes that "even now I feel the bitterness of Haji Mulla Baqer's bastinadoes of the soles of my feet." Later he was placed in the Russian school of the town, where he studied for four years. In the curriculum only superficial attention was paid to the teaching of Azeri.

Mirza Jalil's late brother, Mirza Ali Akbar, told us about events during their childhood: "When he was 13 or 14 years old Mirza Jalil asked his father to put him in the boarding school in Gori to which he did not consent. Because of this Jalil took a stick and broke all the china dishes that were placed on the shelves. His parents seeing his anger did not say anything and just left the room. After this they agreed to send him to the Gori boarding school."

Mirza Jalil's parents died in Nakhchivan in early 1905. This news saddened him and for three days he did not open the door of his room.

The Gori boarding school had a very good influence on Mirza Jalil. He became friendly with the principal, Chernyayevski[4] and he liked his wife very much and showed them great respect and kept their pictures with him. In this school Chernyayevski taught his students as if they were his own children. In the school very often plays were performed and Mirza Jalil took part in them. He even acted in women's roles. By nature he was an outgoing and social boy and he was very successful in the school.

He finished the Gori School in 1877 and after the finals one of his school friends, Isma`il

1. When Hamideh wrote her *Memoirs* in 1934-38, the exact date of Mirza Jalil's birth was not known. According to his own *Memoirs* his date of birth was in 1869. Later, his birth certificate was found by Professor Sharif and it was established that he was born in 1866.

2. This was a war between Russia and Turkey.

3. From 1906 to 1911, Mirza Ali Akbar (1872-1922) was involved in the Constitutional Revolution of Iran and he was a close friend of Sattar Khan.

4. Alexander Ossipovich Chernayevski (1840-1894), who knew Azeri very well, was the chief of the Turkish section of the Gori Seminary for Teachers. He never was the director of the Gori Seminary (when Mirza Jalil was there Semonov was the director). Chernayevski is the author of *Vatendili* a book about how to teach Azeri.

Shafi`beyov,[5] invited him to come to Shusha. Later he remembered this journey with fondness. At that time, Shusha was an important commercial city. In the summer many people came there for their summer vacation. From all windows the sounds of music and songs were heard. Those who came to stay there during the summer spent their time visiting the beautiful sites outside the city. I should add that at the time Mirza Jalil may have met the famous poetess, Khorshid Banu Natavan, daughter of Mehdiquli Khan.[6]

In that same year, Mirza Jalil became a teacher in the village of Ulukhanli and later became teacher in Nahrem, where he stayed for 10 years[7]. In the village of Nahrem Mirza Jalil became very friendly with his colleague Tigran Sergeevich Sambatiyan[8] He taught him Azeri and learned Armenian from him. After learning Armenian he became acquainted with Armenian literature. Mirza Jalil was a close friend of the famous Armenian writer Shirvanzadeh.[9] He gave a copy of his work 'Chaos' to Mirza Jalil and wrote on it: "To my dear pen friend Mamadqulizadeh (*Molla Nasreddin*) with great respect. A. Shirvanzadeh 07/17/1929, Kislovodsk."

In Nehrem, Mirza Jalil married one of the girls of the village who was called Halimeh Khatun[10] and their daughter Munavvar was born in 1897.[11] Mirza Jalil began his career as writer in Nahrem and he wrote: *The Accounts of the School of Danabash Village* and other works in that place.[12]

In 1897, Mirza Jalil came to Nakhchivan and in the summer of that same year he went to Moscow with a friend to see the intellectual hotspots and places worthy of visiting. In Nakhchivan, Mirza Jalil became friends and associated with a large number of intellectuals, among them Eyn Ali Bey Soltanov,[13] Memedquli Kengerli,[14] Qorban Ali Sharifov[15] and many others, as well as the well-known lawyer Memedquli Bey, who became a close friend of his

---

5. Isma`il Bey Shafi`beyov (1869-1918) taught at schools in Yerevan and Shusha, where he died.

6. Mehdiquli Khan (1770-1845) was the son of Ibrahim Khan Javanshir, who was the Khan of Qarabagh from 1758 to 1806. Khorshid Banu Natavan (1817-1897) was the famous poetess who met Alexandre Dumas during his travels in the Caucasus.

7. This is not entirely correct. Jalil after finishing Gory Seminary in 1878 taught from September until December of this year in Ulukhanli near Yerevan and then from December 1887 until January 1890 he taught in one of the villages of Nakhchivan called Nurashin. From January 1890 till April 1897 he was a teacher in the village of Nahrem.

8. Tigran Sergeevich Sambatiyan (1874-1971) after finishing his studies at the Yerevan Seminary in 1895 was appointed teacher in the village of Nahrem where he taught for two years along with Mirza Jalil. Sambatiyan writes in his Memoirs about Mirza Jalil, see *Literary Armenia.* Yerevan 1957, pp. 281-88.

9. Alexander Minasovich Mu'assiyan Shirvanzadeh (1858-1935) was the famous Armenian author and dramatist.

10. Halimeh, daughter of Nagi Mamadqulizadeh (?-1898). Mirza Jalil married her in 1895. Her date of death in some sources is given as 1897.

11. Munavvar Mamadqulizadeh (1897-1965) the first child of Mirza Jalil. After the death of her father she worked as a midwife in Nahrem for a long time and later she became the public health official of that region. In 1946, she became a deputy of the Supreme Soviet.

12. The first work by Mirza Jalil was not written in Nahrem but in Nurashin in 1899 and it was titled *Chay Dastgahi*, an allegoric drama.

13. Eynali Bey Chölbeyi Bey-oghlu Sultanov (1863-1935) was an author, dramatist, drama critic and journalist. He had completed his law studies at Novoruski University in 1913. He was very active in the intellectual circles of Nakhchivan. His play called *Turk qizi* (the Turkish girl) was performed in Nakhchivan in the 1880s.

14. Memedquli Bey Shefi` Aqa-oghlu Kengerli (1864-1905) was a well-educated officer; he was a lawyer and an education reformer.

15. Qorban Ali Haji Alasgar-oghlu Sharifzadeh (1854-1917) was an education reformer, publicist and the father of Aziz Sharif (1895-1988). He helped Mirza Jalil with the publication of *Molla Nasreddin* and sometimes wrote articles under the name of Leylak (Crane).

and under his direction Mirza Jalil prepared to take the exam for the law school.

This group of young intellectuals often had literary meetings and many times performed the plays of Fath Ali Akhundzadeh. Mirza Jalil had a role in *Monsieur Jourdain* and in *The Vazir of Lenkeran*[16] and the role of Mast Ali Shah was played by his brother Mirza Ali Akbar. In these plays Mirza Jalil and Mamed Taqi Sidqi were the directors.

In these years, Mirza Jalil devoted himself to serious study of works by John Stuart Mill, Darwin, Socrates, Marx and others.

* * *

In 1898, Mirza Jalil's wife died and he came to Yerevan, where later he became interpreter of the district office. At that time, he wrote the stories *Yan Tutaki* (reed pipe) and *The Post-box,* and as he himself writes, the author A. Sultanov liked them very much. On 13 June 1900, Mirza Jalil married for the second time. His new wife was the sister of Memedquli Bey Kengerli, Nazli Khanum (her original name was Zeynab Agha Khanum)[17]. Nazli Khanum had been the wife of Aliquli Shahtakhtli and she had a ten-year old son by him called Heydar. Mirza Jalil gave his sister Sakineh to Memedquli Bey in marriage and both marriages were performed on 13 June 1900.

After one year Memedquli Bey divorced Sakineh and the relations with Mirza Jalil became strained. Sakineh married for the second time to a relative of Memedquli Bey, Askar Aqa Kengerli. She bore him two sons (Teymur and Jalal) and a daughter

Pakizeh. Mirza Jalil raised all his sister's children and saw to their education.

Memedquli Bey and Nazli Khanum's father, Sharif Aqa Kengerli had studied and served in government employment in Petersburg and that is why he was able to give his son a good education. Memedquli Bey first served as an artillerist, and then he left the military and entered law school. After finishing it he returned to his homeland. Later with his own money he opened a boarding school for girls in Yerevan. To teach them he brought special teachers who were educated at the Smolni Institute of Petersburg.

Here I would like to mention two events that Mirza Jalil told me about how he had come to know Nazli Khanum.

Mirza Jalil said that almost every day in Nakhchivan he would go to see Memedquli Bey Kengerli and sit in his office for a long time and talk to him. "I was preparing for the law school entrance exam. I was using his extensive and good library. One day I was sitting in his office and I was reading when a beautiful young lady opened the door and entered. I was frozen in my place. This lady, unlike all other young Moslem women, who as soon as they saw a man they didn't know, run away; she did not, and she neither feared me nor lost her composure. After waiting a few seconds she looked at me and with pride and dignity left through the other door. She appeared to me like an enchanting angel and her beautiful face remained engraved in my mind.

"Again one day I was sitting alone in the office of Memedquli Bey, as I was wont to do. I was cleaning my revolver and filling the cylinder. Suddenly the gun went off and wounded my left hand; I started bleeding and I was feeling very bad. In the other room somebody cried and fell down. People came rushing in and bandaged my hand. The bullet had injured my hand and it got stuck there. (This bullet remained in his hand and he went with that bullet to his grave). I was curious to see who had shouted

---

16. These two plays are by Akhundzadeh. For the English translation of Akhundzadeh's plays, see Hasan Javadi, *Dramatic Works of Fath Ali Akhundzadeh* (forthcoming).

17. "Agha," spelled with the Persian letter "غ" refers to a woman, but when spelled as "aqa" with the letter "ق" it's an honorific for a man, similar to "sir."

and fell down. You would not believe it, but Nazli Khanum was watching me from the key hole. When hearing the sound of the gun and seeing me wounded she screamed out of fear and fainted. A few years after this incident we got married."

Mirza Jalil and Nazli Khanum's marriage created many problems. From the social point of view Mirza Jalil was not from a compatible class.[18] He had neither money nor a steady job. All Nazli Khanum's relatives, except Memedquli Bey, were against this marriage. To silence her relatives Mirza Jalil got a job in the district office, although he hated it. Later he left this job and in a serious manner prepared himself for the law school entrance exam.

In 1902, Mirza Jalil's relations with his wife began to sour. His wife loved him madly, but Mirza Jalil spent most of his time on his own work. His wife became angry with him, for months on end she did not talk to him, did not leave the house, became sick and nervous, and as a result, she had an early childbirth and a nervous breakdown.

After 1903, Mirza Jalil with Memedquli Bey brought her to Tiflis to be treated and left her in the neurological clinic of the hospital. Nazli Khanum did not want to eat, nor did she want to see anyone. Day by day she was melting like a candle and before long she died.

The death of his wife grieved Mirza Jalil and left an incredibly bitter memory, but he bore this enormous pain with fortitude. They say that for three years he used to go to his wife's grave every day and built a monument on her grave. After her death Mirza Jalil decided to stay in Tiflis permanently and when he was dying he said that he should be buried next to Nazli Khanum.

In 1903, Mirza Jalil by chance met Memed Aqa Shahtakhtli.[19] He invited Mirza Jalil to work at the Russian newspaper called *Sharq-e Rus* to which he agreed. In 1905, in Tiflis, the progressive newspaper *Vorozhdeniye* was published. Mirza Jalil was working there and in charge of its Moslem desk. At the same time he had good relations with Armenian and Georgian scholars. In Tiflis he was a member and secretary of the Islamic Charitable Society. On 23 June 1905, Mirza Jalil wrote to the office of the censor of the Caucasus and asked for permission to publish a newspaper in Turkish called *Nowruz*, but this was denied. In the same year, Mirza Jalil opened a boarding school in his house in Kransogorsk Street. He had taken the children of his relatives in Nakhchivan and educated and prepared them for school. Also, in that year he became acquainted and befriended Omar Fayeq Nomanzadeh.[20] Together they started to look for

---

18. Nazli Khanum was a member of the Kengerli family that for many decades, prior to the Russian conquest, had held the governorship of Nakhchivan, and therefore, her family considered that she married below her station.

19. Mohammad Aqa Mohammad Taqi Sultan-oghlu Shahtakhtli (1846-1931) was a publicist and scholar. In 1871 he studied philosophy and law in Leipzig University. From 1873 to 1875 he lived in Paris and then he returned to Tiflis. From 1899 to 1902 he studied higher education at the Sorbonne. From 1903 to 1905 he published *Sharq-e Rus*. In 1906, he sold his printing press to Mirza Jalil and his friends. In 1907 he was selected as a member of the Duma from Yerevan. He was the first professor of Turkish at the State University of Azerbaijan.

20. Omar Fayeq Nomanzadeh (1872-1937) was a publicist, teacher, and social worker. In 1882, he studied in Istanbul at the Fateh School and in 1892 he completed his studies at the *Dar al-Shafaq* seminary. In 1892 he returned home. Thereafter he taught at various schools. In 1900, at Shamakhi he taught history, geography, arithmetic and Turkish. In 1902, he went to Tiflis and as of 1903 he worked at *Sharq-e Rus* with Mirza Jalil and others. In 1906, he had a special role in establishing the journal *Molla Nasreddin*, where he was secretary and in Mirza Jalil's absence Omar Fayeq had full authority over the journal. At the same time he wrote articles for other journals. In 1918, he was elected as the chief of the Akhaltsikh and Akhakelek national committee. He asked the Menshevik government of Georgia 3 times for autonomy of these two districts

ways to start a newspaper. In early August 1905, Memedquli Bey with his late sister's son, Heydar Shahtakhtli came from Nakhchivan to Tiflis. He was leaving for good to Paris. They said good-bye to Mirza Jalil and left for Batoum. When they were getting to the ship, on the bridge to the ship, two hired gunmen killed Memedquli Bey in front of the eyes of his young nephew.[21] Seeing this terrible killing the young man fainted and fell down. After regaining conscious he sent a telegram to Mirza Jalil, who hurriedly went to Batoum. He brought Memedquli Bey's body to Tiflis and buried him next to his sister, Nazli Khanum. He took Heydar under his wings.

Mirza Jalil and Omar Fayeq opened a printing press called *Gheyrat*. Mirza Jalil told me that for a long time he felt the need for a satirical journal and that he was thinking about a suitable name, but he could not find one. One time he was walking in Skhneti Street when suddenly he thought about *Molla Nasreddin* and Mirza Jalil was overjoyed with this idea and did not think that there was a better name. He put all his efforts into trying to get permission to publish. Finally, he obtained it. This happened in April 1906. The first issue was published on 7 April with a circulation of a 1,000 copies.

On the evening of 6 April when the first issue was ready for publication Mirza Jalil had only 9 manats in his pockets. Together with Omar Fayeq he had hired a worker to turn the printing press. In the middle of the night they let him go. They

did not have money to hire another worker and therefore, they themselves took turns to operate the press. In this way they worked until daybreak. In the morning, in spite of not having slept all night, they began putting the pages in the proper order, binding them and preparing them for sale. The publication of the journal was a major social event. From all sides there was a continuous stream of congratulatory letters, positive comments and praise. Subscription orders went through the roof. Every week one issue of the journal came out of the press regularly. On the first of January 1907, the 39th issue of *Molla Nasreddin* was published. Very soon the revenues from *Molla Nasreddin* paid for all expenses and debts. The journal was a great success.

* * *

In Tiflis, the *Gheyrat* and *Sharq* printing presses turned out *Towq-e La`nat*-like (Collar of Damnation) tracts and books against the *shari`ah*. Jamshid Ardashir Afshar[22] in his timeless work exposed the immoral way of life of the Moslem clergy in the East and put the stamp of corruption on this harmful class in an everlasting manner and hung it around the neck of the Moslems of the East. The

and therefore, he was imprisoned. In the time of the Republic of Azerbaijan he was inspector in the police department of Baku. In the Soviet period he was editor of several journals. He worked in several positions until 1937 when he was executed as a pan-Turkist.

21. Memedquli Bey was one strong supporters of the Turkish movement in Yerevan. He was active as a lawyer and teacher and he established schools for teaching Turkish. He knew that they were out to kill him and he had sold all his property and wanted to go Paris, but it was too late.

22. Jamshid Khan Ardashir Afshar known as Sardar Majd al-Saltaneh Afshar was the son of Ardashir Khan Afshar. During the constitutional revolution he was army commander in Urmiyeh and during the First World War he founded the Islamic Council (*anjoman-e eslami*) and lived in Tabriz where he published the newspaper *Azarabadegan*; he was a liberal. The *anjoman* of Tabriz sent him to fight the Kurds, who were pillaging West Azerbaijan. After the 1918 massacre in Urmiyeh he went to Istanbul and later he returned to Tabriz in the summer of 1919. He had a very good library, which the Russians took to Tiflis. He was the author of several works, among them *Towq-e La`nat* (The Collar of Damnation), published in Tiflis in 1332/1914 and *Mashallah Khanum*. Towards the end of his life he lived in Tehran where he died.

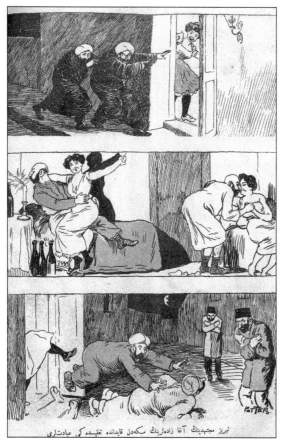

"The sinful life of the sons of the Tabriz mojtaheds" -
From Mecca straight to the brothel
(no. 4, yr. 8, 3 February 1913)

authors gave examples of the so-called "spiritual life of the clergy," which was worse than the acts of the wildest and most savage tribes of Africa.

The author describes a terrible deed by the so-called "the spiritual father" with the dead body of a young girl. The author writes that 25 years earlier, in one of the journals of Iran, it was reported that after the death of a young girl of one of the leading families of Tehran her body was kept in a mosque for one night and three Mullas were supposed to continuously read the Qur'an for her and keep vigil. Among the 'holy trinity' one of them was one of the teachers of the deceased girl. They

performed their duty in turns, one after the other. One of the two who was sleeping woke up and saw that the mulla teacher during his session of the Qur'an reading had opened the shroud and was doing some evil deeds to the girl's body. The third one also woke up and they bound the hands and feet of this savage. The next day the angry public covered him with wax and set fire to him. In this manner they took him around the streets until he died.

This type of publication angered the mullas and sheikhs of Tiflis and they complained to the government. At the same time, they issued *fatvas*. Gendarmes inspected the printing-house and in accordance with the law, they confiscated all the tracts. The tract titled "Freedom of speech, why meetings and discussions are necessary?" published by the Gheyrat printing-house was confiscated, because of its "illegal contents." In Tiflis, during the administration of Shirinkin, Yatskovich and Martinov[23] they said: "look, what kind of disrespectful publications" the cursed revolutionary Moslems are making."

In the turbulent days of 1906, on 12 December, I heard from Omar Fayeq that because of our Moslem informers the police of the sixth district of Tiflis had carried out a search in the Gheyrat printing-house and confiscated Olga Volkenshteyn's tract[24] "Why freedom of speech and assembly

---

23. Mikhail Pavlovich Shirinkin (1873-?), general of the gendarmerie of the Caucasus and deputy chief of police. Vladimir Avksentievich Yatskevich (1832-1917?), lieutenant-general. In 1905, he was the temporary governor of Tiflis and Yerevan. Piotr Ivanovich Martinov (1867-?), commander of the gendarmerie of Tiflis, after 1906 he was in Kiev and in 1909 he was governor of Baku.

24. Olga Akimovna Volkenshteyn was a journalist and the author of many books. She was born in Kishinyovda and went to school in Kiev. In 1898 she went to St. Petersburg. From 1906 to 1908 she worked in the Women's Equal Rights Council. From 1917 to 1918 she was in Rostov, Petrograd and Moscow and published books on politics. Her book "Freedom of speech" was

"The picture that was here was censored and there
was no time to draw a new one"
(no. 8, yr. 4, 22 Feb 1909)

and demonstration is necessary," which had been translated into Azeri in 2,500 copies. All copies of the confiscated tract were taken away. On 12 December 1906, the publication committee, in note no. 1830, ordered them not to publish such tracts, unless there was special permission. The people in charge of the Gheyrat printing house accepted not to publish such works in the future and with this stratagem the whole matter was resolved.

According to an official letter from the gendarmerie of Tiflis, no. 9854, dated 27 December [1906],

in accordance with police regulations, the copies were returned. On 26 March 1907, the chief of the printing-house asked for the return of the confiscated tracts that had been taken away in 1906. In a note no. 787, dated 5 April 1907, the Committee ordered that the Gheyrat printing-house could take possession of the confiscated tracts and distribute them.

In June 1907, *Molla Nasreddin* was closed down by governor-general Timofeyev,[25] because of its 'harmful activities' during martial law. It was proposed to exile the editor of the journal to one of governorates in Russia. In the same month of June, Jalil Mamadqulizadeh petitioned V. Kolobov, the head of the Publication Committee, asking for permission from the general-governor of Tiflis to restart the publication of *Molla Nasreddin*. He undertook to be respectful of His Majesty in political matters. After the head of the Publication Committee accepted certain undertakings with regard to the governor-general, *Molla Nasreddin* was allowed to begin its activities again. *Molla Nasreddin* was republished on 25 June 1907.

What Mirza Jalil wrote in his article titled 'Armenian and Moslem Women' created violent reactions in Baku and other places. They wrote critical and threatening letters to the office. He kept all these letters, but in May 1913 when the gendarmes searched our house they took away those interesting letters as well as other valuable documents.

A few copies that I still have in my possession I want to publish properly, for example, the letter from N. Nikolski to V. I. Kolobov.

To the Honorable V. Ivanovich. Secret. The deputy of the viceroy wants to inform you that there are two journals taking extreme revolutionary positions: *Molla Nasreddin* published in Turkish in

---

published in 1906 and is one of her first books.

25. N. P. Timofeyev was the military governor of Tiflis. On 14 May 1906 there was an assassination attempt on him.

"Modest Moslem versus Immodest European Dress—
A European lady's shameless dress versus the chaste
Moslem dress of Tehrani and Gilani women"
(no. 36, yr. 1, 8 Dec 1906)

Tiflis and *Ikhtar* published in Baku [according to E. Taherzadeh, there is no such a journal; very likely he meant *Iqbal*]. At the same time, about our army, about His Majesty's person and about the king of Iran comments and caricatures are published that are unsuitable. I should mention that these publications are not only very well known in the Caucasus, but in Iranian Azerbaijan as well and they seriously influence the people.

V.I. Kolobov's letter, dated 4 September 1908, addressed to the deputy of the viceroy reads:

> The head of the secretariat in the document no. 168, dated 2 September, informed me that Your Excellency had asked[26] my personal opinion about the Turkish journals *Molla Nasreddin* and *Ikhtar*, which is published in Baku. The illustrated weekly *Molla Nasreddin*

began publication as of the second half of 1907 in Tiflis and in 1907 the governor-general Timofeyev temporarily suspended it because of its harmful activities during the period of martial law. The reason for the closure of the journal was the publication of highly critical articles concerning the high clergy of the neighboring countries, this, from a diplomatic point of view, had created an embarrassing situation. Later the Moslems of Baku wrote to the viceroy that if internal political problems of Moslems are treated cautiously the journal should be allowed to be published. On 27 June 1907, general Timofeyev, having in mind the interests of the Moslems, without any trial or fine, allowed the journal *Molla Nasreddin* to be published again.

Here is an example of an article in *Molla Nasreddin* no. 26 of 30 June 1908, titled: "The same man" which is about Mohammad Ali Shah addressing the people of Tabriz in a telegram on 4 Jomadi II:

> O people of Tabriz! O those people who are dissatisfied with me! I hear that you are displeased with me, that, although I have sworn on the Qur'an, I am betraying the government and the nation and I have gathered enemies of the country around me to destroy the country.

> O people of Tabriz, suppose that all of this is true, and let every one say what he wants, but I don't simply understand it. What do you say and what do you want from me and what do you expect from me? By God, I am astonished about your position. If the people of other provinces are displeased with me they may be right, but I don't understand what you, the people of Tabriz, want from me.

> That is to say, have not you really known me so far? Let strangers say whatever they want, my good people, don't you know me? You

---

26. The date of the viceroy's request is given as being on 5 September, which is impossible, because the letter in which this is mentioned is dated 4 September. This is either due to a printer's error or to a misreading of the original letter.

know from what type of bird's egg I have come out. You know my deeds well.

O people of Tabriz. Just remember that it was only two years ago that I was heir apparent in Tabriz and what I did there and what actions I took. In those days you were just standing and would not say a word.

Remember the Prince's garden![27] There is no doubt that you all know what I have done there. How many sons of very respectable people did not I bring to that garden and what delightful nights did not I have in that garden? How many virgins were not brought at my orders to that garden right in front of your eyes? Just remember it well, how many girls and boys were sacrificed to my dear self. …

In those days you said nothing, why are you speaking now?

At that time, did any one tell me that what I did in the Prince's garden were not good things? Did any of our *mojtaheds* or other scholars call my actions bad? Every month they would publish a religious tract. "How many times is it necessary to cough and how many times is it necessary to massage? That is to say, a woman who puts on her underclothes while standing for three days her wishes will not be fulfilled and at the time of dressing she should say this prayer."

O people of Tabriz.

After I had finished my training as the heir apparent, you made me the Shah and sent me to Tehran.

Now what do you want of me?

I am the same person only "the donkey is the same, but the saddle has changed."[28]

Let the people of other provinces expect more humane rule and better kingship from me.

What are you saying? You know me. Just remember the Prince's Garden

What do you want from me?

Mohammad Ali Shah, when in Tabriz,
and after he had left
(no. 35, yr. 1, 1 December 1906)

---

27. This refers to the killing of Mirza Aqa Khan Kermani, Haji Mirza Hasan Khan Khabir al-Molk and Sheykh Ahmad Ruhi Kermani on 17 July 1896 in Mohammad Ali Mirza's residence.

28. This is a saying in Persian: "The donkey is the same only its saddle has changed." In the text it is given as "*palun-e digar ast.*"

LIVING IN QARABAGH

It was the year 1905, the powerful waves of the revolution had started. In the summer in Shusha Armenians and Moslems clashed and unrest was everywhere and the roads were dangerous.

I was living in the village of Kahrizli, which is situated 18 km from the city of Aghdam in Qarabagh. Here I had a small house and some land.

In the summer of the same year I took the children and my servant Sipyagina[1] to Khankandi to vacation there. I had rented a threshing-machine from the Russians and was harvesting in the village. It was on 8 August that Moslems and Armenians started clashing. The Armenians had taken Ft. Asgeran and had closed the roads. Most Moslem families were in the summer quarters of Shusha and Khankandi and the men, like me, remained in the village and worked there.

The situation was dangerous and I decided to cross the siege lines around Asgeran and go to Khankandi and try there to bring about peace between Armenians and Moslems. My cousin Ibish Bey, whose family was in the summer quarters of Shusha wanted to come with his horsemen. On the way to Aghdam a few small groups joined us.

They were as worried as we were and were trying to help their families. When we arrived in Aghdam we had become a group of 100 horsemen. I stopped at the post-office and learned that peace still reigned in Khankandi, but there was fear that any moment war might break out. Also, the

families were asking us for money to buy provisions. Ibish and his friends asked me many times not accompany them all the way, but rather stay here and solve the problems of money and provisions. They promised and assured me that they would do everything to maintain peace in Khankandi and not to allow any troublemaking and would bring back our families safely. I was persuaded. Our people safely crossed Asgeran and entered Khankandi. They joined with the reasonable young men who did not want to destroy things.

In Shusha and Khankandi our neighbor and friend Soleyman Mehmandarov[2] was the leader of both Armenians and Moslems. His group was keeping the peace. Day and night they took turns and did not allow agitators to create problems between Moslems and Armenians. Fortunately, our people were able to do this.

At the end of September I took my daughter Mina to the girls school in Tiflis and she was going to stay there as a boarder. In Tiflis I met my old friend Sophia Khanum who was one of the very well-educated Azerbaijani women and the wife of the late Isa Soltan Shahtakhtli and we stayed with them.[3] They had two daughters who had studied

---

1. Olga Grigoryevna Sipyagina knew Turkish well and she played female roles in theater performances in Shusha.

2. Soleyman Mehmandarov (1886-1918) was a member of the Communist party since 1907. In 1918 he was imprisoned by Aghvardiyachi in Piyati Qurusak, where he died in the same year of tuberculosis.

3. Isa Sultan Najaf-oghlu Shahtakhtli (1853-1894) was one of the Azerbaijani journalists of the second half of the 19th century. After finishing the gymnasium in 1871 he studied in Paris, London, and Zurich. In 1875 he defended his dissertation in the University of Zurich on an agricultural and forestry related subject. For many years he worked for the government and he was the political editor of the journal *Tiflichiski Viestinik*. In 1877 he published the journal *Kavkazaski Almanakh*.

in the same boarding school. One of their daughters, Layla Khanum, in 1904 had gone to Lausanne in Switzerland to become a physician, but four years later she died there (there is an obituary of her in *Molla Nasreddin* no. 52, 1908 with her picture). The family was living at 29 Krasnogorsk. After placing my daughter at school I was busy with my own affairs. My late father, Ahmad Bey Javanshir[4] left a manuscript, a collection of poems, which during his life he had collected and made into an anthology of poems from original works by himself and also, in translation, works by Pushkin, Lermontov and Andersen. He even had permission for its publication, but he did not have the means to print it. In his will he expressed the wish to have it published so that children might read it. To publish this collection my friends advised me to go and see the owner of the Gheyrat printing house, Jalil Mamadqulizadeh. Because of this Sofia Khanum invited Mamadqulizadeh to her house.

Mirza Jalil was living in the same street in a boarding-house. It was in the evening of the 13th of October that he came to Sophia's house with his friend and partner Omar Fayeq Nomanzadeh. Mirza Jalil was a rather tall and lean man. He dressed very fashionably and he had put on a white shirt with a starched collar and he had a long coat made of broadcloth. He looked very serious and depressed and he could not have been otherwise, because one year earlier he had lost his beloved wife and in 1905 he had lost his parents as well as his brother-in-law and close friend Memedquli Kengerli. Unlike Mirza Jalil, Fayeq Efendi was outgoing, friendly, witty and talkative. I should mention that Fayeq Efendi at that time had participated in a large meeting at Nakhalovka, one of the quarters of Tiflis. On behalf of the Moslems he had made a speech and he talked about his meeting that

evening. I showed my father's manuscript to Mirza Jalil and asked him to publish it. He looked at it and liked it and promised to publish one thousand copies for 240 manats. He took the manuscript and the money for the printing and gave me a receipt. Our conversation lasted long. All evening we talked about the revolution, Armenian and Moslem clashes, and the backwardness of our nation. Mirza Jalil said little, but he asked very interesting questions.

We were talking about our charitable society whose secretary was Mirza Jalil. He said: "Why don't you educated Moslem women get together and create a similar society?"

I very much liked this idea and instantly we decided to try and create it. Since Sofia Khanum was a resident of Tiflis one could say that she knew the addresses of all intellectuals in the city. We started to make a list. She gave the addresses one by one and I wrote them down. The list of women was getting to 45. The next day we took a phaeton and went to the house of Mirza Ali Fath Ali Akhundov's granddaughter, Malek Sima Khanum. We asked her to make her salon available for our meetings and she accepted this proposal with utmost kindness. In her house I became acquainted with Nisa Khanum, the daughter of our beloved playwright Akhundzadeh.

After fixing a date for the general meeting we went to other houses as well. Everyone accepted this proposal with eagerness and they promised to come. Especially Gowhar Khanum Qajar[5] was very delighted and did not spare any effort in bringing about this meeting. The next day with Gowhar Khanum we went to other houses. In the evening we sat and wrote letters to the wife of Fereydun Bey

---

4. Ahmad Bey the son of Ja'farquli Bey Javanshir (1828-1903). The same manuscript that is discussed in the text was published in Tiflis in 1906 and its proceeds were spent on the girls' schools in that city.

5. Maleksima Qajar, daughter of Khanbaba Qajar (1875-?) was married to Aqa Sadeq, the son of the famous Hajj Zeyn al-Abedin Taqiyev, wealthy capitalist and industrialist.

Kucharli[6] and also to the wife Ali Khan Avaraski[7] and invited them to the meeting.

Unfortunately, the day of our general meeting coincided with the strike of the phaeton drivers. There was chaos and excitement in the streets. People were scurrying away in fear. In spite of this we went to the meeting. Because of the strike fewer people came, but we did not postpone the meeting. We discussed some problems. Gowhar Khanum suggested that we should ask the wife of the governor to become our president. We were doing this to safeguard ourselves from the enemies of women's liberation. Because a short while ago, the efforts of the late Hasan Bey Aqayev[8] to create a charitable women's society in Ganjeh was furiously rejected by the reactionaries of Ganjeh and Baku and came to nothing.

On 19 October, Sofia Khanum and I went to see our daughters at their school. When we were returning we saw that there was a large crowd at the Ulqiniski Avenue. People were carrying red banners and there was a big crowd in front of the Duma of the city. They were standing and the speakers were orating and they were pouring down criticism on the Tsar, the ministers and other people.

Then the crowd moved to Buryatisk Street and went towards the Vornosov Bridge. We became interested and followed the crowd and before long we met our friends Mirza Jalil and Fayeq Efendi. They told us that the crowd wanted the prisoners in Metekh Castle prison to be released. If I am not mistaken the next day must have been 20 October and there were clashes with the Qulunisk strikers and there was shooting at the students of the middle school of district one.

The following day, in Nakhalovka, representatives of all ethnic groups were demonstrating; among them we Moslems also were represented and were carrying red flags on which was written: "Long live Liberty." Fayeq Efendi made a speech there.

I forgot to mention that on 14 October Mirza Jalil and Fayeq Efendi had told me of the strike of the railroad workers. In the city serious clashes were happening. Demonstrators, red flags in their hands, were going around. Therefore, I stayed in Tiflis and I was busy with the work of the charitable organization. Once or twice Mirza Jalil and Fayeq Efendi came to Sofia Khanum's house and talked about our activities. At this time they were publishing pamphlets and telegrams in Gheyrat printing house and they were participating in the strikes and talking in the meetings.

* * *

At that time one issue bothered me very much. At the school, apart from different arts, the girls, being from different ethnic groups, were learning their own mother language, but there was an exception in that the Moslem girls did not have a teacher for their mother language. In the past I had discussed this with the school mistress, but she said that we have neither a teacher nor the money to pay one.

6. Fereydun Bey Kucharli (1863-1920) was a great educator, literary critic, and literary historian. His wife was Bade Saba Khanum (1881-1953), the daughter of Mustafa Kucharli. During the Soviet period she was a teacher and for many years she was the principal of a model school.

7. Ali Khan Avaraski was at that time the temporary governor-general of Kutaysi. In 1905-07 he was the reactionary general who put down with force the revolution in the Caucasus.

8. Hasan Bey, son of Mashti Hasan Aqayev (1875-1920) was one of the famous reformers. In 1901 he graduated from the school of medicine at the University of Luminsov in Moscow. He was appointed as district physician and worked for a long time in Ganjeh. At the same time he wrote and worked in different journals. His translation from Russian of the book "Selk Sinif va Ferqeh" (The Road of Class and Party) was published in 1906 in Tiflis by Gheyrat print house. He was killed under unknown circumstances by mysterious criminals in Tiflis on 19 July 1920, and he was buried with much honor by the Moslems of the city.

Finally, I told her that I was ready to pay the teacher's salary from my own pocket. The school mistress thought it best to contact the Sheikh al-Islam to find a teacher. With Sofia Khanum I went to the house of the Sheikh al-Islam. Sofia Khanum was shy to meet the Sheikh al-Islam and she went to the women's quarter and I waited for him in reception room. He received me respectfully and asked me why I had come. After he had learnt what I wanted he praised me. When I said that so far why we don't have a teacher for Azeri,[9] he said that there was no suitable teacher and therefore, to choose a young teacher would not be proper. Then he promised me that until a suitable teacher was found he himself would go and teach the girls grammar. I thanked him and we left.

Later my daughter wrote to me that Sheikh al-Islam had come and had taught a few lessons. The coming of such a high-ranking dignitary to the school was a great event. Every time the whole school board and the mistress would receive him with special respect and see him off in the same way.

At last in the year 1905, the 17 October Manifest was published and it calmed people somewhat. Among the political prisoners freed from Miskhit Castle was our close friend Soleyman Mehmandarov. He was one of the revolutionaries who was actively engaged in clandestine activities and also he was one of the organizers of the strikes. Mehmandarov told me that, "in the coming days the strikes of the railway workers will come to an end and you can return home."

At the end of April 1906, Zaker's relative, the poet Mustafa Bey[10] came from Aghdam to our

Fayeq Efendi Nomanzadeh arrested. "What happened to your boastfulness. All those rousing words? All that fault-finding with the notables. Who was right, you or we? (no. 36, yr. 2, 22 September 1907)

village Kahrizli as our guest. He told me that under the editorship of Jalil Mamadqulizadeh a satirical journal *Molla Nasreddin* was being published in the Azerbaijani language in Tiflis. I told Mustafa Bey that I had become acquainted with Mirza Jalil and I had given him my father's work to be published and I asked Mustafa Bey to subscribe me to the journal and paid him for that. At that time every issue of the journal *Molla Nasreddin* was making a big impact among people.

---

9. The text has 'Moslem language' (*Musulman dili*). At that time, in addition to the appellation "Tatar," it was the expression used to denote Azeri.

10. Mustafa Bey, son of Shahveran Bey Behbudov (1841-?) was a relative of Qasem Bey Zaker and he had studied Russian and Persian. As is clear from Hamideh Khanum's Memoirs, he used to write in

the journal *Molla Nasreddin* under the pen name of Supurgah Saqal (broom like beard). Until recently, it was thought that Abdol-Rahim Bey Haqverdiyov was writing under this pen name.

At the end of May 1906, I went to Tiflis to bring back my daughter. Also, this time, I was a guest at Sofia Khanum's house and met Mirza Jalil again. But this time as if we were old acquaintances and I praised his journal. We talked about how the journal was received with success in Qarabagh and other subjects. He had his head bowed modestly and continued smoking a cigarette. I asked him to write the following words on the back of my father's book: "The proceeds of the sale of this book will go to the Moslem girls' school." Mirza Jalil thought that it would be better if we distributed the book with the help of the office of the Head of Education of the Caucasus, L.Q. Lopatinsky. The help of the latter would increase the sale of the books and the amount of the proceeds to the school. Then Mirza Jalil gave me the list of the agents of the journal, who would sell our book.

* * *

In Tiflis a very progressive newspaper was published by the Georgian Qutva under the name of *Vorozhdeniyeh* (Revival)[11] and I wanted to become a subscriber to this newspaper. By chance I met Mirza Jalil at Quluvinsky and I told him what I wanted. He took me to the office of the newspaper and I paid and they subscribed me.

At the end of August 1906 I took my daughter back to school. Again there was no teacher for Azeri at the school. Again I was staying with Sofia Khanum and there I became acquainted with Mirza Jalil's step son, Heydar Shahtakhtli (he was the son of Nazli Khanum). He told me that it would be better to ask Mirza Jalil himself to teach Azeri to the girls. Together with Heydar I went to see Mirza Jalil. At that time he was living at the foot of Mt.

San`an. Because he did not have time he declined this and suggested that we talk to the editor of *Sharq-e Rus*, Mohammad Aqa Shahtakhtli.

The next day with Heydar I went to the house Mohammad Aqa. He accepted the proposal and I took him to Papuva, the female head of the school. Since Shahtakhtli had lived for a long time in Paris and knew French very well Papuva was very delighted and fixed a salary of 30 manats. I had to pay him this amount directly.

In February 1907, Mohammad Aqa Shahtakhtli was elected to the second Duma from Nakhchivan. He assigned Puladzadeh[12] as his substitute teacher. In total there were 15 Azerbaijani girls at the school and they were taking Azeri lessons together with my daughter.

I received a letter from Sofia Khanum in December 1906 suggesting that I marry Mirza Jalil. She asked my thoughts about this. I thanked her for her suggestion, and said that I could not leave my father's affairs and get married.

* * *

In the year 1907, in Qarabagh the crop was destroyed by locusts. There was a terrible famine and epidemic in the region.

As much as I could, I helped the villagers and gave them millet, flour and wheat. I was doing this in accordance with my father's will, which said that to overcome a sudden famine every year one should store a great quantity of grain. There was a report in the newspapers of that time about the famine and what I was doing for the villagers. The charitable organization of Tiflis was headed by Ibrahim Aqa Vakilov and his deputy Mirza Jalil. They had sent by mail 60 manat under my name to help the

---

11. P. A. Qutva (1873-1936) before the revolution he was a very active intellectual and journalist in Georgia. He was a close friend of Jalil Mamadqulizadeh, Sultan Majid Ghanizadeh and Hoseyn Minasazov.

12. Mirza Asghar Puladzadeh (1873-1953) after finishing the superior religious school of Ganjeh worked as a teacher in Ganjeh, Tiflis and Nakhchivan.

afflicted people in our district. As soon as I received the money I went to the most afflicted villages and under the supervision of government officials and village elders gave every person 1 manat and 50 kopek. After signing the relevant documents concerning the distribution of the money I came back and the next day I followed my daughter to Tiflis, who was going to graduate. When I was passing through Aghdam I learnt that to help the afflicted people Haji Zeyn al-Abedin Taqiyev[13] had sent 1,000 manat under my name. I got the money and I wrote to him that because I had a business that could not be delayed I was going to Tiflis and thus I did not have time to distribute it. I thought perhaps this could be done by Mehmandarov.

Ahmad Bey Aghayev[14] and others had wired some money to help those afflicted by the famine and the epidemic.

* * *

On 21 February 1907, due to people's needs and the arrangement of peace between Armenians and Moslems a special conference was organized. The organizers of the conference Haji Zeyn al-Abedin Taqiyev and Ahmad Bey Aghayev sent a telegram inviting me as representative of the villagers to the conference. Although I did not receive the telegram in time and therefore, was a few days late I went to the conference with a representative of the villagers, Kerbela'i Ja`far. In Baku I learned that some religious leaders and some of the Beys of Qarabagh bitterly opposed my participation in the conference,

because at that time, the participation of women in social affairs was considered to be against the Sharia and the customs of our ancestors. The organizers of the conference had arranged a separate meeting with the people who were not opposing my participation and they wanted me to talk about the situation in our district, but I declined and left Baku. Previously, I had given some of the documents related to this to Samad Aqa, son of Aqa Mali,[15] who worked in our region as an assessor. He published them in a book called *Namus* (Honor).

In the middle of March, in our district and neighboring districts, many locusts appeared like a cloud. The government officials brought a large number of workers to the fields to get rid of the locusts. But since the workers were not properly fed the work was not very effective.

There was a famine among the people. I was baking bread at home and took it to various districts and distributed it to the workers. We had been expecting that this year there would be a bumper crop of wheat and cotton, but the locusts came from the Nile desert. In fact, they came in an extraordinary number. Ten to 15 werst in length and 50-60 *sazhen*[16] in width the wave of locusts increased daily and wherever they passed they ate everything. This was a dreadful and terrible sight.

To safeguard the fields I was working day and night. At the end, realizing that nothing was working, I sent a telegram to governor Kovalyov. In the telegram I described how the situation was becoming dangerous and begged him to take urgent action. Kovalyov came and ordered workers to be brought from other regions. The food supply for the workers was very well organized, but there was not much success, because it was too late. The

---

13. Haji Zeyn al-Abedin Taqiyev (1838-1924), an Azerbaijani entrepreneur and philanthropist, reputed to have been the richest man in Transcaucasia.

14. Ahmad Bey Mirza Hasan Bey-oghlu Aghayev (1868-1939) was a famous journalist, orientalist, diplomat, and teacher. He had finished law school in Paris. He worked in Tiflis with several newspapers, but at Taqiyev's invitation he came to Baku and taught French there. At the behest of Rothschild and Nobel he went to Petersburg to ask the Tsar not to take the right to the oilfields from them.

15. Samad Aqamali (1867-1930) was an important government official. In the 1920s he was the head of S.S.R. MIK of Azerbaijan. He was a fiery defender of the Latin alphabet and he was a tireless organizer of the social revolution. He was the author of several books.

16. One *sazhen* equals 2.1 meter.

"They are not gypsies, they are Moslem villagers. How much do you think the Haji has given to the charity box?"
(no. 15, yr. 8, 7 March 1913)

locusts were flying and at this time they could not be battled. In this way all the fields in our districts, even the gardens and orchards, were destroyed. The famine caused typhoid fever and with it there were numerous deaths. The poor villagers were weeping and raising their hands to heaven asking help from God.

The famous Georgian physician Tupuridze was sent to our district to combat this typhoid fever. I remember one day he was in our house and we were discussing the journal *Molla Nasreddin*. He was full of praise and said: "It is a beautiful journal. The man who writes the satirical pieces of this journal has a unique talent. A man who has such a wise satiric talent does not come around in a millennium. The nation to which he belongs is a fortunate one."

* * *

When I went to Tiflis for the graduation of my daughter I was incredibly tired and beaten up. As usual I stayed with Sofia Khanum and in spite of my tiredness I was busy with my affairs. But gradually I was feeling worse. Sophia Khanum once again raised the issue of my marriage to Mirza Jalil and she tried to reason with me and convince me. Mirza Jalil was sometimes coming to Sophia Khanum's house and he would sit for a long time and talk. I gave him the document of the distribution of the money as he was the secretary of the society. I talked with him about the affairs of the village, the famine, the locusts, the typhoid fever, and how I went to the conference in Baku. I was feeling that he wanted to say something, but he was avoiding it. In those days Mirza Jalil wrote an article about Armenian and Moslem women in *Molla Nasreddin* (19 May 1907 no. 20) which created a sensation. It was this article that made me accept Mirza Jalil's marriage proposal.[17]

Fayeq Efendi told Mirza Jalil not to leave the house, because they wanted to kill him. The great unwashed were angry. Some people had gathered under the leadership of the reactionaries and they were cursing Mirza Jalil and were asking for the death of that infidel. At that time, Mirza Jalil, on purpose, was living in the Georgian quarter in 22 Davidovski Street in the house of someone called Milov, away from where the common people lived.

Fayeq Efendi went to mosque and tried to make some explanations about the article, but the common people considered him to be an infidel and did not allow him to go to the pulpit. But a few young intellectuals took his side and calmed the people and made them listen to Fayeq Efendi's speech. This had a positive effect and they were slowly leaving the mosque; everything remained quiet.

In Baku and other places the common people were angered by the above mentioned article. They sent threatening letters to Mirza Jalil, which he kept. In the year 1913, when the secret police came and searched our house they took these letters with many other valuable documents.

* * *

On 27 May there was a soiree on the occasion of the graduation and among the graduates was my daughter Mina, who received a medal. As I was very sick I could not go to this soiree. At the soiree the Sheikh al-Islam asked my daughter why has your mother not come? She replied that she was *azarlamush* (sick). The Sheikh al-Islam corrected her and said it is better to say *nakhuslamush* (indisposed).

The discussion of the Sheikh al-Islam with the girls gave Mirza Jalil a new subject and he wrote Two Open Letters to the Sheikh al-Islam of the

---

17. In this article Mamadqulizadeh quoting from the Qur'an (24:31-32) argues that *hijab* does not mean Moslem women should cover their faces but rather dress modestly. He says that this rule of modesty applies to women of all nations. He compares Armenian women and Azerbaijani women, saying that forcing them to cover themselves and not allowing them to go far away from home does not make them more chaste. Besides men took part in all sorts of debaucheries and had no right ordering their women around.

Caucasus (*Molla Nasreddin* no. 22, 1907). Because of that, the publication of the journal was temporarily suspended by the government.[18]

The physicians considered my illness to be serious and ordered me to rest for a long time. I finished my work in the village and decided to come to the city. I replied positively to the Mirza Jalil's proposal. I became his wife and helper. We decided to have our wedding in the fall. I invited Mirza Jalil to our village and he accepted.

In the early days of June we went to Qarabagh. On the way he asked me not to tell anyone who he was and to introduce him as my daughter's Azeri language teacher Mohammad Hasanov. Mirza Jalil loved village life. He was not bored, and sometimes he was writing.

My father's friend and confidante Doctor Karim Bey Mehmandarov, who lived and worked in Shusha, had been our family doctor for a long time. We loved Karim Bey very much and we respected him. I sent a telegram and asked him to come to Kahrizli and diagnose my illness. Originally I wanted to talk to him about this great change that was going to take place in my life. Karim Bey came and listened to me very carefully and then he said: "Your wishes definitely don't surprise me. Sooner or later you had to love someone and marry him. I have to say I don't like your fiancé. He is a person of great talent. He has a brilliant future, but leaving his important work in the city and coming to live with you in the village may be the cause of disappointment for him. At the same time, it will be an unfortunate situation, if you leave the village and your useful work for the common people and go to the city. You will be a stumbling block for each other. Intellectual women usually are demanding of their husband, they ask an accounting for everything and that is why they annoy them and make

"If Japanese women had not become used to working with men unveiled in the same office, they, like the Moslems, would have progressed like us," says Molla Abdol-Rashid Ibrahimov (no. 18, yr. 4, 3 May 1909)

them unhappy. You had better be careful. Guard him well and in many affairs compromise."

Later on in the difficult moments of my life I recalled the good doctor's advice. In fact, I compromised on many things and I made myself such that I would not be an impediment to Mirza Jalil's activities.

Mirza Jalil became acquainted with Dr. Mehmandarov and they liked each other and they talked for a long time. The idea of the article, which is printed in *Molla Nasreddin* (1 July 1907, no. 24 entitled "where are the 45,000 manat?")[19] was

---

18. About these letters to the Sheikh al-Islam and the usage of the words "Azarlamish" and "Nakhoshlamish."

19. This article which was signed by *Muzalan* (gad-fly); it is about the money collected for the hungry people of Baku and how it was misused by different people.

suggested by Dr. Mehmandarov. He wrote this in Kahrizli.

I asked the doctor not to reveal the identity of my guest to anyone. When the doctor was leaving he invited our entire family to come that summer to Shusha to rest. He told me: "Come, and help me in establishing good relations with our Armenian neighbors."

The above mentioned old and respected poet Mustafa Bey Behbudov came to stay with us from Aghdam. He was a humorous, witty and sociable man and he was one of the admirers of *Molla Nasreddin*. I introduced Mirza Jalil as Mohammad Hasanov, the teacher of my daughter. They talked animatedly with each other and liked one another very much. Usually, Mirza Jalil did not laugh, but on this occasion he could not stop laughing, because of Mustafa Bey's conversation. Mustafa Bey asked Mirza Jalil:

Do you know the editor of *Molla Nasreddin*?

Yes, I know him.

Are you involved in this journal?

Occasionally, I write for it.

May a curse be on him, he writes so well.

In these last issues he really has become stupid. He is criticizing religion.

Sheikh al-Islam of the Caucasus
(no. 4, yr. 3, 27 Jan 1908)

Mirza Jalil liked his words and he hardly could suppress his laughter. At the same time, he was eager to continue the conversation with Mustafa Bey. Without realizing it he gave Mirza Jalil a few short articles and asked him to give them to the editor of the journal *Molla Nasreddin*. He had signed the articles as Supurgah Saqal (broom-like bearded man). Those articles were published in the same year in *Molla Nasreddin*. Mustafa Bey liked Mirza Jalil so much that he did not want to leave him. When he wanted to return to Aghdam Mirza

Jalil saw him off and accompanied this old and worldly-wise poet as far as outside the village.

Mirza Jalil wanted to return to Tiflis, but since our phaeton was broken he could not go. After a few days Mirza Jalil changed his mind and asked me to tell my relatives who he was and that we should marry. My late daughter Mina in Tiflis already knew that Mirza Jalil had proposed to me and she was insisting that I should accept.

Mirza Jalil wrote letters about our marriage to our friends including one to our friend Mustafa Bey and we both signed them. We sent it by a special carrier and we asked Mustafa Bey to come and participate in our wedding ceremony. The carrier when he returned said that when Mustafa Bey read the letter he was very astonished and became angry and returned the letter saying, "you go yourself and put it into the mail. I will not do the bidding of Hamideh Khanum anymore. And I don't want to go to them." My old friend was very much hurt.

On 15 June 1907 we brought a Mulla from the village of Quzanli and in the presence of my relatives and my close friends he performed the marriage. On this occasion there was no celebration or ceremony. After learning the news, neighbors and villagers became acquainted with Mirza Jalil and he talked to them. He made a good impression on everybody, except on the servant of my house, Sipyagina, who did not like him. "He has a ruthless look in his eyes and he is going to make you unhappy," she said. She cried and begged me not to marry him. Some of the villagers would come and asked with tearful eyes: "Are you leaving us and going to the city?" I reassured them and said I am not going for a long time.

My relatives came and became acquainted with Mirza Jalil. One time I persuaded him to read out aloud one of the works published in the journal. He was in a good mood and agreed to do so and he read with a beautiful voice a poem by one of his favorite poets Haji Aqa Faqir.[20] The poem was nice as well. Everybody was happy about the reading and becoming acquainted with him. He was talking with people and sometimes made notes in his notebook.

Mirza Jalil visited the mill that we had in Kahrizli and other buildings that my late father had built. We had a big library. My father had begun to start collecting books in the mid-1840s. My late brother also had some books related to agriculture.

Mirza Jalil

Mirza Jalil browsed through them with great interest and promised that he would help organize them and make it even bigger.

Our gate opened to the roads to Aghdam, Hindarkh, Aqchabedi, and Lenberan and everybody who came from there, especially government officials, would come, rest and eat in our place.

On 25 June Mirza Jalil received a telegram from Fayeq Efendi that the journal had been closed down. We decided to go to Aghdam together; from there he went to Tiflis and I accompanied by the children went to Shusha to spend the summer there. My marriage had tremendously angered most of the Khans of Qarabagh. To be true to their tradition they wanted to punish me. They even wanted to kill Mirza Jalil in the bazaar of Aghdam. Before

---

20. Haji Aqa Memed-oghlu Faqir Ordubadi (1835-1886); poet and father of the famous author Mohammad Sa`id Ordubadi. It is said that he was a descendant of Mirza Hatem Ordubadi, a famous poet and grand vizier in the time of Shah Abbas I.

leaving one of my relatives who lived in the village of Aftali told me that the Khans wanted to cause an accident to the phaeton of Mirza Jalil to kill him or to humiliate him. I called my close relatives and consulted them. They were angered by this shameless act of the Khans, and my paternal cousin Ibish Bey[21] more than anybody else.

Twenty years ago Ibish Bey, because of his opposition to the government, was imprisoned and spent 12 years in Siberia. Because of the 1905 Manifest he was set free and returned home. He was a man known for his courage, fearlessness and manliness. The Qarabagh Khans were afraid of him. In August 1905, because of him we managed to create peace between the Armenians and Moslems in Khankandi.

My cousin Ibish Bey with 20 armed men accompanied our phaeton until Aghdam. In this way we safely passed the bazaar of Aghdam and reached the station. But it became clear that two influential men from Shusha were waiting there for us. It seemed that the idea of attacking us had already reached Shusha and our friends had sent them to welcome us and take us to Shusha.

* * *

I sent Mirza Jalil to Yevlakh with two trusted armed men, and, accompanied by the children, I went to Shusha. There, in the Tezeh quarter, we were the guests of the late Qasem Bey Mehmandarov. His house was very nicely painted and there was a very big hall. On its ceiling and walls there were paintings of the heroes and characters of Ferdowsi's *Shahnameh*. From the window you could see the enchanting view of the mountains of Shusha.

My Shusha friends had sent rose bouquets and welcoming congratulatory poems. None of the Beys of the province had come to the summer quarters of Shusha. They were afraid of the conflict with the Armenians and because of the closure of the Asgeran Castle. Most of the Beys had gone to summer quarters elsewhere. After a few days I received a letter from Mirza Jalil. He said that after having given proper explanation he had managed to get permission to continue the publication of the journal. As I mentioned earlier, because of the satirical article published in no. 22 of the journal at the request of the Sheikh of Islam the journal was closed down. In the letter Mirza Jalil promised to come to the village on 22 August.

Our old friend, my late father's friend, the playwright Nejef Bey Vazirov,[22] one of the leaders of the Charitable Society of Shusha, Dr. Karim Bey Mehmandarov, the teacher Mirza Ali Akbar Akhundov,[23] his brother Dr. Bahram Bey[24] and Dr. Akhundov's wife Saltanat Khanum[25] came to see us very often. Saltanat Khanum in spite of being a French woman would go out in a chador.

With the encouragement of Kerim Bey and Nejef Bey we decided with the help of aficionados and students to create a society to perform plays and organize concerts and give the money collected to poor students. The performances

---

21. Ibish Bey (d. 1919) was the son of Ahmad Bey Javanshir's brother.

22. Nejef Bey Vazirov (1854-1926) was a famous Azerbaijani playwright.

23. Mirza Ali Akbar Mirza Ja`far Bey-oghlu Akhundov (1872-?) was a teacher and brother of Bahram Bey Akhundov.

24. Bahram Bey Mirza Ja`far Bey-oghlu Akhundov (1872-1932) was a physician and social reformer. He studied biology in Lille and then studied medicine. He received his medical degree from the University of Kharkov in 1904. He was a member of parliament of the Azerbaijan Republic (1918-20). Under the Soviets, Narimanov sent him to Europe as supervisor of Azerbaijani students.

25. Saltanat Khanum (d. 1914) was French; her original name was Celestine Purte.

were being carried out in the hall where we were staying. The leading female roles were played by our servant Olga Grigoryevna Sipyagina and she spoke Azeri very well. The head of the society was Mir Hasan Vazirov,[26] who later became one of the 26 commissars. He was an extremely able, serious, and good-natured young man. The plays and the concerts were performed in the Nikolayeski School. The late Nejef Bey was always the director and performed the lead roles.

We would go to visit the Charitable Society of the Armenians and intellectual Armenians would come to our plays and came to visit us. In this way our mutual friendship was established. About all this I would write very often to Mirza Jalil and he would write back long letters and talk about his life, his work and how he felt. He would also write about the situation with the journal and other affairs. His letters were very interesting and meaningful, but unfortunately when the Secret Police searched our house in Tiflis they, of course, took all these letters before everything else. I would write things about social life in Shusha that would become a topic for the journal. We wrote in Russian.[27]

During the summer we staged a few plays as well as a few concerts. Through them we managed to collect 1,000 manat. We distributed this amount among the poor students of high schools. Before leaving Shusha, we took a picture with the members of our society, in the garden of our house. I still have this picture.

According to the old calendar, on 21 August we left for the village. Young men rode on horses and accompanied us until the Aqa bridge stage.[28] There we lunched together and they left.

The next day I sent a phaeton with an armed man to Yevlakh to bring Mirza Jalil. My daughter Mina, who wanted to study Education in Tiflis, as well as my servant Sipyagina and the children went in the same phaeton.

* * *

On 23 August Mirza Jalil came. This time he had dressed simply. He had a reddish vest and long shirt that he fastened with a silken string.

We organized the work in the village and made preparations to depart for Tiflis permanently. In September the size of our landlord's share was supposed to be determined; there were disagreements with our neighbors. But Mirza Jalil got involved and reconciled us.

Mirza Jalil especially liked village life. He would sit in the driver's place of the phaeton and would take the rein of the horses in his hands and lead them and would love this and get a great kick out of it. He loved the long-winded conversations of the villagers and learnt about their lives, customs and manners with great interest.

While Mirza Jalil was looking into the papers of my late father we discovered a big manuscript collection of proverbs. In a large notebook on one side were written the Azerbaijani proverbs and in front of them there was the Russian equivalent. The Russian proverbs were taken from the book by Dal.[29] This manuscript consisted of four parts. It was ready for publication. Mirza Jalil was thinking of publishing it, but later this manuscript was lost. I don't know whether it was stolen or taken by the Secret Police who were searching our house.

---

26. Mir Hasan Vazirov (1889-1918) was a progressive intellectual.

27. They wrote in Russian, because Hamideh Khanum found it difficult to write Azeri in Arabic letters.

28. The famous Aqa Bridge is in Khocale, at 1 km south-west of Khankandi. It was built by Khojali Memed Aqa, one of the wealthy people of Qarabagh.

---

29. Vladimir Ivanovich Dal (1801-1872) was a Russian writer, lexicographer, and ethnographer. His famous book in 4 vols. is called the Russian Illustrated Dictionary (1863-69).

Every evening after the village slept and there was absolute quiet Mirza Jalil would sit at the writing table and would write editorials, essays and satirical pieces for the journal and he would write them into a thick note book. Mirza Jalil had given the hero of the play *The Dead* the name of our relative and the friend of my father Iskander Haji Hasan-oghlu. Iskandar was living in the village of Husulu[30] where he would make a wine similar to champagne from the grapes of his own garden and did not care for the criticism of the people and would drink it. Therefore, they called him "Drunken Iskandar."

As we said above, that year locusts had destroyed all the crops. We could not even pay our taxes. I told my family to pay the wages of the well diggers of our water system from the income of our mill. With my family we went to Tiflis to live in Mirza Jalil's house. At that time Mirza Jalil was living in no. 24 Davidov Street. We went to Tiflis accompanied by Mirza Jalil. This was around the end of October 1907.

In Mirza Jalil's house apart from his 10-year old daughter Munavvar, there were the children of his sister, who were studying at the Gymnasium. In addition, there were Fayeq Efendi's nephew Ahmad,[31] and Qorban Ali Sherifov's son, Aziz[32] and Ebil Kengerli, the son of Sakineh, Mirza Jalil's sisters. Every Sunday, these children would fold the journal that was freshly printed and would write the subscriber's name on them and would take them to the post office.

---

30. Husulu is a village in Aqchabadi district.

31. Ahmad Pepinov (1893-1938) was a writer and government official, who mainly worked in the Publication Office.

32. Aziz (1895-19??), literary figure, critic and doctor of philology. He was professor at the University of Moscow, at the Lermontov Institute.

Mirza Jalil was in the habit of writing in the night up to 4 o'clock in the morning. Therefore, he would sleep late and then would get up and at noon he would receive people who were coming in connection with the journal. He would help out in the office and answer the letters "to the Editor." Every day, sometimes 30 to 40 letters would come to the editor. Among them strange and humorous letters abounded. He would put such letters on the right-hand side of the desk's drawer of our house. At night he would work on them together with the letters that he had put aside for publication in the journal.

Since he did not sleep well at night in the day time he was nervous and irritable. When he slept well he was joyous and would joke with the children and talk patiently with the people who came to the office. Very often the people who came to the office wasted Mirza Jalil's time with their useless and uninteresting talk. Therefore, he had written on a piece of paper on the wall in large letters, "No shaking of hands," and "No long talking, please." He hung it at the entrance of the office. This would astonish visitors and they hesitatingly would enter the office. If he shook hands with a person whom he did not know he would go and wash his hands.

Very often Mirza Jalil had a headache. He was anemic and his color was somewhat pale. The physicians would often recommended that he go and live in the village, because it had fresh air and would not tire his mind with work. However, he would rarely listen to the advice of the doctors. When we tried to persuade him to rest, he would say "I cannot leave the work and go. The journal has subscribers and I have to print one issue each week."

Mirza Jalil was very disciplined. He would keep all his promises. He would print the journal regularly on Sundays, because the children were home on that day and they would fold the journal and send them to the subscribers. Some of the

The Charitable Society Before and After Its Establishment
(no. 12, yr. 4, 22 March 1909)

issues of the journal, due to censorship, would sometimes be late, because the topics that were censored would have to be replaced with new items.

I would say that Fayeq Efendi came every day to Mirza Jalil and they would talk for a long time. They would read newspapers and journals and plan for the coming issue of the journal. They would joke and laugh. Mirza Jalil was the journal's editor, but when he went to the village everything was left to Fayeq Efendi.

* * *

The cartoon of the *mojtahed*s published in the issue of 20 January 1908 of the journal enraged the clerics and from everywhere threats and curses were aimed at us. The *mojtahed*s of Najaf had signed a *fatva* and condemned Mirza Jalil to death. It was said in this *fatva* whoever killed Mirza Jalil the killer's place would be in paradise and the copy of the *fatva* was sent to Mirza Jalil himself.

In the journal's issue of 3 February of the same year, a cartoon of the Mullas of Maku was published by Mamed Amin. A Mulla was sitting in Aqa Javad's mosque on the pulpit and because it was unclean he was holding an issue of *Molla Nasreddin* with the tips of his fingers in his left hand and in his right hand he held a copy of the Qur'an, and while he was crying he was cursing its writer, and was calling the Moslems to take revenge on the heretics. Because of this caricature 30,000 Moslems of Baku sent a letter to the viceroy and asked for the closing down of *Molla Nasreddin*, since it was criticizing religion. This was not enough for the people of Baku and they hired three killers from Tiflis to assassinate Mirza Jalil. As soon as Mirza Jalil's friends heard of this they sent someone to inform him.

In those days in Tiflis near Yerevanski Square a suspicious man wrapped in a felt coat who had three revolvers in his belt was arrested. It became clear that he was one of the killers who were sent from Baku. At that time, Mirza Jalil had a small pistol for protection; its number was 371966. This is the same pistol that I gave to the Museum.

After planning the caricatures of the journal, Mirza Jalil would go to Schmerling and Rotter and would describe the characters in the cartoon.[33] Rotter did not know Russian very well. Therefore, Mirza Jalil made him understand his ideas with all kinds of gestures and was forced to show him the characters that lived in Shaytan Bazaar. The first and main illustrator of the journal was Oskar Ivanovich Schmerling and because sometimes he could not finish the illustrations on time he had recommended Rotter to Mirza Jalil. I have carefully saved a few letters that Schmerling sent to Jalil. Schmerling was a great favorite of Mirza Jalil's and he would often say that *Molla Nasreddin*'s success to a great degree was due to him. Schmerling would immediately understand the ideas that Mirza Jalil described and would amaze him with his beautiful cartoons. Because with his wonderful brush he was creating something that made the common people laugh. Mirza Jalil lived with the desire that one day he would be able to recompense him properly. They corresponded until very recently.

At that time Mirza Jalil was using the water treatments developed by Dr. Miller and Kneypp.[34] Throughout the year he would swim in cold water and even in wintertime he would leave the windows open while sleeping.

---

33. Oskar Ivanovich Schmerling (1877-1938) was the cartoonist of *Molla Nasreddin*. Most of the illustrations before the October Revolution were drawn by him. In his memoirs Mirza Jalil gratefully remembers him. Josef Rotter (18??) was another illustrator of *Molla Nasreddin* from 1906 to 1914. For further information on these illustrators see the Introduction, see Appendix 2, p. TK.

34. K. Miller, *Domashnii Gomeopaticheskii lechebnik*, this book was very famous at that time. Sebastiyan Kneypp (1821-97) was a German priest. His book *Treatment with water* was very famous. In 1848, he allegedly cured himself of tuberculosis, see Appendix 2, p. TK.

سوال از سران روحانی درباره روزنامه ملانصرالدین و پاسخ آنان
(تصویر کوچک شده نسخه اصلی)

Text of the *fatva* the *mojtaheds* of Najaf signed condemning Mirza Jalil to death.

Mojtaheds in Najaf
(no. 3, yr. 3, 20 Jan 1908)

In the winter and spring of 1907-08, I was working for the Women's Charitable Society. Its president was Gowhar Khanum Qajar, an educated, down-to-earth, and capable woman who went out without the veil. Her husband was in the military. She would frequent the clubs of the high society and would go to the parties of the wife of the viceroy. With her connections as well as her wisdom and politeness she would help us with our meetings and gatherings.

At first, our society was very poor because there were not many people interested in it. To organize our events (such as concerts, lotteries, dances, etc.) we faced many difficulties. For each event we would need permission from the government and in getting this from the officials the late Yusef Bey Taherov[35] was helping Gowhar Khanum. The treasurer of the Society was an educated Moslem woman called Mina Khanum Taleshinskaya. The gatherings of the society took place in her salon. For such a difficult job like collecting money through a lottery Mina Khanum and I would collaborate and from the Men's Societies the late Ibrahim Vakilof and his assistant would help. When some donation had to be collected people would hide from us. At that time, *Molla Nasreddin* published a caricature.

On one of the days of the winter of 1908, because of the criticism of the head of the municipality of Yerevan, Mirza Jalil received a letter from the sixth district informing him that he was under investigation and that he had to go to Yerevan for an interrogation.

Mirza Jalil was astounded, because he had not written anything offensive about the person of the mayor. We did not know what to do and what action to take. We were afraid that after the interrogation he would be arrested. Therefore, I suggested that I accompany him and if need be I would bail him out. He said, "last year I published a poem by the poet Haji Agha Faqir in the Journal and that is why they have called me."

This was a poem that Mirza Jalil had recited for us as a song last year. The content of the poem was like this:[36] A poor Kurdish woman, beautiful Fati, made a beautiful horse blanket and gave it to her husband Shamovu to take to town to sell and to

---

35. Yusef Bey Taherov was an intellectual, who was closely associated with the activities of the Charitable Societies of Tiflis.

36. For the text of the poem, see Faqir Ordubadi, *Aghlar Qalam Alimda*, Baku 1989, p. 161 (*Hekayat-e javanmard-e Kurd*).

Woman's burden (no. 28, yr. 3, 14 July 1908)

buy necessary things for the children. However, as much as he tried and went around the bazaar he could not sell it. Eventually he took it to the mayor's office hoping that he would give more money than it was worth and he gave it as a present to the mayor. The latter three times told him: *Khorosho* (Good), and, one time *Molodoz* (Bravo). Shamovu dejectedly returned home and tells Fati that nobody bought that horse blanket, but "I gave it to the mayor and he in return gave me three *Khoroshos* and one *Molodoz.*"

Mirza Jalil told the investigator that he had not written the poem. The poem was written by a poet called Faqir ten years earlier and had nothing to do with the mayor of the city. After giving assurances that he would publish a full explanation in the press Mirza Jalil was allowed to go.[37]

The journal *Molla Nasreddin* was supervised by the departments concerned. A letter dated 1 September 1908 no. 7526 states: "The office, in accordance with the request of the governor, asks you to send the ten last issues of the journal *Molla Nasreddin*, which is published in the Tatar language in Tiflis. After the committee has examined them the issues that are not needed will be returned to you." After having examined these ten issues it seems that Lozino-Lozinski had suggested to leave publications in Turkish alone. When they returned the issues of the journal *Molla Nasreddin* the Press Committee in a letter dated 13 September 1908, no. 7790, wrote that the viceroy of the Caucasus orders that henceforth it should not publish anything critical of the king of Iran.

It was said about the periodicals of the Caucasus: "*Molla Nasreddin* is a humorous and satirical weekly journal published in the Tatar language in Tiflis. Its editor and owner Jalil

Mamadqulizadeh has completed the seminary courses. The journal has a run of 2,000 to 3,000 issues. Sometimes you see very nice illustrations in the journal. In its pages backwardness and conservatism of the Moslem society is constantly satirized. The clerics are seriously satirized. Polygamy and the suffering of women are humorously criticized. The journal can be rated as middle-of-the-road liberal. In rare cases it touches upon internal politics. If it touches political subjects, it does so very carefully. Of late, the barb of his satire is aimed at the shah in particular. But now, after having given a warning to him, he does not deal with the Iranian situation in a scathing manner. It is the third year that he publishes *Molla Nasreddin* and among the Moslems of Russia it has raised a great interest.

In the winter of 1908 the Women's and the Men's Charitable Society organized a joint concert at the Hall of the Actors' Society for fund-raising purposes. Beforehand, invitations were sent to the notables of the various cities. In Baku, Haji Zeyn al-Abedin Taqiyev had received an invitation and sent 1,000 manat. The wife of Vorontsov[38] had come to the concert and gave a few hundred manat. This was the first concert to be organized by the Moslem Women's Charitable Society and many young men had come even from other cities. Usually, Mirza Jalil did not want to go to ostentatious concerts and parties, but even he came. The concert took place with considerable success and in total 10,000 manat was collected.

About that time the drama society of Azerbaijan was properly established and I presented a complete set of Qarabagh women's silk-cotton (*atlas*) clothes to the society.

In the winter of the same year we organized several plays and concerts for charitable purposes. I was assistant to the president and actively involved

---

37. The poem called 'Fati' by Haji Agha Faqir was published in *Molla Nasreddin* on 10 October 1907, no. 34. On 23 December 1907 in no. 48, Mirza Jalil explained that the mayor concerned was not the current mayor.

38. Count Illarion Ivanovich Vorontsov-Dashkov (1837–1916) was a Russian official and from 1905 to 1915 was the viceroy of the Caucasus.

and had no time to take care of house work. Mirza Jalil energetically took care of the household chores; he ordered lunch, gave money to the cook, and looked after the accounts. He was a spendthrift. For him every kopeck had its own value. He always warned me against excessive spending.

At that time he was busy writing the play "The Dead." Many years later he told me that he had not made up the story of the Sheikh bringing the dead back to life. In the past, in the town of Yerevan such an incident had occurred. Old people had told him of that and the models of the characters that are portrayed in the play may be found in Nakhchivan.

* * *

March 1908 was approaching. Mirza Jalil very much liked the festival of Nowruz; it is the beginning the year. Some people want to associate this festival with religion, but this is not so. This festival has remained from the time of idol worshippers. This is the time when night and day are equal and nature awakens from the sleep of winter. A similar festival exists among the people of Russia. The Russians call theirs the Ivan Kupala festival.[39]

He made preparations for Nowruz and would say that his father would buy new clothes for the children, prepare sweetmeats, and celebrated Nowruz with much fanfare. Mirza Jalil would buy presents for his relatives, brother, and close friends and would display a colorful table arrangement. I was pregnant. The house being small, I decided to go to the Sobestianski hospital. On 18 March at 3 o'clock in the morning Mirza Jalil took me to the hospital. The next morning at 11 o'clock Mirza Jalil was informed that he had a son and he came to the hospital. His joy had no limit; he was sitting on a stool and was looking with astonishment at

با کوره حاجی جواد مسجدینك ، ملا یحجلوایین .

Baku Molla (no. 5, yr. 3, 3 Feb 1908)

the baby. After 10 days he took us home. Mirza Jalil liked the baby dearly and he himself took care of him. He even bathed him himself. Mirza Ali Akbar [his brother] had come from Nakhchivan.

---

39. A summer solstice festival is celebrated on the night of 6/7 July.

Sakineh [his sister] was 23 years old and she was a very beautiful and quiet-natured lady and at that time had two children. Her son Jalal was three year's old and Teymur was only ten-months old. Mirza Ali Akbar was about 35 years old and later in southern Azerbaijan he became one of the famous revolutionaries[40] and fought alongside Sattar Khan and spent seven years of his life in several prisons. Mirza Jalil told us that at one time Mirza Ali Akbar was arrested and handed over to the Russians who chained him and put him in a cart. Together with 100 Cossacks they sent him to Nakhchivan. While on the road, a French traveler saw this happening and asked who he was and drew a picture of him and wrote his name in notebook.

Mirza Ali Akbar knew Azeri and Persian very well. He was humorous, funny, quick-witted, pleasant and good-natured. He played the *tar* very well and sang. Mirza Ali Akbar was an active man and before long he returned to Nakhchivan, but Sakineh stayed with us until wintertime.

At one time Mirza Jalil took Sakineh and her children for a walk to the cable railway.[41] He returned very agitated and said that he would never go with Sakineh anywhere. She was dressed in the clothes of the Nakhchivan women and went without a veil at the wish of her brother. People were drawn to her by her appearance, and in groups kept following her. After this incident we made modern clothes for her. Sakineh when talking about the life of her brother said: "In all his marriages my brother was very lucky. His first and second wives were very good women, they loved him from the bottom of their heart. But my brother never appreciated how fortunate he was. He made these women unhappy."

---

40. Mirza Ali Akbar is one of the characters in the novel by Mohammad Sa`id Ordubadi, *Dumanli Tabriz*.

41. In 1900 the city government of Tiflis commissioned the Belgian engineer Alphonse Roby to construct a funicular. The 500 meters long line was opened in March 1905.

* * *

I received a telegram from Kahrizli from Muzaffar. He said that there had been a quarrel about the harvest between my cousins and they even wanted to kill each other and they were asking me to come immediately. I was not yet completely recovered from childbirth. At the end of April 1908 I took the baby with the wet nurse and went to Kahrizli.

After I was able to make peace between my cousins I began taking care of the unresolved affairs of the farm; I began planting cotton and other crops as well. After having taking care of all these things I returned to Tiflis at the end of June. My daughter Mina had gone to Abbastumani[42] to stay with her friends and I wanted to go there and rest during summer. I asked Mirza Jalil to come with me. He said that he had work that could not be put off till later and did not come. At this time he was working on "The Dead." But he said that he would accompany us until the village of Akara near Akhaltsikh where Fayeq Efendi was living. I took my son Midhat and the wet nurse and by the Borzhom road we went to Akara and we were the guests of Fayeq Efendi for one week. The late mother of Fayeq Efendi whose name also was Hamideh received us with great hospitality. Their house was next to the fast running river Kur on a beautiful spot. The house was surrounded by fruit orchards. Mirza Jalil was very happy with the garden, the fruits and especially the pomegranates with big seeds pleased him. He spent much of his time resting and playing with his son. After resting one week Mirza Jalil returned to Tiflis and we went via the Akhaltsikh road to Abbastumani.

At the end of August we returned to Tiflis and I went to Kahrizli. My daughter Mina entered the advanced course for women, which had recently opened. In 1908, Mirza Jalil did not go to the village

---

42. Abbastumani is a health spa in Georgia.

Nowruz in the household of the poor and the rich: "Father, the neighbor's kids have new clothes. They say it is Nowruz, where are our clothes?"
(no. 10, yr. 6, 5 Sept 1911)

to rest. He stayed in Tiflis and regularly published the journal and he managed to send the annual 52 issues to its subscribers.

In the 1909 year, the number of subscribers of the journal had increased somewhat. It seems that this was as a result of the caricatures and the satirical articles, which were written about the reactionaries of Turkey, Iran and Baku. The governments of Turkey and Iran had strictly forbidden the entry of the journal. It was suggested to Mirza Jalil that he should accept ads of such things as gramophones, boots, and other items. Since he was against such things he would not consent. Later, because of the financial situation he was forced to accept them. As at this time the number of subscribers had decreased and the financial situation of the journal had deteriorated.

For a long time I wanted to start a co-ed school in Kahrizli. The school building was already constructed. Mirza Jalil liked my idea and to make it happen he went to work. He called the carpenter Tiqur and ordered 20 desks and the blackboard, which he painted with oil color (Mirza Jalil liked colors and whatever needed painting he did). Then he called a meeting and convinced the villagers and their wives to send their children to the school. The villagers respected me and believed in me. Therefore, some of them consented to send their daughters to the school, but some did not do so, because the daughters were looking after the babies at home. My relatives thankfully agreed to send their daughters to the school.

In the beginning 30 boys and 10 girls came to the school. Mirza Jalil himself and my late daughter Mina were teaching them. Later we invited from Georgia, a teacher called Khomaladze. Apart from his salary we provided him with food, beverages, and a house. The Azeri language was taught by Mirza Safi Akhundov. The next year we invited Salman Bey Alibeyov[43] and made him the Azeri

Border closed: *Molla Nasreddin* not allowed into Iran (no. 8, yr. 1, 26 May 1906)

teacher (in secret Salman Bey was a Bolshevik. I had a picture of him and the horticulturist Sharashidze together with the students outside the village). In general, I helped as much as I could whoever in the village was in need, I treated them free of charge, gave free medicines and other things. We would give the poor children clothes and shoes.

Mirza Jalil and I decided to manage the orchards in a scientific manner. An agricultural specialist in the *Vorozhdenie* (Revival) journal had put an ad and

---

43. Salman Bey Alibeyov (1877-1919) was a village

teacher, active revolutionary, and because of his revolutionary ideas he was expelled before finishing the Gori Seminar. In the 1905 revolution he was the leader of the revolutionary activities in the Javanshir district of Qarabagh. Especially between 1917 and 1919 he was very active as a revolutionary. In 1919 he was killed by the Beys of Sarija (Sheki).

offered his services. We invited him to Kahrizli and fixed a salary of 25 manat per month for him. His name was David Gitoyevich Sharashidze; he had a saintly face, was very polite and a scientific person. We wondered why he wanted to come and work in a remote village for a wage of only 25 manat. Later we found out that he was a revolutionary. In Iran he had participated in the Revolution and he was sent to the London Conference as the representative of Georgia. You would not believe that he and his family were hiding in our village.

Shariashidze had a positive effect on the villagers, everybody loved him. He learnt the Azeri language well and talked to the villagers and he did not spare any effort to help them with cultivation. During his five-year's stay he made our old orchard thrive. He prepared a piece of land to start a new orchard and ordered a few hundred saplings to be planted. But due to the negligence of the mail these saplings remained in Yevlakh[44] where they dried and became useless. Later, Mirza Jalil and Fayeq Efendi went to Gori and brought a few hundred saplings for the orchard. I still have the letters that he sent from Tiflis concerning this matter.

The following year we ordered a few types of apples, pears, and apricots from Rostov and brought them. Mirza Jalil's uncle, Alishdani Kishi, sent good varieties of fruit trees from Nakhchivan. These saplings started very well in our orchard and came to fruition quite well. From the saplings that we brought we gave some to the villagers.

Mirza Jalil liked working in the orchard and looking after the trees and he paid special attention to the ones sent by his uncle, which he liked very much. One day, when he was in a very good mood, he told me: "When I come to Kahrizli and I see the rows of the poplars and recognize our farm my heart starts beating out of joy and I ask the carriage driver to go fast so that I can get sooner

to my own family, my dear friends and relatives. I only feel happy here in this quiet corner of nature. The beautiful springs in these places, its enchanting moonlit nights, its shady gardens, the fragrance of the flowers, the song of the nightingales, the song of other birds, and the beautiful sound of the shepherd's reed, which is heard everywhere settles my tired nerves and gives wings to my thoughts. After I am done with the journal, then I want to spend my last years in this quiet corner. ..."

Mirza Jalil also liked to play the *kamancheh* and the flute. I remember, one day, the daughter of Kerbela'i Ja`far, one of the village notables, was getting married. Our whole family went there. Mirza Jalil's brother, Mirza Ali Akbar was with us. The people in the wedding had heard that he had a good voice and asked him to sing. Mirza Ali Akbar did not refuse. At that time, Mirza Jalil went to the musicians and got the flute of one of them and replaced him and he began to accompany them in a lower key. While he was playing the flute he made his cheeks swell up so much that the people were amazed. I understood why he was doing this and I especially begged Mirza Ali Akbar to sing. Mirza Ali Akbar smiled and got up and sat next to his brother and took the dulcimer and began singing. In this way we were able to enjoy his beautiful voice.

In 1903 there was an incredibly horrifying smallpox epidemic and this illness caused mass fatalities. Many children and young people died and the people who survived were mostly blind or disfigured. The government did nothing. In a space that covered hundreds of kilometers there was not a single physician or health worker. Most of the people did not know that children could be saved by inoculation. I decided to learn how to inoculate. I went to Tiflis and learnt it from physician B.N. Aghabeyov whom I knew and acquired a sufficient amount of the necessary medicine and returned to Kahrizli. I obtained a large amount of lymph nodes from the veterinarian, who lived in Prozorovski

---

44. Yevlakh a town in the republic of Azerbaijan, 265 km, west of Baku.

Street. I believed that I was going to save the children from this dreadful disease, but after returning to the village I witnessed a very strange scene. The villagers were not allowing their children to be inoculated. Was it because of ignorance, or what it intentionally? Somebody had spread the rumor that I wanted to start a new disease among the children. All my begging and supplications had no result. I was horrified. At last a lady who liked me very much, brought her daughter called Asiyah to me and she said: "I believe in you. Take her. Whatever you know, do to her. Either save her or let her die." I inoculated the child.

A few days after this, the physician Karim Bey Mehmandarov, by chance was passing through our village and was going to Aghjabadi for an autopsy. I showed him the place of inoculation of Asiyah and he said that it had taken very beautifully and the child was saved. After this the children were brought from other villages to me for inoculation. Of course, I did not ask for money, and, in a notebook, I wrote down the name and age of the children and where they were coming from.

From this time on every spring I would order special medicine and would inoculate the children. At last, the number of people who wanted to be inoculated became so large that I could no longer cope. Later, I did the same for villagers living 50-60 werst away, who would come to us. Therefore, I taught the skill of inoculation to some of my relatives. Among them were Mirza Jalil and his brother Mirza Ali Akbar. As much as we could, we tried to treat other diseases as well. We always needed quinine and other medicines. Doctor Mehmandarov encouraged me and taught me the treatment of other illnesses. I read a number of medical books and I had a small pharmacy in my house. When I was living in Poland I had learnt to treat some illnesses with herbs. There, I also had medical books and a small pharmacy.[45] After the

Revolution these books were lost. When Mirza Jalil was going to Moscow and other cities to propagate the new Latin alphabet he brought me a medical book and he had written on it the following words: "A gift from *Molla Nasreddin* to Hamideh Khanum, who has treated the villagers all her life. Moscow, 22 October 1924." I still have this book.

In the summer of 1910, I went to Khankandi with the family. We were resting in the house of Markar Shikhiev. Mirza Jalil with his daughter Munavvar joined us in July. We went around Khankandi to walk and all day we were walking and amusing ourselves. Mira Jalil was very happy and pleased with the relaxation. Every day he would go with the children and other youths known to him to swim near Agha Bridge. Once, between two rocks he was caught in a current and almost drowned. A young man called Shirinbeyov dashed into the water and somehow saved Mirza Jalil. That young man is now an engineer and lives in Moscow. That day when Mirza Jalil came home he was pale and dejected and after that he never returned to that spot to swim.

Once we decided to go on an outing on horseback and we left to go for a picnic to Malbeyli village. We had heard it had good minstrels and Mirza Jalil wanted to listen to them. Qahraman Shirinbeyov, as well as an Armenian who was working as prosecutor there and my daughter Mina were with us. Near the village of Khanbagheh when we were on a slope my horse suddenly bolted, I don't know why. Since we had rented the horse I did not know its character. In spite of my efforts the horse, which was an English breed, was galloping like a bullet and those behind me were racing to reach me and they were shouting. At this time I remembered that one had to pull one side of the horse's bridle and I did that and the horse stopped immediately; it tried to throw me up into the air, but I held on to the saddle.

45. From 1893 to 1899, Hamideh Khanum and her first husband lived in the Polish city of Brest-Litovsk.

Molla Shokr Ali after destroying the girls school in Baku: "I did a good job!" (no. 6, yr. 6, 20 Feb 1911)

The first to reach me was Mirza Jalil; he was extremely pale and nervous. After that he did not allow me to ride on the same horse and therefore, we exchanged horses.

Malbeyli village was on the slope of the mountain in a very beautiful place, one could say that nearly all of the village men were in the business of cart driving. The women were weaving beautiful rugs. Our arrival astonished the people and roused their interest. When they saw the prosecutor who was with us they thought that we had come for a judicial case. They immediately surrounded us and the people around us were mostly women and children. The village chief welcomed us and took us to his house. The notables of the villages also came with us. Someone from our group said that *Molla Nasreddin* was here and he pointed at Mirza Jalil and everybody stared at him. The men started whispering among themselves. Mirza Jalil inquired whether the minstrels could come. At this time the villagers agitatedly looked at each other and they sent somebody to call them and again they started whispering. We waited long but the minstrels did not come. We had tea, we talked about the school, and about this and that, but there was still no sign of the minstrels. The minstrels believed that Mulla wanted to trick and ensnare them and then to draw their picture and print them in the magazine (they were very afraid of caricatures). Therefore, they had hidden the minstrels and said that they were not in the village.

The common people were very scared of the pictures of *Molla Nasreddin*. In spite of behaving very cautiously their village was not spared from the view of the Mulla, and at that time (7 February 1911, no. 6) he printed a satirical cartoon of the village's Mulla sitting backwards on a donkey. Also, his opposition to the opening of the girls' school was made fun of. It seems that this was another reason why the villagers were wary of *Molla Nasreddin*.

* * *

In the spring of 1910 we were living in Tiflis. I heard that our talented poet Saber was very sick. Mirza Jalil wrote a letter to him and asked him to come to Tiflis for treatment. Saber came and we gathered all around him and we did our best to get him treated. Saber was a very saintly-looking and affectionate man. We all were fascinated by his wit. Sometimes he would share the poems that he composed extemporaneously and he would comment on them. He would say that his mother was a very religious woman, she liked to go on pilgrimage and her sons to please her would go with her, one each time, to Karbala or Mashhad. In this way Saber had gone 7 or 8 times on pilgrimage. Therefore, in Shamakhi she was looked upon as if she were a holy person like the daughter of the prophet, Fatima Zahra.

Saber said that his wife had given birth to seven daughters one after the other and all of them in the month of Ramazan. This had become for his mother a source of great grief. She had vowed to stop this calamity and that she would go on another pilgrimage. After seven daughters Saber's wife had given birth to a son and it so happened that the son was also born in the month of Ramazan. The son who was born after seven daughters became a source of delight for Saber's mother and the whole family.

Saber loved tea and he drank it strong and hot; once, because of some event, his tea came late. For this reason Saber immediately extemporaneously this poem:

Mulla, samavarindan derda, hazar derda
Bir istikani indi, bir istikani farda

O Mulla, on your samovar sorrow and thousand
   times sorrow
One glass today and one glass tomorrow.

Mirza Jalil called the physicians for a consultation; they found that Saber had a kidney stone and
they thought that to remove it they would have to
operate on him. However hard we tried, Saber did
not agree. Perhaps he did not believe the physicians or he was afraid of the operation. After two
months living with us, with great sadness we bade
him farewell.[46]

In October 1910 Mirza Jalil came to the village
and told me that his brother Mirza Ali Akbar had
been arrested because of his revolutionary activities and that he had been in jail for the last six
months. His case would be heard in the court of
Yerevan. If he was not going to be hanged he would
be condemned to hard labor.

Mirza Jalil was horrified and said that he could
not stand such a great pain. If they would send
his brother to Siberia he would follow him there.
His state of mind affected me greatly. To obtain
the freedom of the prisoner we had to hire two
well-known lawyers and somehow I got 1,200
manat together and gave it to Mirza Jalil. He went
to Yerevan and hired two lawyers. One of these
was one of the most well-known lawyers, Malik
Aqamalov. The lawyers delayed the trial until
spring.

Mirza Jalil returned to the village; he was sick
and his back and left foot hurt. At the advice of the
physicians, I rubbed a medicine on them and put
his feet in hot water. However, this did not help; he
was in pain and became thinner and looked older.

---

46. Mirza Ali Akbar Saber (Taherzadeh) was a famous
satirical poet (30 May 1862– 12 July 1911). For more
information, see Appendix III.

We had a craftsman whose name was Grigor and
Mirza Jalil was very dear to him. He went to his
village and brought for us essence of mulberry,
which was mixed with red pepper. Twice we would
rub this on his foot and to keep it warm we would
wrap it. Before long Mirza Jalil regained his health
and after one month he had totally recovered and
was completely healthy and returned to Tiflis to
look after the affairs of the journal, which had been
neglected for a long time.

In 1910 we were expecting a good cotton
harvest; this year there was no locust, no drought
and no blight. For planting cotton we did not have
enough land of our own. I leased different plots
from neighboring farmers on the condition that I
provided seed and water which I gave to be planted.
I should mention that since I was a woman the
landowners would not lease me the plots. In spite
of not having water the land would be left arid and
of no use. I was very angry because of this. I had
spent much time on this. Then they changed their
minds and I could rent. For this reason, the cotton
plots were in different and faraway places. To look
after the crop and to reap it on time and to bring
it home we needed reliable people. Meanwhile, I
wrote a letter to Mirza Jalil and, with the help of
his Georgian friends, he found some people and
send them to Kahrizli. They were very honest and
happy campers. With the help of these Georgians
that Mirza Jalil had sent, we gathered the crop on
time and collected it without any loss. One of them,
whose name was Lavrenti Qogeliya became very
attached to our family. He lived for a long time
in our place and even in the year 1922 he came
from Tiflis to Kahrizli and helped us repairing our
house and mill. Another man lived for a while in
our house, Pavel Mjivanadze, and later on married
the teacher of the school, Olga Alexievna Kolakova;
she was a revolutionary and had been imprisoned
in Kazan. Later she escaped with someone else's
passport and had come to Tiflis. There she became
known as Sharashidze. She talked to me and to
avert the attention of the government officials, she

Ashura in Mashqata village near Baku (no. 5, yr. 4, 1 Feb 1909)

asked me to find a job for her in the village. At my recommendation she found a job for a while as a teacher[47] in the family of Mir Jabbar Aqamirov.[48] After that she came to us and asked for employment with us. She helped me for a while with my work on the farm. She was a very intelligent and able woman; she was so afraid of imprisonment that later when she saw the inspector and other officials she became agitated.

Kolakova did not hide her past from me. She became familiar with village life and she even learned to speak the Azeri language. For a few years she was the teacher in the school and she was also the administrator of the mill, and later she married Pavel Mjivanadze. Their wedding took place in our

house. Later she became very familiar with my farm work and even when I was not there she would manage it.

David Gitoyevich Sharashidze kept a regular diary. He recorded the changes in the weather, and wrote some articles in the Georgian press about our village life. Some of the neighboring Beys did not like what I was doing. Sometimes, there were disputes between us about the plots and they conspired to have one Bey oppose me. He sent a telegram to the mayor of Ganjeh, whose name was Kovalyov, saying: "the husband of Hamideh Khanum, Mirza Jalil Mamadqulizadeh incites our peasants and raises agricultural issues. We ask you to take steps."

Mayor Kovalyov, who later became governor, told me that he used to receive telegrams from the hostile Beys concerning me with similar contents,

47. Vazir instead of 'teacher' has "wet nurse."

48. Mir Jabbar Aqamirov was the son of the poetess Khorshidbanu Natavan and Sayyed Hoseyn.

but since he knew my good work he did not interfere.

The Beys also were inciting my family against me, who would not hesitate to create all kinds of problems for me. For example, we had planted Tehrani vines near our house. I had received them from the agricultural engineer and wine maker, Pirim Pirimov. The vines grew very well. Mirza Jalil and I were very delighted and we thought that in one or two years this type of grape, which was very rare in our parts, would produce fruit. One night the neighboring Bey had taken away the fence and sent his cattle and as a result the young vines were completely destroyed.

In general, the neighboring Beys did not spare any efforts to destroy our farm, gardens and orchards. No fence, no obstacle would stop these bipedal animals.

In those days Samad Aqamali-oghlu who worked as a land assessor in Qarabagh lived for two months in our house. When he found out about what these ill-wishers had done to me he thought it would be best that I should sell everything and go to the city. If I had not promised my late father to manage his farm I would have done so. Once in the journal *Molla Nasreddin* a critical cartoon concerning the ceremony of Ashura was published. This cartoon enraged the Moslems, especially the people of Hindarkh village. Some trustworthy people told me that the people of Hindarkh had sworn in their mosque that they were going to kill Mirza Jalil. Usually, Mirza Jalil going to Yevlakh would pass Hindarkh and the woods of Soltanbud, which was the place of brigands and smugglers.

At this time Mirza Jalil was in the village with me, but he had to return to Tiflis shortly. I accompanied him to Yevlakh personally and to guard against all possibilities I took a rifleman with us. We safely saw Mirza Jalil off from Yevlakh.

In March 1911, I went to Tiflis; my daughter was getting ready to marry. I was preparing a dowry for her and I also had this idea to buy a small house with garden and give it to the journal *Molla Nasreddin* so that we would be free from space problems. Jalil liked this idea and would occasionally go and look for houses. We were looking for a house that would be cheap and with a mortgage at the same time. Apart from the office for the editorial staff we wanted to have an office for Mirza Jalil. He liked to work alone; the slightest noise would make him nervous and make him stop working.

* * *

7 April 1911 was the fifth anniversary of the publication of *Molla Nasreddin*. I remember in the years 1907 and 1908 many people tried to boycott the journal and tried to have it closed down. Mirza Jalil would tell me: "If the journal is allowed to be published at least for five years I would have no grief in the world."

On the day of the fifth jubilee I bought a wall clock for the journal and when Mirza Jalil was absent I hung it on the wall. When he entered and heard the tick-tock of the clock he was amazed. Mirza Jalil was sleeping in the same room. The next day when I entered the room I saw that Mirza Jalil had wrapped a cloth around the clock hammer. He had put a handkerchief around it. I asked the reason for it and he said the tick-tock and the bell of the clock made him nervous and did not allow him to sleep or work. I was sorry and took the clock down and hung it on the wall of the dining area of the office. I still have this clock.

Mirza Jalil particularly liked Oriental and minstrel music. He was especially friends with the minstrels of Gulabli, Najafquli and Abbasquli. We invited these minstrels to our daughter's wedding and they came to Tiflis, but when I was getting married to Mirza Jalil, since we were against any kind of elaborate ceremony, we did not have anything special. In those days Moslems were getting ready to celebrate the jubilee of the late dramatist Fath Ali Akhundov and Mirza Jalil was actively involved in this. The jubilee's ceremony was going to be in Dvortsov Street in Bankovski Theater. At the invitation of Mirza Jalil the minstrels performed in the ceremony and they were a great success and they received a substantial amount of money. The minstrels also sang for us in the evening in our house, and the next day they left.

In the early days of June I thought I was going to give birth, so I could not go to the Cadaster Office. Therefore, in my place Mirza Jalil, around 20 April, accompanied by the little and lovable Midhat, we went to the village. The first of May I became very ill, it was frightening, and I was going to have an operation. I sent a telegram to Mirza Jalil and asked him to come back. He managed to get back to me on 11 May and it was on the same day that my son was born. I was very ill, and they were even afraid to take me to the hospital. So it was on 13 May that the best surgeons of Tiflis gathered in our house and had a consultation. My situation was so bad that they could not move me to the hospital and that is why, led by the surgeon Kimont, they operated on me in the house. After the operation my fever came down, but my blood was poisoned. After consultation, the physicians agreed on a second operation. Because my heart was weak they decided to do it without anesthetics. I called Jalil and made my testament. At this time he was crying and could not speak to me, he was just holding my hand. He sent a telegram sending for my relatives, the manager of my property Karbala'i Ja`far and the notables. They came and said farewell to me. I asked Mirza Jalil to look after my children.

The surgeon Kimont operated me for a second time; I passed through incredibly dark minutes, but again my fever came down. In those days Mirza Jalil received a telegram in the first days of July that the illness of our great poet Saber had become critical, and on the 12th of July a telegram came that the poet had passed away. This tragic news had a devastating impact on Mirza Jalil and my condition was

gradually getting worse. The physicians thought it better that I should be taken to the summer quarters in the Baku area. They thought that the cypress woods and the cool air there would be beneficial for me. In those days of sickness midwife Tokhadze was looking after me. She loved me very much and she was like one of my family. Mirza Jalil paid her wages with a special arrangement. He and the midwife took me on a cart to the train station. From there we went to the summer quarters of Baku. Here we found a suitable place which accommodated me and he entrusted me to Tokhadze and returned to Tiflis. In the Baku region we learned that at 7 km distance from there, in the village of Chikhijavari there were sulfur baths, and if I would go and bathe in there I would become healthy.

Tokhadze was taking me there twice a week and gave me a bath there. Gradually I was getting better, my fever came down, my appetite improved, and before long I was walking with crutches. We wrote to Mirza Jalil about this and before long he came and brought various gifts, among them was a small gramophone for the children. The Baku region had a beautiful climate. The air was pregnant with the odor of cypress trees, you could breathe easily. Mirza Jalil was feeling extremely well there. He was having a good time and was joking with the children. He especially liked to walk with his bare feet on the grass. Once he was walking bare feet along a swift brook near our house. His 3-year old son Midhat grabbed the gramophone and was able to start it and was playing a record of Azerbaijani dances. As soon as Mirza Jalil heard the music he started dancing and the children began clapping.

The same summer the composer Uzeyr Hajibekov[49] with his family and brother were

---

49. Uzeyr Hajibekov (1885-1945) was one of the leading personalities of 20th-century Azerbaijan and his compositions are well-known. He also played an important role in the development of the Azerbaijani press. He was the editor of *Taraqqi* (1908-09), *Haqiqat* (1909-10), *Yeni Iqbal* (1915-17). He also wrote in other

relaxing in the Baku area. We talked to them and we agreed that we would go together to the woods. One morning we got provisions and we all went to the woods. They put me under a tree. Mirza Jalil liked Mirza Uzeyr greatly and they had many interesting discussions and they were running along with the children and playing with them. First we decided that they were going to prepare lunch and were going to make *bozbash* [a yoghurt meat stew]. They went and gathered firewood and made a fire, they put three stones around it and put the kettle on it. Uzeyr and Mirza Jalil were not going away from the fire. Sometimes they would add wood to the fire and sometimes they would taste the *bozbash*. Mirza Jalil said that never before in his life had he tasted such a tasty *bozbash*. Finally, lunch was ready and the ladies spread a cloth under a cypress tree and they brought bread, vegetables and other things there and called the children. Everybody was hungry and was waiting for the lunch with impatience. At this time, somebody unintentionally, struck the stone of the fire and that delicious *bozbash* fell into the fire.

Mirza Jalil returned to Tiflis. My health was getting better day by day. My fever had come down and I was walking unaided with the help of my crutches. At the beginning of September Mirza Jalil took us to Tiflis to our house. There, I again became very ill. Poor Mirza Jalil was getting tired of looking after me; at last I became better. At the end of September I became well and we went to Kahrizli, because my affairs there were very much neglected. When I was ill we had spent our money for my treatment and the plan for buying a house was totally out of the question.

I forgot to tell that the trial of Ali Akbar, Mirza Jalil's brother was fixed at the end of May at the time that I was ill. Therefore, Mirza Jalil had to leave me and go to Yerevan. As a result of the efforts of the lawyers, the provincial court gave Mirza Ali Akbar

a sentence of only 2 months prison, and because Mirza Jalil put up bail he was freed immediately. They both returned to Tiflis and Mirza Ali Akbar went to live in Kahrizli.

In the summer of 1912, I convinced Mirza Ali Akbar to come with us to Shusha to the summer quarters and spend his 2-months' prison sentence in its prison. Mirza Ali Akbar did not want to go to prison, but with lots of effort I convinced him and put him in a carriage and sent him off. All the time I was afraid that he would leave the carriage and flee. Every day I sent food for him to the prison and asked the physician of the prison to look after his health and treat his ailments.

That same summer Mirza Jalil came to us to relax. I had been sick for a long time and the boycott of the journal had brought the financial affairs of Mirza Jalil to a very dire situation. He was managing them with great difficulty.

* * *

Mirza Jalil once told me about himself, "I have not been created for family life, I am essentially a dervish-like person. I have a difficult character. I am nervous. I confess that living with me is difficult. I don't have the patience to raise the children. You have made me a family man."

One time he told me the following about his life in Nakhchivan. "It was 1898; I was still living in Nakhchivan. My daughter Munavvar was one year old. I was busy with serious work. Since her mother was sick there was nobody to look after the child.[50] I left my work and I was trying to console the child, but whatever I tried I could not make her be quiet. I became so agitated that I almost threw her into a well. Later I was shocked and would tell myself, what was the fault of that little child that I was so angry with her?"

periodicals and published his articles under no less than 66 pseudonyms.

50. At that time Munavvar's mother died.

Mirza Jalil was a very well-intentioned person. He would give his last piece of bread to somebody else. He was mostly absorbed in thought and he was very pensive most of the time. He would focus his eyes on one point and the slightest movement or noise would upset him. When eating, if someone was eating noisily, if the person was a friend he would criticize him, if he was not close then he would find an excuse and quietly leave to another room. He was very sensitive to noises and smells. He would immediately notice the slightest steam from the stove or samovar and this would give him a headache. He could not tolerate untidy persons. He heard the whisper in the next room. He was very cautious and suspicious and would not easily trust someone. He always wanted the door of the room in which he was sleeping to be open.

In the summer of 1912 we rented a house in the Armenian quarter of Shusha in the house of Daniel Beyov. I had not yet completely recovered, the children, especially the poor new born, were sick. At the advice of the physicians I took the children and went for two weeks to Tursh-Su (the mineral water spring).[51] From there we went to Kechel Dagh in the waters rich in iron. It had wonderful water to swim in and its beautiful nature and climate would resurrect the dead. My poor son who was very sickly improved and became well in this climate. We were all astonished. After we returned to Shusha our neighbors amazed when they saw the child. So far he remains very healthy. I myself also became very well. There I met the teachers the late Farhad Aghazadeh[52] and Yusef Aliev[53] and we became friends. We returned from Shusha in the first days of August. When I was there I received from Vatatsi, the governor's assistant, an official letter with a survey related to cotton cultivation and with the request to fill it out and send it back. I wrote down all the answers to the questions and sent it. After a while, I was invited to a conference of cotton farmers, which was going to take place in the fall of that year. According to the letter of invitation, I had to write my paper first and send it and had to explain my ideas about the expansion of cotton cultivation in our province. I wrote a detailed letter and was waiting for Mirza Jalil to come. First, he looked at my letter with a measure of disbelief and did not want to read it, and said: "Oh man, does a woman write a conference paper?"[54] I did not understand whether he was joking or whether he was serious, but later when he was in good humor he read it and in the habit of editors said, "this is too long" and shortened it in some places. But after the conference he accepted that he had shortened it inappropriately.

Later I rewrote it again and sent it, and when the conference time was approaching I myself went to Tiflis. Mirza Jalil stayed in the village and was resting and taking care of farming issues.

In the conference, Vatatsi, the head of the cotton cultivation office, suggested that I read the paper myself. During the break one of the young Beys asked me, "Are you going to read the paper? Do you have such courage?"

---

51. Vazir has here Istisu or sulphur spring.

52. Farhad Aghazadeh Sharqli (1882-1931) was a scholar, a very famous teacher, and a Methodist. He graduated in 1900 from Gory Seminar, came to Baku and for 30 years he worked as a teacher. He was one of the organizers of the first and second Congress of Azerbaijani teachers in 1906 and 1907 and he was one of the ardent supporters of the change of alphabet to the Latin alphabet and he wrote a number of works about this. He also wrote a book on the importance of the *journal of Akinchi* (the Farmer), the first newspaper entirely printed in Azeri as well as the first newspaper in Russia printed in a Turkic language..

53. Yusef Adishirin-oghlu Aliev (1888-1966) was a well-known teacher and author of dictionaries. He graduated from Gory Seminar in 1907 and became a teacher in Baku and wrote various books for students. During the Soviet era he did remarkable work in the area of compiling dictionaries and he participated in the editing of Russian-Azeri dictionaries.

54. These words were in Azeri in the original text.

"Women, know your place." *Left*: "Lady, where are you going?" "I am going to the lamentation gathering"
Right: "An educated Moslem girl with her diploma" (no. 22, yr. 9, 19 Feb 1914)

They could not imagine that a Moslem woman, especially in such a big conference would get up to the speaker's chair and read her paper.

The conference was taking place in the big hall of the actors' society. The elected members of the Transcaucasian officials and landowners were participating in this conference and the number of participants was about 500. Without hesitation and without losing my composure I read my paper successfully and they clapped for me. When we came to the salon a high official who had a white beard came to me and shook my hand, and said: "Finally I witnessed an educated Moslem woman

participating in social life and I am happy from the bottom of heart."[55]

After the conference Vatatsi also praised my paper and invited me to the reception. I thanked him, but I could not go to the reception. In the conference there was another female participant, an Armenian lady who talked about the water to the Kur and the dry lands of Van, but she did not read her paper. The contributions to this conference

---

55. For the translation of the paper of Hamideh Khanum, see Annex 1.

were published in a book titled *The Thirteenth Conference of Cotton Farmers*.

Mirza Jalil after reading newspaper accounts of my presentation in the conference wrote a very passionate letter to me and in the letter he called me "the brave one."

* * *

After my serious illness I had not recovered completely. At this time an unfortunate incident was added to my property affairs. It seems that a piece of land that apparently was mine originally had belonged to a certain unknown person, Hamid Bey Qasem-oghlu, with a loan of 1,900 manat, which was in my name. This was wrong. However, I wrote to the inspector of the loan office of the municipality of Nakhchivan, but nothing came of it. The local officials were asking for the payment of the loan or else they threatened to sell my property to get the money.

Finally, I received an extension from the government, and in spite of my illness, taking my female ward Manya, went to Yerevan where the office was. The director of the loan office, Lesnyak had seen me in the conference and he knew me from there. At his order thick books were brought and they looked in them. It became clear that there was a property under the name of Hamid Bey Qasem-oghlu, but after his death his neighbors divided it among themselves. It seems that the officials of the loan office had seen that my name was similar to his. They crossed out his name in red ink and instead had written my name Hamideh Khanum, daughter of Ahmad Bey. The director ordered this mistake to be corrected and I breathed a sigh of relief and returned to Kahrizli. Mirza Jalil went to Tiflis to pursue the affairs of the journal.

* * *

On 13 January 1913 when I was living with the family in the village I again became very ill. I sent a telegram to Mirza Jalil and asked him to come. At that time the journal's state of affairs was not very good and in fact he wasn't too concerned about my case. However, he came to the village and called a physician from Aghdam. The doctor A. Eritsyan told us that my case was serious and advised us to take me for treatment to Aghdam. In Aghdam he gave us two rooms in his own house and started treating me.

Mirza Jalil willy-nilly had to remain. Sometimes he stayed with me in this family of strangers and sometimes he went to the village to look after our property. At that time his brother Mirza Ali Akbar was living in Kahrizli and was helping us.

March came, but my fever was not going down and my situation was getting worse. At this time we received a letter from Mirza Jalil's sister Sakineh in Nakhchivan that after being afflicted with tuberculosis she was spitting blood and asked that her brothers came to see her.

My illness became very serious and in spite of the fact that I had been ill for 3 months my fever was not going down from 40°C (104° F). Poor Mirza Jalil was totally at a loss what to do; he could not leave me with two young children in my sick condition and go to Nakhchivan. He sent his brother Mirza Ali Akbar to Sakineh. The physician Karim Bey Mehmandarov while passing through Aghdam had heard about my sickness and came to see me. After seeing me, he said that I should be taken immediately to Tiflis and to be operated on again. The physician Eritsyan agreed to accompany me to Tiflis. The next day, Mirza Jalil took me and the physician to Tiflis.

We stayed with my late daughter Mina. The famous surgeon Kimont, who had operated on me twice, started treating me. At his advice, Mirza Jalil put me in a private clinic of the Physicians Society in Reutovski Street. My condition was so bad that after getting a letter from Mirza Jalil they accepted me to the clinic. The letter vouched, "If my wife dies, the physicians will not be held responsible for her death."

I was operated on at the end of April 1913. The operation was successful. My foster daughter Manya stayed with me. Mirza Jalil was living with his daughter Munavvar and his two young sons in a rented house in Chavchavadze Street. Every day they would come to see me. One time, Mirza Jalil told me that the police had come to the house at night and had searched; they had taken all his letters as well as other papers; the children were sleeping. The police asked: "Whose children are these. What are their names?"

There was a telegram from Nakhchivan that Sakineh's condition was very bad and they were expecting Mirza Jalil to go there. Mirza Jalil entrusted our children to my daughter Mina. My condition was still critical; my fever would not go down. After two weeks Mirza Jalil returned; he was very depressed. Sakineh was afflicted with a very severe case of tubercolosis. Jalil had brought her 5-year old son Teymur to Tiflis to raise him with his own children.

My condition was gradually improving. Mirza Jalil went to the Baku district to find a house. He was delayed for a few days. I was very anxious and was wondering what might have happened to him en route. On the 31 May we received a telegram that Sakineh had died.

Mirza Jalil came the next day. What had happened was that the Baku train had overturned, which was why Mirza Jalil had been delayed. By the end of June my health improved and I was released from the clinic. A few days later I took the children and went to the village.

To put the affairs of the journal in order Mirza Jalil had to stay in Tiflis. Some time prior to that, he had invited Aliquli Nejefov, whose pen name

was Ghamqusar,[56] to become the second editor of the journal.

Since *Molla Nasreddin* had been banned in Iran and Turkey it was boycotted by the reactionaries and the number of subscribers had dropped significantly and it could not pay for its expenses. Lately, due to my illness, my property had been neglected and as a result we had to borrow money. We had no one close to us to help us and Mirza Jalil was doing all the work himself.

In the summer I took the children and went to Shusha. In the Armenian quarter of the town I rented rooms in the house of D.S. Shakaryan near the Boulevard and the park. I used to sit on the balcony of the house and listen to the music, which would delight me and breathe the fragrance of the flowers.

I was still weak and I was being treated and resting. Many of our friends had come to Shusha to relax. Among them were the writer Abdol-Rahim Bey Haqqverdiov,[57] the composer Uzeyr Hajibeyov,[58] and his brother, Azad Amirov[59] who was a student at the time (now he is a professor),

---

56. Aliquli Najafov Ghamqusar (1880-1919) was one of the most active members of *Molla Nasreddin*. Under different pennames he wrote satirical pieces in prose and poetry. As of February 1913 until 1914 he was the co-editor of the journal *Molla Nasreddin*.

57. Abdol Rahim Bey Haqqverdiov (1870-1933) was a famous playwright and publisher, and he was one of the close associates of the journal *Molla Nasreddin*.

58. Uzeyr Hajibeyov (1885-1948) is a great composer, musical theorist and writer. One of his well-known works was the musical "Koroghlu."

59. Azad Amirov (1889-1939) was one of the most respected educators in Azerbaijan. From the early 1930s to the end of his life he was a professor at the Medical Institute of Azerbaijan.

he had gathered the abovementioned friends and read his play "The Dead" to them.

After a while Mirza Jalil first went to Kahrizli and from there to Tiflis. I took the children and went for treatment to the mineral waters. Uzeyr, his brother, and their nephew, and engineer Aghalar Aliverdiov,[62] and the *tar* player Yusef (who has since them became a physician) came with us.[63] We pitched tents and lived there.

* * *

In the summer of 1913 the intellectual youth in Shusha led by Azad Amirov performed some plays and organized conferences. The proceeds were given to poor pupils and students. At the end of the summer, the physician Mehmandarov invited us and some other friends to the Jidir Plain for an outing. After lunch, in accordance with the old tradition of the poets of Shusha, the men engaged in poetical contests.[64] At the end, the late Abdol

"*Molla Nasreddin* is published again" (no. 1, yr. 8, 27 Jan 1913)

the actor Sarabiski,[60] Ghamqusar's brother Rezaquli Nejefov,[61] and many others would come to see me.

Eventually, Mirza Jalil arrived. I prepared a room for him, so that he could easily work there and receive his friends. His window had a view of flowers and this excited him very much and encouraged him to work. At that time in Shusha

---

60. Hoseynquli Malek-oghlu Sarabiski (1879-1945) was an actor, director, and one of the founders of operatic theater in Azerbaijan.

61. Rezaquli Nejefov (1885-1937) was a writer. In 1913-14, while his elder brother was the second editor of *Molla Nasreddin*, he was collaborating with the journal as well. Later he became the deputy-editor of the journal *Yeni Fekr* (New Thought) in Tiflis and editor of *Dan Olduzi* (Star of Dawn). He was the deputy-head of the committee in charge of changing the alphabet. He was the director of the state drama theater of Azerbaijan in Tiflis.

62. Aghalar Bey Karbala'i Ali Akbar Bey-oghlu Aliverdiov (1880-1953). His father was a milk-brother of the famous poetess Khorshid Banu Natavan. Kerbela'i Ali Akbar Bey's daughter Shirin Khanum, from his first marriage, was the mother of Uzeyr Hajibeyov. Thus, Aghalar Bey was Uzeyr's maternal uncle. Aghalar Bey studied at the Technology School of Petersburg in 1901. Later he graduated from the Civil Engineering Institute of Warsaw. In 1913 he returned to Baku and worked as a road engineer. He also was a good musician and was teacher of voice at the Asaf Zeynali School of Music. He was Uzeyr's first music teacher.

63. Yusef Mashhadi Hoseyn-oghlu Salahov/Salahi (1897-1963). The Azerbaijani government sent him to Europe to study. He studied medicine at Heidelberg and Munich. In 1927 he received his doctorate from Munich. During the war he became a prisoner of war and then he ended up in Turkey, where, later, he became a professor of medicine.

64. For a description of these poetic contests, *see* Willem Floor, *Games Persians Play*, pp. 45-48.

Rahim Bey Haqqverdiov took a picture of everybody and Azad Amirov still has this picture.[65]

It was the summer of 1914; we were living in room 41 in the Donksy guesthouse in Yessentuki and we had our dinners there. Mirza Jalil was writing very frequently to me.

In the fall of 1914,[66] I was living with the family in Kahrizli. Mirza Jalil was continuing the publication of the journal with Aliquli Ghamqusar. Again I fell ill. The physicians advised me to go for treatment to Tiflis. I had to call Mirza Jalil. He came to the village and took my place. I went to Tiflis and stayed with my daughter Mina. This time I was treated by doctor Ostorovski. I became well and returned after one month.

To recuperate from my illness, the physician advised me to go to Yessentuki. We had to get some money for that. Mirza Jalil could not come with me, he had to be in Tiflis and the village and look after the family. I decided to go to Yessentuki with my 14-year old son Muzaffar. This spring, the village was in full bloom, everywhere was green. The fragrance of the flowers would intoxicate you. Everywhere you could hear the song of the nightingales. The small park in front of our house and old orchard was covered with grass. Mirza Jalil was also in high spirits. My friend, an intellectual young woman from Moscow, had come as a guest and was staying with us to rest in the bosom of nature. She was a talkative woman and our days were spent in happiness. The beauty of nature and the environment had a very good impact on Mirza Jalil. He had taken a book of Guy de Maupassant and was reading it, sometimes in the park, sometimes in the garden amidst the flowers, and sometimes lying on the grass. He would say: "To live in the world you cannot imagine a place better than this one. I want to live all my life here."

Fortunately, there was neither sickness nor famine this year; we were expecting a good harvest. One could say that we had vaccinated all the people against small pox. Normally, our courtyard would be full with people who wanted to be vaccinated. Mirza Jalil was helping me with this work. Mirza Ali Akbar was looking after the farm and mill. Therefore, Mirza Jalil and I were feeling very free. In June, I took Mirza Jalil with the children to Khankandi[67] for relaxation. We rented a place in the house of the Sheikh of this town. My old friend Dimitrieva Ohanova, who was an old lady, was living there. I asked her to look after the children and I set out with Mirza Jalil and Muzaffar to Yevlakh. From there Mirza Jalil was going to Tiflis and we were supposed to go to Yessentuki. One day before our departure there was a rain storm and all the rivers were swollen. Our carriage managed to cross the Khojaleh River with difficulty. The water in the river Tartar was so high that we feared to cross it in the carriage. Everybody was crossing the river with carts. We rented a cart and put everything in it and sat in there and crossed the river. Mirza Jalil did not listen to my pleadings and crossed the river in the carriage. We met in Yevlakh and then we parted. Mirza Jalil promised that he would go very often to Khankandi and look after the children. My daughter Mina and her children were living in Zhelnovodosk and she was being treated there. Occasionally we would go there and see them. Mirza Jalil was often writing letters and would frequently go and see the children and write

---

65. In Mehraban Vazir's edition (pp. 155-61) follow two letters, one from the Viceroy's office (Aug. 1913) and the other from the Press Commissionair in Tiflis (Sept. 1913) concerning an article in *Molla Nasreddin* that satirized Babis (Baha'is), whose center was in Ashqabad and Merv and who complained about this article. They asked for the suppression of no. 20 of the journal.

66. Since later Hamideh Khanum writes that is is July 1914, this date is either wrong (e.g. 1913) or, because the Diary is written on unnumbered pages, this paragraph has been wrongly inserted here.

---

67. Khankandi is the capital of Upper Qarabagh and after the Armenian takeover it was called Stepanakert.

news about them. This is one of the letters that he wrote on 7 July 1914 from Tiflis:

While we were living in room 41 in the Donksy guest-house in Yessentuki, and we had our dinners there, Mirza Jalil was writing very frequently to me.

My dear Hamideh,

Don't worry, if Ali Akbar had not reported to you the latest news of what happened it would have been better for you. After you have finished the treatment and come back we will discuss this. For the moment, forget this problem. I wish to become a bird and fly to my children to see them. Ali Akbar has promised to send a phaeton to me and surely I will go there shortly.

How do you feel yourself? When does the treatment finish, how is Muzaffar? Tiflis is very hot and I cannot write, and that is why the journal has been delayed. It is very likely that the actors in Baku will perform my play in September and they will invite me there. Of course, I want to go there with you; the troupe has promised to perform the play in Tiflis. Ali Akbar writes that there has been heavy rain in the village, the wheat ears have become blackened, but the cotton has not been damaged. When I am going from Yevlakh to Khankandi I will send you news. Anvar has completely recovered. Ali Akbar sent them money through Aghalar; I sent some small gifts through the mail for the boys and girls.

The affairs of the journal are not bad, but I don't yet get involved with its finances. I hope that next year I will be able to make the journal stand on its own feet. Yesterday, Zeynal sent a telegram asking 120 copies to be sent to Yessentuki. I don't understand how he is going to sell so many copies in that place, Good-bye Jalil.

Mozaffar was serving me. My daughter Mina was staying with her children in Jeleznovodska and getting treatment there. Occasionally we were going there. Mirza Jalil was very often writing letters. In between, to see the children he would go to Khankandi. In early July 1914 the pages of the newspapers were full with news of the war and the start of the war was expected any day. There was a hectic preparation for it. I witnessed a heart-wrenching scene in the railway station; it was the farewell scene of the soldiers with their families.

* * *

Muzaffar turned 15; he was a very bright child, he was reading the newspaper and was interested in the news of the war. He was even absorbed by it. To tell the truth this was making me apprehensive. On 7 July I was sitting in the park with Muzaffar listening to the music. Among the crowd there were many officers. Suddenly, there was an outcry that the war had started. Some people had the latest newspapers in their hands and everybody gathered around them and was listening to them. At this time, the band started to play the national anthem and everybody got up; then the *Marseillaise* was played and since Russia was an ally of France everybody stood up. All this was having its impact on Muzaffar. He was talking about the war with enthusiasm and I was trying to get this out of his head and was talking about the horrors of war. I said that humanity deserved peace and similar things, but, of course, this had no effect on him. At this time, I took the novel of the famous pacifist female author von Suttner titled "Lay down your arms." I took it from the library and gave it to Muzaffar to read.[68] He read the book and his excite-

---

68. Bertha Felicitas Sophie Freifrau von Suttner (1843-1914) was an Austrian pacifist and novelist. In 1905 she was the first woman to be awarded the Nobel Peace Prize, thus being the second female Nobel laureate after Marie Curie.

ment was cooled. That same day, by chance, I came across my friend Maria Philippovna Lebedinskaya from Brest-Litovsk. Maria's brother was a revolutionary and for that reason he was hiding from the government. This lady agreed with her brother's ideas. Maria Philippovna had taught my daughter Mina for a while and her ideas influenced me as well. In the same period, from 1893 to 1899, I and the late Colonel Ebrahim Bey Davatdarov lived in the same Polish city of Brest-Litovsk. My treatment in Yessentuki was finished and to continue it I went to Kislovodsk together with Maria Philippovna. My money had finished and I needed money to return. Here was a lot of people coming and going because of the war. Somehow we managed to get ourselves to the station of the mineral springs (Mineraln'iye Vody). Soldiers were being transported from the south to the north and from the north to the south. The trains were full of soldiers. In the station we could not find a porter. Muzaffar with much trouble managed to carry the luggage himself. With great difficulty we managed to find a place in the train that was going to Vladikavkaz and all the passengers were soldiers. They didn't give us train tickets in Vladikavkaz. We stayed in the hotel and we were forced to go via the Military Road of Georgia. It became clear that all cars had been requisitioned by the military and were taking only military personnel. With difficulty I managed to get two tickets; the car was for 12 people and all the passengers consisted of officers and physicians who were going to the southern front. The next day at 4 o'clock we reached Tiflis. It was dreadfully hot. Mirza Jalil was not there; he had gone to Khankandi. My son-in-law Memedbeyov got two train tickets and we went to Yevlakh. I sent a telegram to Mirza Jalil. The car in which I was going to Yevlakh was breaking down all the time. Eventually, we arrived in Aghdam in the evening and the next day we went to Khankandi. Mirza Jalil and the children welcomed us at the Aqa Bridge halting station. For the sake of the affairs of the journal, Mirza Jalil was restless to go to Tiflis. Two days later he left. This

was around the middle of August. It was on one of these days around four o'clock that there was a complete lunar eclipse.[69]

In the middle of September we went to Kahrizli. Mirza Jalil had come and was helping me with my work. During my sickness my property affairs had suffered greatly and it was necessary to put them in order. In the summer of 1915 we went to Shusha. Mirza Jalil was staying in the village and was looking after our property. He would come

Taqiyev Theater burning. The actor Arabinski says: "I showed so much of people's misery in the theater that it happened to me" The reactionaries are rejoicing, saying: "God be praised that this abode of jinns has burnt." (no. 9, yr. 4, 1 March 1909)

---

69. There was a total lunar eclipse on 21 August 1914.

* * *

every few days to take a rest and then would go back. This year the people who came to the summer quarters were quite numerous. The writer Fereydun Bey Kocharli with his wife Bad-e Saba Khanum[70] was relaxing there. I and Fereydun Bey decided that we would start a literary group. I wrote to Mirza Jalil and asked him to come and read one of his works to the group. I had invited all the poets and writers who lived in Shusha. Apart from Mirza Jalil, among those who came were: Khan Qaradaghski,[71] Khosrow Bey Puladov,[72] Samad Aqa Ghayebov,[73] and others. Mirza Jalil arrived about one hour before the start of the session. In spite of having traveled 65 km, he came washed up, dressed, and ready. The poets recited their poems. The recitation by Khosrow Bey was more impressive than of all others. Mirza Jalil read the story of "Mulla Fazl Ali" and he greatly enjoyed the meeting.

Two days later Mirza Jalil returned to the village. He was not only doing our work, but with his strong logic and polite manners, he had a good impact on the unsophisticated villagers and helped them in every way.

At the beginning of September we returned to Kahrizli and few days later Mirza Jalil handed over his work to me and returned to Tiflis. At this time he was attending the High Pedagogical Course as an "auditing student."

The boys and girls school that I had started in the village continued its activities. This same year I invited a teacher from Samara.[74]

Our eldest son had become seven years old. I dressed him well and with his father I sent him to Mina in Tiflis. Mina took him to a French lady Mme Eberin to teach him. Mme Eberin had a daughter of the same age as Midhat; he was to live in their house to be educated there. Mme Eberin was looking after him as if he were her own child. Mirza Jalil and Mina only went to see him on holidays. Later, Mina told me that whenever they went to see Midhat he would embrace Mirza Jalil and father and son would kiss each other fervently.

In the spring of 1916, Midhat and Muzaffar came from Tiflis. Midhat had brought medicine for small-pox; again spring was beautiful, flowers and grass were everywhere. Mirza Jalil was feeling very great. Very often he would take the children fishing. He would go riding; occasionally he would go hunting. We had subscribed to the newspapers of the capital. In the evening we would sit on the balcony that was surrounded by roses and we would drink tea, talk, and read newspapers.

Because of a family matter I had to criticize Mirza Jalil; he took it very badly. In general he would be hurt easily. Since I felt that I was right I did not apologize and in this case Mirza Ali Akbar sided with me. Without making peace with me, Mirza Jalil gathered his things and unexpectedly left. At this time, he was getting ready with his assistant, Aliquli Ghamqusar to go to Baku to get paper for the journal. In Baku his friends had promised to arrange for the performance of his play

---

70. Bad-e Saba Khanum (1881-1953) married Fereydun Bey Kocharli at the age of 16 and was a teacher and school principal in various towns.

71. Hasan Ali Qaradaghi (1848-1929) was a poet, teacher, and one of the first who started the new system schools in Shusha. He was the first to write a schoolbook in the Azeri language in phonetic spelling. Apart from writing numerous school books, most translations of poems and books for children are by him.

72. Khosrow Bey Puladov was an official of a credit company and an intellectual.

73. Samad Aqa Ghayebov was an educator and in the early-20th century was one of the well-known Azerbaijani intellectuals. He wrote for *Sharq-e Rus* where he was a colleague of Mirza Jalil.

74. Samara, known from 1935 to 1991 as Kuybyshev, is the sixth largest city in Russia and the administrative center of Samara Oblast. It is situated in the southeastern part of European Russia.

"The Dead." When he was in Tiflis on 30 March 1916 Mirza Jalil wrote me this letter:

I live with Eyn Ali Bey's family. I have received permission to publish the journal anew. Concerning the affairs of the journal I will go to Baku. I will stay in the Islamiya Hotel. I don't know where I will go from there. How are Ali Akbar and the children? Jalil.

Apart from not having settled our disagreement he was looking after my affairs in Baku and Ganjeh and he would send the necessary documents whenever this was needed.

The performance of "The Dead" in Baku at the Taqiyev Theater had an incredible success. He sent a telegram, with no signature, about this:

The play had an exceptional success. The theater was brimful and at every interval they would applaud the playwright. Two thousand five hundred manats were earned with the performance. Now I am going to Eshqabad.

Greetings to every one!
Baku, 30 April 1916.

Of course, we all were happy for his success and we were waiting to see what was going to happen.

I organized my affairs in the village. At the end of July, I took the children and went to the summer quarters in Shusha. We took a place in the house of L.S. Shakarian in the Armenian quarter of the city as we had done previously. There was no letter from Mirza Jalil. I was getting worried. It is the past and I cannot remember the exact date, whether it was the end of July or the beginning of August I received a letter from Mirza Jalil. He said that from Eshqabad he had gone to Samarqand and from there to Orenburg, to Samaria, then to Astrakhan, and then to Vladikavkaz. "Shortly, I will go to Petroskova and then I will return home."

Almost around the middle of August, Mirza Jalil with Aliquli Ghamqusar came to Shusha. As soon as I saw him I said: "I am deeply happy for

so much fame that you have gained." He replied to my compliment by saying: I wanted to be worthy of you." In this way we made peace.

Our friends and acquaintances came and they suggested that we should perform "The Dead," in Shusha. They gathered volunteer actors and Aliquli was busy with them. They met in our house and they would read their parts and learn them by heart. For the performance we rented the school building, which was in the Khan's palace. Before the play Mirza Jalil went to the village. The play was performed with great success and its proceeds were spent on needy students. Apart from Munavvar and I there were no women in the audience. From the 'Beys of Qarabagh' only the Mehmandarovs and the Hoseynbeyovs came (The Hoseynbeyovs are cousins of Haqverdiyov). Later we found out that the other Beys had boycotted the play. Since the times were turbulent Mirza Jalil and I decided that this year we would not send Midhat to Tiflis. We placed him in the school of the educator Nikolai Nikitich Vasiliev. Shusha was nearby and when I had time I would very often visit him and send him provisions.

In the beginning of September we returned to Kahrizli. Aliquli was helping us in harvesting the cotton and recording it in the books. Mirza Jalil took Muzaffar and Teymur to Tiflis. Aliquli also went there in October. They were getting ready for the publication of the journal in 1917. In the fall our daughter Mina had taken her children and had come to Kahrizli. Again, Mirza Jalil had sent some Georgians from Tiflis to help us harvest the cotton. They were very good people. With their help our work was going very well.

In the summer of 1917 I took the family to the Arzumanovs. Although they tried to persuade me not to rent a house in the Armenian quarter I rented a summer-house there from Arzumanov. After a while, Mirza Jalil came to Shusha to see us and then he returned to the village and from there he went to Tiflis.

Mirza Ali Akbar had gone for family affairs to Nakhchivan. Mina with her children was spending the summer with us. Manya, the sister of Mirza Jalil's old office worker was living with us as well as Munavvar. I had educated Manya. She had a teacher's diploma and she worked for a while in the school of our village. When she wanted to get married, we gave her as much of a dowry as we could manage.

At the end of the summer Mirza Jalil with Muzaffar and Teymur returned from Tiflis. Again we left Midhat with Vasiliev to be schooled.

In the middle of September we returned from Shusha to the village. It was difficult to live in Tiflis, because of the high prices. Therefore, Mina did not go to Tiflis and stayed in Kahrizli with her children. The political situation was upsetting people and it seemed as if life was better. But exactly the opposite proved to be the case. After the fall of Nicholas II the instability of the new government provided opportunities for highwaymen and smugglers and they had more of a free rein. They plundered poor people without any pity and oppressed them. The roads were incredibly unsafe.

Midhat needed provisions. The people of Arran fearing the bandits could not go to Shusha. They avoided taking provisions. Because of this, there was scarcity in the city and there was the beginning of a famine.

My servant Sakineh Memedova in order to see Midhat dared to travel by cart on the road. When returning she was going to buy sugar cubes; the cart going to Shusha was filled with provisions. I told the driver that above all he should take her to the person that I trusted, namely Hamid Ali Akbaroghlu. To defend themselves, I gave him a rifle and ammunition. I gave Sakineh about 1,000 manat for buying provisions. Out of fear for the bandits Sakineh sewed the money into her dress.

When our neighbors heard that Sakineh was going to buy provisions everyone gave her some money, 40 to 50 and even 100 manat so that she

might buy provisions for them. When Sakineh was receiving this money she hurriedly put it in her bosom or pockets. Near the village of Qaradagh the bandits held them up and whatever they had they took from them. They put a gun and a dagger to Sakineh's head and breast and threatened her and asked for the money. It seems that they had been alerted that Sakineh was carrying money. Whatever she had in her bosom and pockets she gave to them, but my money, because it was sown into her inner lining, was not discovered. When Sakineh returned she gave all the remaining money to me. She was a very faithful and trustworthy woman. She was a Jewess, but her husband was a Moslem. In the famine years I kept all her family in my house and I took care of them.

I was very worried about Midhat. I did not know what to do. There was no news either about Mirza Jalil or Muzaffar. The postman on the road to Yevlakh was robbed, therefore, there was no information.

In Shusha a committee was recently established to keep law and order and they had sent 100 horsemen. The commander of the company was Soleyman Mehmandarov and his deputy was Idris Mirza. I don't know why the whole company had come to our property. Idris Mirza wanted to marry Munavvar, the daughter of Mirza Jalil. Munavvar was willing. At this time Mirza Jalil was in Tiflis, since we did not know whether he would agree with this we could not give our consent. I sent a long telegram to Mirza Jalil and asked him to give his view about the marriage. Two days later he sent a short telegram: "I agree." After this the people of Idris Mirza came and the engagement took place.

* * *

I think it must have been January 1918 when a phaeton came to our house. In it was the *yuzbashi* Bahador from the village of Efatli. He wore a large felt great-coat. Suddenly, Midhat jumped out from under his great-coat and he embraced me. I was so delighted that I did not know how to express my gratitude to this good man Bahador. Now I will tell how Bahador brought Midhat to me. We had a very good friend, the revolutionary Soleyman Mehmandarov. In 1928, I read in the newspaper *Zarya Vostaka* that Soleyman Mehmandarov had informed Stalin that there was a plan to assassinate him in the Baku train station. He had sent him safely from Bilajar[75] to Moscow.

In the winter of 1918, the same Soleyman was in Shusha with his uncle Karim Bey Mehmandarov. He heard from Karim Bey about the difficult situation my son Midhat was in. He took Midhat to Aghdam; from Aghdam, after having been assured of the reliability of Bahador, he entrusted Midhat to him. He had said that nobody should see him and that was why the child was hidden in his great-coat. The bandits might have seized him to ask for ransom. Such incidents were quite common in those days.

After a while, Soleyman visited us. He told us that he had an acquaintance, nurse Makarova; she had been treating Soleyman in Kislovodska. Now she was out of a job. He vouched for her and asked me whether I could give her a job. I agreed and Soleyman wrote a letter to her in Kislovodska. After a while, in a miraculous way, the woman came to my house. I am calling it 'miraculous' because that same year the troops from the Moslem fronts[76] were withdrawing. Therefore, there were disturbances, chaos and revolt everywhere.

In Barda, bandits had surrounded her phaeton, searched each passenger and whatever they had they had taken. One of the bandits let her go to Aghdam. Nurse Makarova was from Siberian Cossack stock. She was about 50 years old, but she looked younger than her age.

All her life she had been devoted to her profession. She became a prisoner of war while working at the Austrian front. From there she had gone to Paris, where she had been helped to return to Petersburg and from there she had come to Kislovodska, where she had met Soleyman. We became friends.

Because nurse Makarova had saved the life of many wounded she had received several medals. One day, she showed her special heroic quality to us as well. In those days, we were in a strange situation; it was as if we were living on a volcano. There was no government. They could have attacked our house whenever they wanted, even in the middle of the day; they could have killed or plundered, without any consequences.

Unfortunately, in those days the dispute over our land with my cousins was in its most critical situation. It is true that I did not trust them, but at the same time I did not expect them to stab me in the back. I was expecting help from another side. Knowing my usefulness for the villagers, I depended on them. Our watchmen were from among the villagers. At the head of them was Qasem Moharram-oghlu, who was a favorite of Mirza Jalil, and he was very brave and faithful to us. Day and night he was guarding our house with his arms at the ready. I and my late daughter Mina had our weapons ready all the time. If there was a sudden event we were ready. One night we heard incessant gun firing.

The fire that was blazing from the northern part of the village could be seen from our window. Mina and Muzaffar opened the front door and we looked at the fire. Qasem who was all the time on guard duty, seeing us, cried: "Lady, what are you doing? The light is falling on you and they will shoot you. Go inside and close the door." Hurriedly, we went inside and closed the door. At that time there was continuous shooting. One of the bullets hit the door quite close to me with a whoosh. Qasem and

---

75. Bilajar is a railhead village near Baku.

76. Moslem fronts means the troops that had been fighting in Iran and the Caucasus against the Ottoman army.

our other guard exchanged fire with the bandits. Eventually, the plunderers withdrew empty-handed.

At another time, Qarash Bashi, a bandit who was from the village of Bayat, passed with his gang close to our village at noon time. One of his mortal enemies, who was a guest in one of my relatives' house, saw him and recognized him. He took his rifle and starting firing and cried: "Don't let him get away, I will kill Qarash right now." To stop the bandit Qarash, the same man ran across our garden, which was a short-cut. Of course, his friends followed him. All our guards, who were from our village, including Qasem, were siding with those opposing Qarash.

During this fire fight my guest, nurse Makarova, suddenly came out like a bullet disregarding the people who had not been hit, began bandaging the wounds of Qarash. Later it became known that Qarash had only fainted from one bullet. This event seriously impacted the relations between our village and that of Bayat. The villagers of Bayat often sent threatening messages that they would plunder and burn our village. We were cautious and all the time had our fingers on the trigger to defend ourselves. My situation was even worse, because there was not one adult man in the house. There were in total 10 women and four young boys, the oldest of which, Midhat, was nine.

In 1918, anarchy reigned in Qarabagh. The people called this 'Freedom." I was living with my family and servants in Kahrizli. Because there was no news of our friends in Tiflis, we were very worried. We heard dreadful accounts of the disturbances that were happening in Tiflis and on the rail road. It seemed that we were not going to see our friends there again. My late daughter Mina and her children were living with me. Her husband, the late Engineer Memedbeyov was working in Tiflis. Mirza Jalil with his son Muzaffar and his nephew Teymur were also in Tiflis.

It was February when we went with my daughter and the children to the mill. We suddenly saw that a rider was coming very fast from the village to the mill. The rider got close and gave us good news. Mirza Jalil, his son-in-law Yusef Khan, Muzaffar and Teymur, whom we had been awaiting for anxiously, were safe and had arrived. In the train they had been stopped and checked several times, but after ascertaining their identity they were let go. En route somebody called Mosayyeb Aliyev had helped them greatly.

One and a half month later my son-in-law Mohammadbeyov had to go to Ganja for his work and started preparing for the journey. A phaeton was made ready and his luggage was placed aboard. He said his good-byes. At this moment, my cousin came galloping from the village and said: "Don't let your son-in-law leave, because on the road to Aghdam,near the village of Saricali, there are bandits at the cross-roads lying in wait." They wanted to take my son-in-law hostage and demand a ransom. I did not let him go.

Anarchy was increasing. You could not even go from one village to another one. All night we kept watch behind doors. We had heard that the bandits of the village of Bayat were getting ready to attack us, but they were unable to do so. They could not get to our house, but instead they took some of our good cows and buffaloes.

Later, two Afatli villagers, Allahquli and Ahmad, since they liked me very much and cared for me, used their influence to force the bandits to return the animals.

Mirza Jalil said that he had tried and received permission for the publication of the journal, but since the post office was closed he had decided to stop the publication. After a while the news spread that the Turks were coming to Azerbaijan. A few notable people came to Shusha and Aghdam and a governor was appointed. From Iran, Enver Pasha's brother, Nur Pasha, who was known to many, came across the Khoda Afarin bridge. He stopped en route and spoke with representatives of the people and gave instructions.

It was summer. During the wheat harvest and there was cholera in the village. In our village in one day six people fell ill and died. I immediately went to Aghdam and obtained the necessary medicine from Dr. Bahador Aliverdi and started treating the sick. Our treatment was not bad, some of the people who were afflicted became healthy again. Mirza Jalil who was afraid that the children would get sick thought it wise to take them to Shusha. He decided to stay himself at home. Mina and I took the children to Shusha.

We had hardly traveled three werst when suddenly, one after the other, two phaetons passed us. In each one of them there were Moslems with a lot of luggage. At that moment we heard shooting. Armenian horsemen were pursuing them and firing at the phaetons. Suddenly, a few armed men appeared, riding into the same direction. Our phaeton was going very slow, because there were children in it. A few of the pursuers came next to us and jumped onto the step. My poor daughter Mina, thinking that they were going to kill us, clutched the children to her breast and screamed. The baffled Armenians tried to explain that they were only pursuing the two fleeing phaetons that were transporting arms to the Moslems in Shusha (later we learnt that these two phaetons safely reached Shusha).

Above Aghdam, in the cemetery of Qarahaji, the Armenian guards stopped us, saying that we could not continue. But after they recognized me, with great respect, they allowed us to go on. Also, the Armenian representative Khan Baqqi (Minasbeyov) showed us great respect and even offered us a place to stay overnight. The next day he gave us a letter and sent us to Shusha. In Shusha the Armenian and Moslem situation was very tense. We were advised not to rent a house in the Armenian quarter. Nonetheless, I rented a house near the Armenian quarter, in the Khoja Mirjanli quarter in the house of Bala Haji Sadeq.

Relations between the two sides was worsening day by day. The Moslems and Armenians had placed guards at the borders of their quarters. The Armenians had closed Asgaran castle and they had banned the sale of foodstuffs to Moslems. As a result, prices had risen and there was bread scarcity.

The governor of Shusha, the Moslem Hasan Efendi, was very peace-loving and was trying to persuade the people not to fight.

For some time I had no news from Mirza Jalil. I was very worried. Our flour was almost finished. I decided with my late daughter Mina to go to the military governor of the Armenians and get permission to buy five or ten *pud*s of flour and five *pud*s of potatoes.[77] Fortunately, the governor gave us permission and wrote a letter.

When we were getting the flour, one of the Armenians shouted: "Why are you selling flour to Moslems?" Somebody else replied saying: "She is the daughter of the Russian Ahmad Bey." The one who was shouting became quiet and said: "She is OK." We got the flour and with the porters we crossed the demarcation line. On the way nobody bothered us. At home, after baking bread we were at ease for a while.

One day Heydar from the village of Gulabli brought a letter from Mirza Jalil. Heydar was a very brave man. He would go on foot at night over the mountains and would bring letters and money to a number of people. This courageous young man, this heroic Heydar, was treacherously killed in 1920. Heydar was a Bolshevik.

There was talk that the Turks were coming to establish order in the region and open the road to Shusha. Everyone was waiting for the risk to come and there was a big preparation to welcome them. The city was decorated. At the gates of the castle there were several victory arches. I had erected one of them in the name of the Women of Shusha. On a banner there was a crescent and a star with the

---

77. One *pud* = 40 *funt* = 16.38 kg

following text: "the sun will come, the sun of the truth will rise, the captive Mother of the East will gain her independence."

First, Jamil Jahed Pasha entered the city in a car. He first went to a mosque. Then, with his attendants walked to Khan Bulagh. At this time, from the Armenian side, in a car, many representatives of the government with flags and banners came to the Moslem side and showed their submission. Later, long speeches were given and there was talk of peace, friendship, and neighborliness.

Part of the armed Turkish force was billeted in the Armenian section. Jamil Jahed Pasha stayed in the Khan's palace.

Mirza Jalil was very anxious about us; every day he would go to Aghdam and try to get news about us. He even thought of going on foot to Shusha, but Heydar managed to dissuade him. Later on, Heydar brought us letters and money.

On one of those days, Mirza Jalil came to Shusha and we had a big feast. A few days later, the husband of my daughter, Memedbeyov came for two days. In my house I had started an intellectual circle, where educated Shushans came.

On the Armenian side, in the square they had hanged two Armenians. They said that in their houses a large quantity of arms had been found. On the Armenian side, everywhere Moslem soldiers were patrolling and doing guard duty. The Armenian intellectuals had given a party in Jahed Pasha's honor to which party the Moslem intellectuals had been invited as well. We were also there; it was a lively party. The Pasha was very pleased. A beautiful Armenian lady was hovering around him. Very soon the Pasha became friendly with her.

At that time, I went to the house of my Armenian friend, who was living on the Armenian side. Near the Winter Club I came across an acquaintance and I started talking Turkish with her. Then one of the Moslem guards who was passing by harshly asked me: "Are you Turkish.?" I said: "Yes." He said: "Why are you walking in the Armenian

Once upon a time, there was no one in the world except Allah. Then there was a stupid Armenian and an idiot Azeri, and except for them, there was a devil. And one day, the devil...(no more room left to write). (no. 13, yr. 2, 13 March 1907)

side?" I said: "First of all, this is not forbidden. And secondly, this is none of your business." The news of this encounter reached the Pasha and he scolded and even reprimanded the guard.

I should mention here that we invited Jamil Jahed Pasha to our house. Of course, he already had heard about Mirza Jalil and the journal *Molla Nasreddin*. From his behavior it was obvious that the Pasha enjoyed meeting Mirza Jalil. They talked for a long time and the Pasha told me that in Turkey women still wore the veil. He looked at us with astonishment and said that our future would

"With my rag-tag army I will destroy the Ottoman army" (no. 21, yr. 9, 28 July 1914)

be bright. My late daughter Mina and Mirza jalil's daughter Munavvar were sitting at the table as well.

Mirza Jalil later told us that he was very worried because the Armenians had closed Asgeran castle and he was afraid that they would kill us and that he would not see us any longer. In this terrible time his only consolation was Heydar from Gulabli. Poor Heydar endangered his life and was bringing our letters to him.

At that time the line of battle crossed the village of Gulabli. Moslems and Armenians had made entrenchments and they were shooting at each other. People from the surrounding area came to visit and watch the shooting and they were hoping that the Moslems would break through the Armenian front and soon enter Shusha. One day the unfortunate Behbudov was killed while watching the shooting with binoculars.[78] Since he was a peaceful man the Armenians liked him. They even mourned him.

It seems that he was carefully targeted because he was hit in the heart. Jalil said that he usually stood in that place and would look at the fighting. On that day, one of our villagers Hasan Nasiroghlu went to him asked him to leave that place otherwise he might be killed. This action by Hasan moved Jalil greatly.

In Aghdam Mirza Jalil was staying with somebody called Soleyman, who had a caravanserai and rented horses. Mirza Jalil befriended this old man and he would talk continuously about interesting events in his life and tell stories and make witty remarks. Mirza Jalil who rarely laughed in his life would really laugh his heart out at Soleyman's stories, which he told with a deadpan face.

Once, Soleyman told Mirza Jalil: "You know Mirza, any man from Baku who comes to work in Shusha gets a girl from Shusha and takes her away. But every Iranian who comes to Qarabagh to work buys a donkey and takes it back home."

After one week Mirza Jalil went back to the village. At this time he was thinking about the play "My Mother's Book," and was getting ready to write it.

We came to the conclusion that we would not take the children to Tiflis, but rather put them into the Real School.[79] Here I have to mention that there was a truce with the Armenians. But I could not entrust the children to anyone. Therefore, I decided to stay myself in Shusha. To spend the winter I rented a house on Mashhadi Mohammad Taqiyev's property, which was a warm and comfortable house.

In Shusha under the leadership of Dr. Mehmandarov we had a Charitable Society, which was located in Mardinli street. I helped Dr. Mehmandarov and he would give me the list of all poor families, widows, orphans and invalids. In this list there were a total of 965 families. We would gather money, wheat and other things from ourselves and other people. At this time, all goods were very expensive in Shusha and the bazaar had been burnt down. Sugar cubes were scarce and its price was 25 manat per *funt*. This was why the poor were suffering. In the Armenian quarter of the city the situation was the same and the poor suffered.

I wrote about this to Mirza Jalil. From the village he sent two carts full of flour. One part of it I distributed to poor Moslems (worth about 300 manat) and the same amount I set aside for the Armenians. Since we did not have the list of the Armenian poor we baked bread and wanted to

---

78. Lotfali Bey Rahimbeyoghlu Behbudov (1879-1919) was trained as an engineer at the Institute of Technology at St. Petersburg and worked as manager for Haji Zeyn al-Abedin Taqiyev's Fisheries. In 1918 he became the representative of the Moslem Army in Qarabagh. According to some Azerbaijani sources, he was accused of trying to destroy the Army of the Caucasus and therefore, Jahed Pasha arrested him and he died in prison, but what Hamideh Khanum writes proves that this was not the case.

---

79. Real school is a high school.

distribute it among their poor in the church. We announced our intention and the poor gathered in the courtyard of the church. I went to the Armenian side with my late daughter Mina, my son Muzaffar and our cook Sakineh. The bread was carried on the back of the Armenian porters and we distributed it among the poor. It was said that this event put the Armenian rich to shame and they resented it. After this they began to help the poor.

The famine in Qarabagh had even become known in America. From there, a special commission led by Dr. Hartman came. They brought much money, provisions, fabrics, medicines and other necessities. The Americans stayed in the Armenian side in the house of a wealthy Armenian Jamqarov.[80] It was said that America was only going to help the Armenians. I talked to doctor Mehmandarov and we decided to try our luck and see what would happen.

Our charitable committee sent me to talk to Dr. Hartman. I was asked to give a list with the Moslem poor and ask him for help. I went there. With the help of an interpreter I talked extensively of the need of the poor in the Moslem sector, who were hungry, sick and in need. The doctor listened to me attentively and immediately ordered to take action. On his orders they gave me much money; if I am not mistaken 40,000 Kerenski manat.[81] Later they helped us with sugar, tea, coffee, various pulses and provisions. Apart from this, they gave a lot of fabrics and a large suitcase with medicines. After receiving all this I gave a receipt and thanked Dr. Hartman from the bottom of my heart. I got a phaeton and brought all this to our house. Our committee had assembled there. The provisions, fabrics and medicines were received and recorded. We made a list of the poor and distributed the main part of this gift. The medicines were given to Dr. Mehmandarov. He started treating the sick and gave free medicine to the poor. Following this help, the Americans gave us money and goods several times.[82]

From the time of the Tsars there was a small textile factory in Shusha, where woolen and cotton fabrics were made. The master weaver was Vasiliev. The looms had been made by a master called Simonyans. The worn out metal parts of these looms could be brought from Tiflis. After looking at this textile factory, I thought, if we could bring the parts for 10 or 12 weaving looms, a number of poor girls and women could come and work there. I wrote a very detailed letter to Mirza Jalil and asked him to come to Shusha and look into this matter. Mirza Jalil came and after looking at the factory he liked my idea. Master Vasiliev promised to help training them.

We first ordered four looms from Simonyans, which cost, I think, about 360 manat. Then we ordered eight more. Through the intermediary of Mehmedbeyov, my son-in-law, we obtained the metal parts for 12 looms from Tiflis. All of this cost 24,000 manat.

Mirza Jalil was getting wool from the village for the factory. In Shusha, I was separating and dividing the wool and gave them to Moslem and Armenian women. Instead of money I paid the wages of the

80. Isaak Isaakovich Jamqarov (1845-1902), was a banker and merchant and a charitable person, who had good relations with the Turks. The Dashnaks kidnapped him and asked for 13,000 manat. Apparently he did not keep his promise to pay and moved to Moscow. The Dashnaks issued a death warrant for him and Matevos Minasian killed him in front of the Armenian Church in Moscow.

81. Alexander Fyodorovich Kerensky (1881-1970) was a lawyer and major political leader before the Russian Revolution of 1917 belonging to a moderate socialist party, called Trudoviks. The manats were issued during the time (6 August to 8 November 1917) that his government ruled Russia. Later its value dropped and people preferred the old imperial manats.

82. The famine struck the whole of the Middle East and the story of the American relief effort, which started in 1915 to help Armenians, is told by James L. Barton, *Story of Near East relief (1915-1930)*. New York: MacMillan, 1930.

"Dear Sir, we are also animals, so please be so kind as to give us some oats as well!" (no. 46, yr. 2, 9 Dec 1907)

women in flour. This was to their heart's desire, because they were working and earning. Gradually they became more proficient in working the looms. First, I placed four looms on the veranda of my house and the women started working there. When the number of looms increased Dr. Mehmendarov managed to have people accept placing them on the second floor of an old mosque, which was next to a caravanserai at the end of the bazaar.

I took charge of the looms that were going to be placed in the mosque and I put eight looms there. The trainer Vasiliev taught the weavers how to operate the pulleys. The overall operation was gradually getting better. Eventually I had a few rolls of coarse wool. Slowly the quality of our product was getting better.

At that time, the military commander of Shusha, Semed Bey Mehmandarov[83] inspected the factory and praised us greatly. He promised to order cloth for military uniforms from our factory.

Engineer Farrokh Bey Vazirov's Property

Five werst from our village there was Hinderakh village, which was the property of Engineer Farrokh

---

83. Semed Bey Mehmandarov (1855-1931) studied at the artillery school in Petersburg and became general of the artillery in 1915. In the period of the Azerbaijan Republic he was a member of parliament and military commander from 1918 to 1920. He was not a member of a party. The Communists imprisoned him and made him clean the streets. He wrote a letter to Nariman Narimanov and in August 1920 he was sent to Lenin in Moscow. Afterwards he taught military tactics at the War College. In 1921, he returned to Baku and taught artillery at the Azerbaijan Military School.

Bey Vazirov.[84] Hinderakh was a large village, but Farrokh Bey did not live there. There was a manager, Behbudov, who had an assistant called Dargha Ja`far. There were many mechanics and other workers there.

Farrokh Bey Vazirov had built a very beautiful, impressive and large building in Hinderakh. In jest his villagers called it the Washington White House. In addition, there were many other buildings in this compound such as servant quarters, large stables with glass roofs, a motorized mill, a cotton mill, a post-office, and a telegraph-office, for the Russian workers with families living in small village houses; it was a big and elaborate estate.

Farrokh Bey Vazirov had erected various buildings to serve as a bazaar near the village on the road to Shusha. It was expected that the railway station would be built there as well. In addition, near his house, Vazirov had planted many fruit trees from Turkey and Europe and had created a very wonderful park. The entire property was very modern. He had brought from Europe various machines to improve production.

In the village there were three strong foremen. One of them was Ja`far, who was the *darugheh* (village police man). As a result of his service, Ja`far had amassed much more wealth than his colleagues. Out of jealousy and envy, the two other foremen, Asad and Mashhadi Adil joined in rivalry against him to bring about his downfall.

---

84. Farrokh Bey Mirza Hamid Bey-oghli Vazirov (1857-1920) was a charitable man and landlord. He received his engineer's degree from St. Petersburg School of Mining in 1886. In his village of Hinderakh he bought much land and constructed European-style buildings. He also started a cotton plantation and a cotton factory, according to the new system. To improve the horse breed of Qarabagh he began a stud farm. In Hinderakh he started a school, a dispensary and free schooling. In 1906 he moved to St. Petersburg and there also was engaged in social and charitable works. He always defended the rights of all Moslems in the Caucasus and Central Asia.

Ja`far had six sons who could bear arms. His rivals had the same number of sons and many friends and relatives. Mashhadi Adil and Asad were going around in phaetons surrounded by armed men as if they were Khans of Qaradagh. They were in touch with the local bandits and had a hand in many of the estate-wide plundering.

Vazirov's mechanic was a very able and talented Pole, called Porfiri Klimentovich Shidlovski. One day, he returned from Baku with his eldest son, the surgeon and the agronomist. Shidlovski was accompanying the surgeon and agronomist to the Vazirov estate to work there. On a back road from Yevlagh's railway station to Hinderakh suddenly the bandits attacked. They killed all four of them and cut them into pieces and buried them in a ditch. Shidlovski's poor widow almost lost her mind. She lived with her brother Iosif (Yuzya) Peslyak in one of the houses that Vazirov had built for his workers. By night, the bandits of Hinderakh attacked Shidlovski's house and they took whatever there was of value. The widow wrote a letter to me begging me to save her. I asked Aghalar, my water distribution supervisor, to take my phaeton and a cart to Hinderakh and bring back Shidlovski's widow and her brother and whatever was left of their belongings.

Aghalar brought those two poor people safely to us with whatever was left. Poor Shidlovski's widow and her brother were almost naked. I gave them clothes, a separate room and whatever they needed.

There was a rumor that the bandits were planning to plunder the Vazirov estate. The telegraph line had been cut. This news was sent to the recently formed committee in Shusha. This group under the command of Soleyman Mehmandarov, the chief officer Ziyadkhanov and Major Idris Mirza (at that time, Idris Mirza became acquainted with Mirza Jalil's daughter Munavvar and as a result they got married).

Hundreds of this group came to my house and stayed there. Nurse Makarova was managing my

village affairs and she performed her tasks consci-
entiously. To feed hundreds of people, lodging
them and providing for their horses for three
days was not an easy task. I continuously talked
with Mehmendarov and Ziyadkhanov and gave
them advice so that the matter would be resolved
peacefully.

I sent my trusted fried Aghalar (who was a good
friend of Salman Bey Alibeyov) to Mashhadi Adil
and Asad. I told them to put down their arms and
not shed innocent blood, in exchange, in spite of
what they had done and had shed so much blood,
I would get them amnesty.

That same day, a very respectable and noble
person, a distant relative of mine, Hoseyn Bey,
came to see me. He also agreed that it was better to
resolve this dispute peacefully. Aghalar brought the
answer: "You and Ziyadkhanov are invited to talks."

Ziyadkhanov, I, Hoseyn Bey and Aghalar went
there. Near Hinderakh, we saw Mashhadi Adil and
Asad's people, who were carryingh all kinds of
arms. They had also dug trenches on the way that
were hidden. Since they knew that we were coming
they let us pass to go to the village. We dismounted
at Mashhadi Adel's son's house, whose name was
Islam. The negotiations lasted a few hours. Finally,
we reached agreement that the following day the
armed horsemen would enter the village and that
nobody from the other side would be arrested. In
addition, they would go to the mosque and swear
that they would no longer be engaged in plunder
and highway robbery and make peace with the
people of Dargha Ja'far. It was also agreed that
Mashhadi Adil and Asad would lodge and feed the
army and provide for their horses for three days.

We returned home in the evening. The following
day, nurse Makarova, Aghalar and I in one phaeton
and Ziyadkhanov and Hoseyn Bey in another one
were followed by the entire army of horsemen,
with their cannon and machine gun, under the
command of Soleyman Mehmandarov. We reached
the village without any problem. The army settled

in Vazirov's huge courtyard. To negotiate between
the two sides we once again went to Islam's house.
That night we stayed at the house of Georgi, the
post and telegraph master. He was a very polite and
pleasant young man, and originally a Georgian.
Later he was treacherously killed in Aghdam.

The following day we brought all of them almost
by force to the mosque. Here they made peace and
kissed each other and vowed that they would not
resume hostilities. We had just finished the peace
talks when the Commissioners from Shusha came
by car. After hearing what had happened they were
very much astonished that this conflict had been
peacefully resolved.

In the evening, the Commissioners asked me to
go to their office on the following morning to give
an official report how this peaceful solution had
come about and under what conditions.

The following day in the meeting that took
place, apart from the representatives of the two
sides, the section commanders, the Commissioners
of the Russian, Armenian and Moslem communi-
ties all participated in this meeting.

I described what had happened in great detail.
I listed one by one the conditions of the peace
agreement. Everything was written down. The
Commissioners willy-nilly came to accept the facts
and nobody was imprisoned. Everybody signed the
agreement. Everybody was happy with this good
conclusion and then each went his way. But unfortunately, the peace did not last. Two, three months
later the conflict became worse. Mashhadi Adil
and Asad's gangs forgot all the agreement's conditions and their promises and, to take revenge on
Dargha Ja'far, they first plundered and destroyed
Farrokh Bey's prosperous, modern and very well
organized estate in such a way that not one stone
was left unturned. They even destroyed the Post
and Telegraph office; the flour mill, the cotton mill,
and other workshops were leveled. They cut down
and destroyed the park, the garden and the forest.
They destroyed all the buildings. When they were

destroying the metal roofs with sledge hammers they were making such a noise that five werst away we heard them.

After this, the people of Hinderakh came to our mill which was at one werst distance and they would stand in line for weeks to grind their wheat.

***

The coming of the army to our village was not without result. Major Idris Mirza asked for the hand of Mirza Jalil's daughter Munavvar. Without Mirza Jalil's consent we could not do anything. Mirza Jalil was in Tiflis with my son Muzaffar. I had no news from them for a long time. As in other cases, I wrote a telegram in such a way that he would like it and asked for his consent. Two days later a very short telegram came from him saying: "I agree." After this the groom's people came and made the betrothal official.

Apart from this, one of Yuzbashi Soleyman's horse soldiers fell in love with Sonya Alexandrovna, who was Mina's daughter's wet-nurse. Sonya fell in love with him and consented to marry him. I took upon myself to arrange the wedding. Nurse Makarova gave her blessing to the bride.

***

This summer I was in Shusha. Finally, I received a letter from Mirza Jalil.

25 August 1918, from Kahrizli.

My Dear Hamideh

Yesterday I received your letter of 22 August. I am getting ready to go tomorrow, 26 August to Aghdam to meet Heydar and talk about your recommendation. Everything is OK with us. A little fever and some stomach aches discomfort us. The good news is that there are no deaths to report. However, cholera continues in Aghdam as before.

I continue harvesting. I have threshed the barley. Now we are almost done with the wheat. Now, the peasants will have bread. Our partners are threshing the crop and they will be busy for a while. We have gathered the millet in the courtyard. The haystack is completely full and even outside, it is full of hay. There are so many heaps that you cannot walk anywhere. In this time of high prices I know that this amount of harvest will be enough for us.

They have promised that today or tomorrow they will release Aghalar, for the time being he is inside.

What is happening in Baku we don't know. An aeroplane landed in Minakharli. When we were in Aghdam we saw it. They were English, it was flying to Khankandi.

The flour mill is working somewhat. Pavel is not there. He is mostly drunk or sick. I have given up on him. I operated the mill as much as I can, but I don't have much time because grinding takes much of my time. Our onion crop has been gathered and is finished. Now, they are doing Abdul-Qasem's harvest. His crop is many times more than ours. We have stored many melons and water melons in our barn; I have kept them for you. Also, dried apricots, plums, figs, and cornel cherries. We have two pounds of grape syrup and other provisions. We will have a few sacks of walnuts for the winter. We have plenty of pomegranates as well as sour plums. Currently, we are bargaining and still at it.

Qasem works very well. He is a very good worker. We've never had such a worker before.

Our work seems to be going well. The closing of the road to Shusha troubles us very much. The letters that I received from the children made me very happy; I kissed them.

Tomorrow I will go to Aghdam and I will give a little money to Heydar to bring it to you. In such dangerous road conditions can one sent 1,000 manat? I will send something for the children.

What has happened to Adika, why is she feeling unwell?

Shahverdi Khan and Idris Mirza are in our house. Idris is ill, but now he is feeling somewhat better. Everybody in our house is sick. Ebrahim Bey is also sick, Qasem is sick. Occasionally, I also don't feel well.

How are you? Well, when are the roads going to be open again? I have to go to Tiflis. I am waiting for you to come and then I will go. With Heydar I am sending you 400 manat in small notes.

Jalil.

***

Early December 1918 Mirza Jalil had finished his work in the village and came to rest in Shusha. He wanted to finish his play and to do that he needed a quiet atmosphere. I gave him my room and I went to the children's room. Later he said that he wanted to buy a *kamancheh* and learn how to play. I sent our servant Sakineh to the Armenian quarter of the city and with the help of one of our acquaintances she bought a *kamancheh* for 500 *manat*; and its bowl was studded with mother-of-pearl. I asked the musician Bakhshi to teach Mirza Jalil, who was very grateful and in good humor. He was taking lessons from Bakhshi and at the same time he was writing his play. At that time, he told me that to write this play he needed many dictionaries. We learned that we could find these dictionaries with the help of the post-office clerk Rasul Bey. It became clear that

the heirs of the Qajar Bahman Mirza[85] of Iran were selling his dictionaries and rare books. With the help of Rasul Bey we bought many dictionaries and valuable books. Mirza Jalil was greatly delighted and began working with enthusiasm. We even had a special shelf made for the newly acquired books and put it in Mirza Jalil's room. Many years later Mirza Jalil took these books to Kahrizli. When we went to Iran the regimental officers who were staying in our house, took these same books in two ammunition wagons to the nearby Armenian village of Hadrut..

After February 1919 Mirza Jalil finished the play "My Mother's Book" and read it to me; he did so with a beautiful voice and diction. I listened to it with great interest. It impressed me so much, when I was listening to it as if bewitched and I was living the events of the play. After Mirza Jalil finished reading the play I was tearful and absorbed in thought and I could not speak. I congratulated him; I expressed my gratitude to him and I asked permission to get a copy of the play and to keep it for myself to which he agreed. The teacher of the children, Mirza Khosrow, copied both "The Dead" and 'My Mother's book." I still have these two manuscripts.

In the spring of 1919 there was the wedding of Mirza Jalil's daughter Munavvar to Idris Mirza. Several times I wrote letters to Mirza Jalil to invite him to the wedding, but he refused to come, but he sent money and provisions. With the help of our servant Sakineh we prepared the necessary dowry. The bridegroom organized his wedding party in Khankandi and came to Shusha and took the bride. We did not want to organize the bride's wedding, because my cousin Ibish Bey had died recently. This

85. Bahman Mirza Qajar (1808-1884) was the brother of Mohammad Shah, who was the third ruler of the Qajar dynasty (1834-1848), and since his relations with his brother became strained he emigrated from Iran and resided in Shusha until his death. His tomb is in the cemetery of Barda.

was the same Ibish Bey, who had rebelled against the government officials and for that he was sent to Siberia for 12 years. In the early days of my marriage to Mirza Jalil he had warned me that the Beys wanted to humiliate us.

After a few days I went to Khankandi and visited Munavvar and her husband. When I saw my cousin's family in great grief and tears I could not contain myself and began crying loudly, and I fainted. This was the first time in my life that I had fainted. Poor Mirza Jalil was sitting next to my bed the whole night. I came to myself in the morning. When I returned to Shusha I went to see Dr. Karim Bey Mehmandarov and described my situation. It became apparent that I was very tired and that my nerves were frayed.

After my health was restored I went back to my social work; the work of the textile factory was improving increasingly. In the factory, as before, the Armenian and the Azerbaijani women worked together. They were making warm sweaters, socks, gloves and they were using the waste for other purposes. Later we thought of making floor covering and kilims. Mirza Jalil promised to get enough wool for this.

At the end of July, Mirza Jalil had completed his work and he came to Shusha. I don't know whether at that time or a little bit earlier the representative of the Armenian community invited me and Mirza Jalil on the occasion of the anniversary of the school's opening. After the gathering a picture was taken of all participants.

In spite of the increasing better quality and quantity of production of the textile factory the revenues were insufficient. The only benefit was that a number of poor women were taught a craft and were earning wages.

The front of Zangezur was quiet. The arrival of Andronikin[86] had made the situation tense.

Therefore, the British general Shettleworth[87] with his entourage had come. When he was going back, Sultanov,[88] the governor gave a party in his honor to which the notables of the city of Shusha and I also had been invited. In the party the general through a translator asked who I was and what I was doing. Then he said, "you remind me of the British suffragettes."

In the fall of 1919 Mirza Jalil was engaged in the agricultural activities of Kahrizli. He personally supervised the plowing and sowing of the seed. In the big fields they were planting wheat and barley. He finished his work in December and when he came to Shusha he told me: "May your eyes be gladdened, congratulations Hamideh. This year the sowing of our crop will yield very good results, because we have plowed the fields at the right time. Next year you will not find a place to put a seed. I wish that in our parts there won't be any famine or need. The peasants following me sowed at the proper time. If there are no locusts, no big hail or drought we will have an excellent harvest."

That year the cotton harvest was not different from previous years. With much difficulty, Mirza Jalil was able to produce 400 *pud*s of cotton, but he was unable to sell it. That same cotton remained in the warehouse until we returned from Iran. After we returned, I sold it and used the money for the

86. General Andronik was one of the field commanders of a group of Armenian irregulars who committed a massacre on 20 August 1918 in retaliation of earlier massacres by Azerbaijaini armed forces that had been formed by the retreating Ottomans.

87. General Shettleworth was the commander of the British forces in Qarabagh in 1919. He asked the Armenians of Qarabagh to accept Azerbaijani rule, but they refused.

88. Khosrow Bey Pasha bey-oghli Sultanov (1879-1941) was a politician. He had graduated from the Medical School of Odessa and was a member of the Caucasus Parliament (Seymi) as well as of the Azerbaijani Parliament. In the first government of Azerbaijan in 1918, he was Minister of Defense. From 1919 to 1920 he was governor of the regions of Shusha, Zangezur, Jabra'il and Javanshir.

repair and cleaning of the *qanat*s, which were in terrible condition.

At the end of 1919 and the beginning of 1920 the relations between Armenians and Turks again worsened. I did not believe that this conflict could go on and this is why I continued giving wool to Armenian women for weaving, who continued to come to the workshop every day. At the same time, I continued with my charitable work.

The famous Bolshevik revolutionary Salman Alibeyov early on had taught at the school of Kahrizli. The Beys were after him and even threatened to kill him. Alibeyov was hiding in the Armenian side of the city. His wife and three children were going hungry. Many times he sent me letters asking me to help his family and I sent money and flour to them. Each time, I wholeheartedly satisfied his request.

We had taken our youngest son to a physician in Aghdam. At that time, I went to visit the field hospital to see the wounded. I saw dreadful things. The wounded were on the floor without a mattress, blanket and pillow. They had neither food nor medicine. The nurses were complaining about the terrible conditions. I promised that I would help them to the best of my capabilities. That same day I bought several rolls of coarse cotton cloth and chintz and went home. In the workshop we had some wool left over from different weavings from which we quickly made some pillows and mattresses. We also called many women from the village and prepared food for the wounded. By the evening we had prepared bedding for six people. That evening, I sent all the food and bedding to the field hospital. In the morning, together with Mirza Jalil, I took a considerable quantity of milk, eggs, and cold yoghurt soup to the wounded.

After a few days, Idris brought Munavvar and left her with us and went to Baku. The dreadful things that had happened in Khankandi had greatly disturbed and affected Munavvar. As I was hearing what was happening in Shusha and Khankandi it

seemed that everybody had lost their senses! That human beings should become so savage is beyond belief! This was a terrible catastrophe and disaster!

At the end of April it was said that the Bolsheviks had entered Baku without meeting any opposition. This astonished us.

***

To get the mail and buy provisions Mirza Jalil often went to Aghdam. There he learnt from the people coming from Baku that the Bolsheviks had been brought to Azerbaijan by the representatives of the Turks. One of them was Nuri Pasha the brother of the well-known Enver Pasha.

About the middle of May, as he was in the habit of doing, he went to Aghdam. In the evening he returned with a young man whom we did not know. Can you imagine, it was Nuri Pasha.

Later I learnt that Nuri Pasha had come to explain to the local people the advantages of the coming of the Bolsheviks. Nuri Pasha gathered the people and gave speeches in praise of the Bolsheviks. Mirza Jalil had become friends with him in Aghdam. During their conversation, Nuri Pasha had told him that he had not rested for the last two months and that he was very tired. He just wanted to relax for a while. Therefore, Mirza Jalil invited him to the village and thus, they came together.

Nuri Pasha was a young handsome man. He only stayed for two days in our house and then he got ready to travel. At that time, he asked if he could draw our portraits. We found out that he was also a painter. My late brother (he was also a painter) had left some drawings, as well as paper and pencils. I gave them to Nuri Pasha. First, he drew my portrait and then, with great difficulty, we managed to persuade Mirza Jalil to sit for him. In general, Mirza Jalil did not like picture drawing. Sitting for a portrait for him was torture. He was sitting uncomfortably as if he was unhappy. Somehow, the painter made a drawing of him sitting with me. Later Nuri Pasha asked that our sons would come so that he might draw them as well with us. In the end, the children did not come. They were shy and went off hiding in the garden.

Nuri Pasha put his name and date on the drawings and gave them to us. Mirza Jalil accompanied him until Aghdam and after that we did not see him again.

***

The seeds that Mirza Jalil had sowed last year had grown good ears of wheat. There was the promise of a beautiful spring. In spring I rented a good piece of land and divided it among the villagers   and we planted the early cotton harvest.

At the end of May, or perhaps the beginning of June, the revolt in Ganja happened[89]. Accounts of destruction and dreadful events had created great anxiety among the people. People, wrapped in fear and dread, were fleeing by the thousands wherever they could and thus, this wave engulfed us as well.

***

At the end of February 1920 Mirza Jalil wrote to me. He said you are helping the poor of Shusha, but you have forgotten the people of the village, they are offended. The villagers are asking that you come and spend the feast of Nowruz with them. He himself was asking that I take the children and come to the village at Nowruz. In the letter he mentioned that he was sending a phaeton.

I bought gifts for the family, relatives, neighbors and people that I knew. Eventually on 6 March the carriage arrived. On the way I stopped in Khankandi; after the illness I took the children and Munavvar to the village. I was thinking that I was going to return after one week, but our forefathers have said: "Man proposes but God disposes."[90] I left Shusha with a houseful of people but I never saw it again.

On 6 March 1920, when we were approaching the village and saw our house we became happy. Mirza Jalil welcomed us in front of the house, and the children happily embraced him. Mirza Jalil was happy with the gifts that I had brought. One could say that for the sake of the Beyram festival they were baking Beyram sweets, and we spent the festival of Nowruz joyously.

* * *

The Ganja Uprising

Mirza Jalil and our entire family were living in Kahrizli village, at 18 werst from Aghdam, on the property of Ahmad Bey. In May 1920, the news spread that there was a revolt in Ganja. The troops that were in Shusha and Aghdam were marching to the railway station of Yevlakh. In Qarabagh, small military units that were withdrawing were attacked by bandits and they killed the poor soldiers and took their arms.

There were rumors among the people that the situation in Baku and Ganja was not good and that the Bolsheviks were leaving. In the beginning of June, the sound of artillery began to be heard from the post office of Shirvanlu and from Barda. Later, firing was heard from the villages in the mountains.

89. The Ganja revolt was an anti-Bolshevik uprising that lasted from 26 to 31 May 1920. It was savagely suppressed. After the city fell it was looted and sacked for a week and thereafter hundreds of people were executed. The revolt gave rise to other uprisings such as the one in June in Shusha led by Nuri Pasha.

90. In Azeri the proverb literally translated says: You count what you count and see what Fate counts.

Everybody was troubled and anxious. Rumors were spread in order to sow unrest. They were saying that the military divisions that had caused the Ganja uprising had returned in anger to Qarabagh and were destroying and leveling to the ground any property they came across.

Everybody was getting ready to flee. There were dreadful rumors going around. They were saying that the troops were killing every young boy, above five or seven, who wore a hat. The common people believed these rumors and left their houses. You would say that the whole place was replete with rumors. People were abandoning everything they had as well as their houses and left in any direction without knowing where. Mirza Jalil and I went to the village and gathered the people in one place. We assured them that no harm would come to their life and property from the Soviet government. We explained that the people that were coming were not their enemy. "On the contrary, they are your friends, they are workers and peasants. For you, poor people, they are no threat." But the saboteurs did not stop, with accounts of dreadful events they frightened people and urged them to flee.

After our words, the villagers were somewhat reassured, but after one or two hours we saw that they were getting ready to flee. Everybody was getting more and more anxious and the number of refugees was increasing daily. This was the busiest time of the year. The harvesters had threshed the barley and were finished. In some places they had started to cut the wheat. In our village there were many day-workers from Iran, whence they had come for seasonal work. The villagers needed bread to feed them. I distributed wheat from my storehouse. Last year's harvest had been abundant in our district.

Because the people of the neighboring village of Asgeran knew that I opposed fleeing en masse they asked me to lead them and talk to the Bolsheviks on their behalf. At that time Mirza Jalil's brother, Ali Akbar, came unexpectedly from Nakhchivan.

He thought it would be better that we should go to Tabriz for a while, so that after the situation had quieted down we might return to our homeland. Mirza Jalil and I decided that we would not leave our house. The sound of gunfire and artillery was coming closer. At this time, the number of refugees from all sides was increasing. There were dreadful stories about killings and massacres. Suddenly you saw that all the villagers and relatives totally disregarded what we had decided about not leaving our houses and were hurriedly loading whatever they could on carts and taking their cattle as well. They followed the long line of refugees. Within one hour the village was absolutely empty and the barking of the abandoned dogs was heard everywhere.

After a while, Qorban, our shepherd, joined the stream of refugees and, without asking anyone, herded our cattle into the courtyard.

Mirza Ali Akbar was insisting on his idea and was saying: "At present the government of Tabriz is in the hands of the democrats and they will receive us gladly. There, we will continue the publication of the journal *Molla Nasreddin* and no doubt this will have excellent results. After the Soviet government has been established in Azerbaijan no doubt they will remember you and they will invite *Molla Nasreddin*. Now it is better not to say so, let us go. I am responsible for your safety."

Mirza Ali Akbar spoke assertively whenever he believed in something, he would not change his mind; he was not afraid of anybody and would not give away to anything.

Without asking me, Mirza Ali Akbar started loading the carts and wheel barrows readying them for departure.

He was loading bedding and food on pack animals. Mirza Jalil looked and I looked at each other and concluded that we could not do anything. We could not stand in front of the wave of refugees. As the saying goes: "There's no sound from one hand clapping." Willy-nilly we gave up and left.

Everybody was collecting things to take with them in a haphazard manner. I gathered my late father's unpublished works, which contained precious material that he had collected over many years about the history of the Caucasus and Qarabagh as well as the Russian translation of Molla Vaqef Panah's work and other poets' works. Later I and Mirza Jalil decided that we should leave these in our house because we hoped that we would return soon.

The other things as well as the library I entrusted to our gardener Tat Polad and told him: "whoever comes from the government give the keys of the house to him." The poor old man cried and he begged me to take his 13-year old daughter Khanom Jan with me. I agreed and took the girl with me. (Later I took her with me from Iran to Baku; she got married with one of her relatives, an electrician, and remained in the city). My old relative Shukur Bey, who was managing the mill, remained behind. I gave the keys of the warehouses to him in case some villagers might come back, so that he could give wheat to them. Shukur wept.

At that time we had a guest from Baku, M. S. Akhundov who, by chance had come to us. He begged us to take him as well. He had many books and a lot of book-keeping paper. He did not want them to leave them behind and he took them with him in our cart.

Mirza Jalil was stunned and did not join in making speculations like we did. But Mirza Ali Akbar was preparing everything diligently. An old Polish mechanic, Qosper Peslyak, who was living with us, while weeping and being agitated asked me to allow him to go with us.

Mirza Ali Akbar made him sit next to the driver on the cart. Finally we left. Two or three old men were left in the entire village. From everywhere the sound of the barking of the abandoned dogs was heard and at a distance the sound of gunfire and artillery was heard. It was around noon, at about 2 or 3 o'clock, 11 June, a Friday. The weather was very hot. Strangely, it was suddenly quiet. It was the quiet before the storm.

I had submitted to fate and was not very anxious. I was hoping that they would send people to ask us to return. Mirza Jalil was also hopeful, because he knew the late Nariman Narimanov very well. In general, ideologically he was pro-Bolshevik.

We joined the general wave of refugees to the south and went towards the Aras River. The roads were filled with people on foot or on horse or in carts, which were filled with adults and children. Most of the women were weeping and beating their breast. The men, while looking back, were driving the cattle. Even the Iranian guest-workers with sickles in their hands were following the wave of refugees.

This was a spontaneous exodus. While I was looking at these lines of refuges, I remembered what my late father had said. He said: "The Caucasus is a gate between Asia and Europe. Time passes. Every hundred years there is an exodus of people from North to South or from South to North, and that is why our people are so wild and poor. Because before they come to themselves and start managing their affairs and property wars, exodus and flight happen. People are forced to flee to the mountains or Iran, or to take refuge in caves and hide-outs. If you look at the history of the Caucasus you see that this is really true. Compared to us, the Armenians are more fortunate because they live in mountainous areas."

***

We arrived in the evening at Elikahriz. The people who were with us said that it would be better to stay there for the night. We ate whatever light food we could find. In the middle of a field we slept in the open air. Mirza Jalil could not sleep. He was saying: "these poor people, what are they afraid of, why are they fleeing?" In general, seeing this spontaneous exodus flabbergasted him.

At day break we woke up, gathered every-thing and we continued our way. Mirza Ali Akbar was managing our caravan. Mirza Jalil was not interfering with anything; he was just observing everything without saying a word. It seemed that in the depth of his heart he was mulling over these things. I was traveling with Mirza Jalil, his 21-year old daughter Munavvar,[91] his 9-year old son Anvar, and his 13-year old nephew Timur[92] traveling in the phaeton. Our driver was Jamal, from our neigh-boring village Dashkasan. In the uncovered cart were Memed Sadeq Akhundov and another guest who had joined us in the confusion. In the other two carts were Peslyak, the wives of our Iranian servants, as well as Khanom Jan. The muleteers who came behind us were also Iranians. Mirza Ali Akbar and his servant Sadeq were armed, and escorted us on horseback.

Among the people who were armed and on horseback was my cousin Shirin, whom I had raised. Some of our reapers and well-diggers from Kahrizli as well as their families were following us. Qorban the shepherd came with 10 sheep for eating during the trip. At every stop, Ghoncheh Nene, the *yukha* baker with all her might was baking bread to feed this crowd of people. At noon we reached Khanshan near Karyagin.[93]

We stopped near a stream. After letting the horses rest for a while we continued. In the middle of the night we reached the village of Veysali. Following the other refugees we decided to stay for the night. Together with the children we wanted

to sleep in a hut. Somebody, whose name I cannot remember now, warned me against staying there and said: "he people of Veysali are terrible bandits; they will cut you to pieces during the night. Nobody will come to your aid." He thought it best to sleep in the carts, in the phaetons, in short in the caravan. By listening to this well-wisher we managed to survive the night.

Early in the morning I had bread baked. Mirza Jalil and Memed Sadeq were walking in the village. Suddenly we saw that from the West, from the mountains, a group of more than 100 soldiers were coming. But these soldiers were not coming like soldiers; they were riding pell-mell as if they were fleeing from some people. Mirza Jalil and Memed Sadeq were asking questions: "Who are you, where are you coming from and where are you going?" It became clear that they were part of the Baku division; Mirza Jalil took some of the newly baked bread from me and gave it to the soldiers.

***

The road was passing over the mountain slopes and without a guide it was dangerous to continue. A very respectable sayyed agreed to guide us for two manat. Fearing the bandits, all refuges tried not to be separated from the caravan. When we arrived at Veysali our old student Hamayel, who was a very able and very competent person, found us. After this, he helped Mirza Ali Akbar escort our caravan. We gave him arms and a horse. Like our other guards he escorted us and was ready to meet any event.

Passing from the Veysali valley was very fearful. Every minute people could have attacked us. Mirza Jalil and I carried weapons. We had Mausers and bandoliers. About noon we arrived at the village of Qervand and wanted to rest there. Hamayel quickly slaughtered a sheep and wanted to make kebabs. Ghoncheh Nane opened the baking plate (*saj*) and

---

91. Vazir, p. 205 gives her age as 12, which is incorrect; she was either 21 or 22 at that time.

92. Timur Asghar-oghli Kangarli (1907-1944) was the son of Mirza Jalil's sister Sakineh. He married Hamideh Khanom's relative Qamar Alieva (1903-1984). He worked as a technician in Baku.

93. Karyagin is the name of one of the Russian commanders during the conquest of Azerbaijan and his name was given to this district; today it is called Fuzuli district.

Types in Qarabagh. *From left to right:* cleric, 2 peasants, merchant, landlord, officer, writer, teacher, millionaire. (no. 22, yr. 9, 8 July 1914)

other utensils and whirled the dough (like a pizza). From our halting place, the smoke of the fire and the delicious smell of roasted meat spread everywhere. For one minute everybody forgot the danger and started eating to their heart's desire.

Mirza Jalil and I were standing on our toes looking with hope at the road that we had traveled. Every moment we were hoping that somebody would come after us. My cousin Alish Alizadeh had promised that as soon as affairs quieted down he would come after us and make us return. If it had not been for Mirza Ali Akbar I would have returned and would not have gone to Iran. Because, if we were to fall into the hands of Kurdish bandits I knew that our life would be in danger.

We had just finished eating our bread when the news started circulating that the place in where we were was dangerous and that we needed to leave hurriedly to Qarakhanli village. We arrived safely at Qarakhanli where we stayed the night. The people welcome us nicely and they put the village school at our disposal to spend the night.

We left a guard outside and slept. At daybreak we continued our journey. Throughout the journey the number of refugees was increasing. Some Beys came to our caravan and asked to our astonishment: "Why are you fleeing?" At midday we crossed the Quru chay. In the evening we arrived at Dördchenar and we camped on the slope of a mountain with a beautiful view, plenty of water and many gardens.

Here the late Javad Agha Javanshir came to our caravan. This old man kissed my forehead and wept. He was the grandson of the poet Ja'farqoli Khan and a distant relative of my late father. Apart from that he was one of the admirers and subscribers of *Molla Nasreddin*. He greeted Mirza Jalil and talked to him and then he turned to me and said: "Daughter of my dear brother, where are you fleeing to? Why are you fleeing? The Bolsheviks will not do anything to you. If you encounter the Kurdish bandits in Iran you will not be safe. To get whatever you have they will cut you, and even the children, to pieces. Come, listen to me. Go back." He invited us to his house, but we thanked him and refused, because we did not want to be separated from the caravan.

I noticed that whenever we arrived in a village that the villagers became worried and hurriedly packed up their things and followed us.

Javad Agha's words did not leave me untouched. I discussed them with Mirza Jalil and Mirza Ali Akbar and asked them not to go to Iran. I suggested staying in some quiet place nearby until the troubles had died down. Mirza Jalil was silent. Mirza Ali Akbar said: "If we hide here they will betray us and we will be killed." He also quoted this proverb that: "until the fox proves that he is a fox he will be skinned alive." Mirza Ali Akbar said that: "I am not afraid of the Iranian bandits. We are not few. We have arms and ammunition. The difficult part is to reach Ahar. I have friends there. From there until the district of Amir Arshad there is no danger. In Tabriz, the government is in the hands of the Democrats and they will welcome us with open arms. And we will publish *Molla Nasreddin* there." He said: "we will see how all this will bear fruit. After the Soviet government is established and firmly implanted in Azerbaijan they will remember us and most certainly call back *Molla Nasreddin*.

And don't hesitate; let us continue our way and I will be responsible for your security."

The late Mirza Ali Akbar was talking with certainty and assurance. He was devoted and courageous. You might call him real committed fighter (*feda'i*). He was a fearless person; if he decided something nobody could dissuade him. In friendly discussions he was very humorous and good at repartee. He was a master in relating interesting events and in telling jokes. He was a well-known revolutionary in Iran. Because of his beliefs he had suffered seven years of imprisonment in Russian jails.

***

In the village of Dördchenar, Mirza Ali Akbar managed to put the caravan in such a way that everything was visible in front us, so that nothing could be stolen. All around us he put guards. You could say that he almost never slept on the way. He was looking after everybody. For Mirza Jalil we erected a shade near the carts so that he could sleep there with the children. We and the children lay down without taking off our clothes. Although we were very tired sleep was not coming to our eyes. They had told me that "in these parts there were bands of bandits, wild as animals. They follow you and whenever an opportunity presents itself they surround you and would kill you."

At daybreak we rose and we continued on the road over the mountain slope into the direction of the Aras. We had to pass Dashkasan village. Our driver, Jamal, originally hailed from this village. He said good-bye and left with his family to his village. The rest of the journey Mirza Jalil sat in the driver's place and drove the phaeton.

Shirin was sitting to Mirza Jalil. At noon we reached the Aras we turned right and followed the river bank. The guides hired in the village of Dördchenar turned our caravan to the right side of the river and said that if we would follow the slope of the mountains the road would be better. Everybody agreed. We continued, but suddenly, I don't know what happened, but the man at the head of the caravan turned and said that it would be better that everybody follow him on the left side of the river. Later, it was said that the guides had turned us on purpose to the right, so that we might be plundered in the mountains and the valleys. It seemed that they were in cahoots with the bandits, who were waiting for us in the mountains. There was a young man among the guides who saw his niece among the refugees. He told her of this ambush. She told her husband and he told the other people. When this plot was discovered they changed course in good time. In one of the bends in the road suddenly one of the wheels of our phaeton dropped off and broke. Mirza Jalil did not know what to do and called the mechanic Pislyak. They took a wheel from a cart and put it onto the phaeton and we continued somehow on our way.

Along the river bank, in a place where we thought the railway was going, wheat was growing. From afar a reed bed could be seen. The river flowed into this reed bed. On the right side of the river there were rocks that were not very big. We stopped for a while in Maralbine to rest the horses. Without resting, to get to Hoseynbeyli village as soon as possible, we continued our journey even though we were hungry. Our phaeton passed other vehicles; we were the first to arrive at the house of Ahmad Bey Hoseynbeyov. The owner of the house welcomed us with joy.

However, the things that he said made us want to leave. We collected our things and left. After much trouble we crossed Khodafarin Bridge over the Aras and stepped onto Iranian soil. Mirza Ali went back and brought with him the phaeton, the carts, and the cattle. We were very thirsty. We were drinking avidly the lukewarm and muddy water to extinguish our thirst.

We crossed the Khodafarin Bridge on 17 June. It was about 10 or 11 in the evening. We continued our way following the instructions of our guides downwards along the bank of the river. We were tired, worn out, exhausted and hungry. The poor children were traveling with much difficulty. After 2 to 3 km we decided to spend the night there. Ghoncheh[94] gave each one of us a piece of bread on which there was butter and honey. The guides promised that they would not sleep until morning and watch over our belongings. After much excitement and suffering we slept as dead in the carts. We got up early in the morning; everything was in its place. One of the villagers of Hoseynbegli village, Ahmad Bey, had written a letter to his uncle Ali Murad Khan, which he had given us so that he would help us. Ali Murad Khan was living close by. After having breakfast we traveled to his village. The roads were very bad and we were all walking. The guides were walking in front and showing us the way. On both sides of the road, in the fields, they were harvesting. On the way two bags with the clothes of Mirza Jalil and Mirza Ali Akbar and the children were stolen.

When we arrived at the village of Larjan, which was the home of Ali Murad Khan we gave the letter to one of the guides and sent him to the village. The Khan came and welcomed us himself. By the Khan's order they took us to a house and made us comfortable. The next day at the Khan's invitation we went to his house and we had tea on his balcony. From the balcony we had a beautiful view of the Aras River. Ali Murad Khan told me that on that day he was going to guide the people who had crossed from the other side. I begged him to search for my son Muzaffar among the people who had fled from there and if he found him to bring him to us. Muzaffar had gone to Shusha and had not returned. We were very worried about him.

___

94. Ghoncheh was a servant girl in Mirza Jalil's household at the time.

The Khan promised to do so. A few hours later they brought the news that the Khan had brought Muzaffar.

Two days later Mirza Jalil and I went to the Khan and asked him to send us reliable guides. From the Khan we learnt that there was fighting near the town of Ahar between Khan Amir Arash and the Khans of Qaradagh. The road to Ahar was dangerous. Therefore, the Khan for the time being thought that it would be better that we'd go to Samsam Khan in the village of Nugahdeh. We had no other choice and willy-nilly we accepted this. We were near Ahar; he hired for us two guides and three mules. In the morning he sent us on our way with many compliments. When we arrived in the village of Nugahdeh it became clear that Samsam Khan had gone to war and his family was in the summer quarters. We spent the night there and in the morning we learnt where Samsam Khan's wife was staying. We wrote her a letter and asked her to accept us as guests. Around noon the wife's answer arrived. With great kindness she invited us to the village of Aliabad. She had told the letter carrier, who came on a horse, to accompany us to her place. We quickly took everything and left. We reached Aliabad in the evening when it was dark. There they told us that Khan Aqa was a very good person, "she will not allow one strand of hair to be taken from you."

We arrived at Aliabad on 24 June; it was night. We stayed in the house of a Kurd. I and Munavvar were invited by the Khan's wife. I took Anvar with us. When we arrived at the building they told us to go to the roof, but since there was neither stairs nor a ladder to climb, we were left bewildered. At that time a Kurdish woman bent and told us to put our feet on her back and climb to the roof. Whether we liked it or not we climbed to the roof in this way; in front of us there was an incredible scene. There were expensive carpets, and on silk mattresses there were beautiful cushions. Two ladies were sitting. Big lamps lit the roof as if it were daylight. One of the ladies wore a multi-colored dress, she had much jewelry. The other lady wore a bright colored dress and much make-up. We looked at each other with much curiosity. After greeting each other they invited us to sit next to them. The lady with jewelry was Samsam Khan's wife, Khanum Aqa (her original name was Malika Khanum); she was very beautiful. In the absence of her husband she was managing everything in the village. At that time these small Khans of Iran were under nobody and they lived independently and were continuously fighting with each other.

The other lady was Agha Khanum, the wife of Samsam's brother who had died three years previously and she was not very beautiful. Next to them a pretty woman, without much make-up, was seated; she was a famous singer in the Qaradagh district. This woman with her beautiful voice and interesting conversation would entertain the ladies.

Khanum Agha kindly asked after our health and before long they brought chicken polow in 20 copper trays. We ate the polow with our hands from the same tray as the ladies. Polow was also sent, at the lady's orders, to Mirza Jalil and company

We stayed the night with them. The next day at the lady's order they erected two felt-covered tents next to a spring that was outside the village. Not very far from there, near a waterfall, they erected tents for themselves. Khanum Agha invited me, Munavvar and Anvar to live in her own tent. For ten days we were her guests at lunch and then she gave us one milk-giving buffalo and ten *pud*[95] of flour. I sent her several *girvanka*[96] of expensive tea and sugar cubes.

This region was mountainous and heavily forested, but the flat areas were very green. The air was clean and fragrant. The water of the springs was cool and delicious. In short, we began to feel ourselves at ease. Mirza Jalil was no longer

---

95. One *pud* equals 16.38 kg.
96. One *girvanka* equals 8.88 kg.

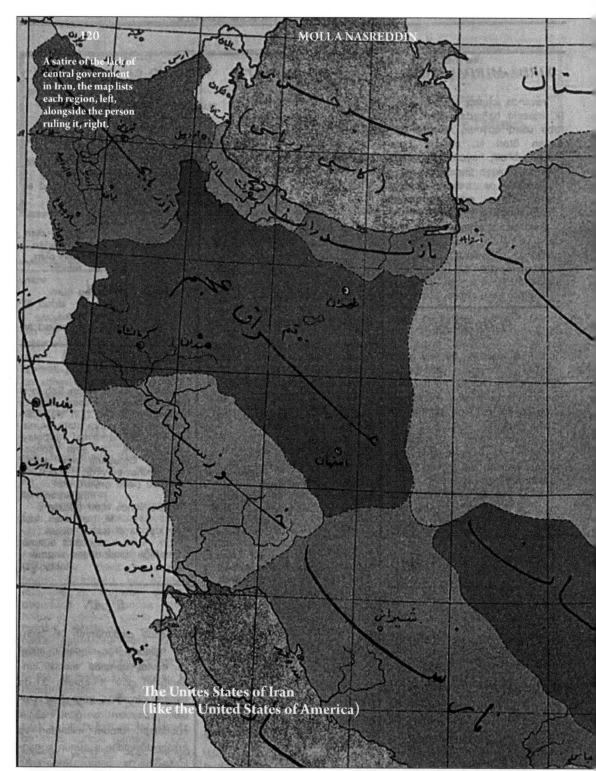

The United States of Iran Torn Apart by Rival Warlords (no. 14, yr. 3, 6 April 1908, image from *Slaves and Tartars Presents, Molla Nasreddin: the magazine that would've, could've, should've*, Zurich: Christopher Keller Editions, 2011)

121

IRAN

States	Governors
The Sultanate of Maku	Eqbal os-Saltaneh
The Kingdom of Tabriz	Mir Hashem
The Emirate of Maraghe	Haji Samad Khan
The Governate of Ardebil	Mirza Ali Akbar
The Empire of Urmia	Mohammad Beg Dashli
The Caliphate of Gilan	The Shariatmadar
The Princepate of Quchan	Salar-e Mofakhkham
The Emirate of Astarabad	Sepahdar
The Principality of Shiraz	Qavam [ol-Molk]
The Tehran Khanate	Mohammad Ali
The Qom Empire	The Motavallibashi
The Esfahan Khanate	Aqa Najafi
The Sultanate of Eraq	Haji Aqa Mohsen
The Salmas Principality	Simko
The Qaen Khadivate	Heshmat ol-Molk

The officers of the Tehran Khanate:	
Prime Minister	Amir-e Bahador-e Jang
Minister of the Interior	Mojallal [os-Saltaneh]
The Foreign Minister	Arfa ol-Dawleh
Minister of the Treasury	Shapshal
The Sheik ol-Eslam	Sheikh Fazlollah
Minister of the Navy	Aslan Khan

low-spirited. He was looking at everything and he was talking with people for a long time and was taking notes in his notebook. Of course, the Kurds were thinking that he actually was *Molla Nasreddin*; they were taken it literally. They had no idea about the journal *Molla Nasreddin*.

* * *

One time Mirza Jalil told me smilingly, "today a white-bearded Kurd came to me and asked me to write a prayer for his daughter who was suffering from chest-pain, and I refused. He thought that I did not want to write it for free and said, 'you write the prayer and instead I will bring you two pairs of socks with a flower pattern.'" These Kurds were very poor, their women and children were in tattered clothes and very young children were walking around naked. They were talking to us in Azeri and among themselves they were talking in Kurdish. One could say that most of the men had gone fighting and in the village there only remained the *kadkhoda,* old men and a few of *farrashes* (servants) of Khanum Agha.

The poor Kurdish women were doing household and field work. The children were guarding the grazing herds and they were helping to cut wood and other chores to help their mothers. Every family had one or two or even three cows and a few goats. Even during the summer they would bring and keep the herds in the stable that was behind their house. The stable door was inside the house. In this way they would take the animals through the house to the stable. The stable had a latticed door. The Kurds, out of fear of thieves had made them like that.

The Kurds were only cultivating millet, barley, and hemp. Their bread was dark but tasty. Especially the butter and cream, which were very good. The Kurdish villagers very rarely ate butter. When the women were churning the butter the

The Khan: "Give me half a manat, otherwise I will take you to the Nayeb and he will take 5 manats from you." The Peasant: "May I be your sacrifice. I have just managed to escape from Rahim Khan's plundering. Apart from my clothes I have nothing."
(no. 15, yr. 4, 12 April 1909)

Khan's servants on the Khan's wife's order would go there and demand the butter. If the women asked for proof of the order they would go and bring the Khan's rosary. Then the women would apologize and give the butter without saying anything. But after the servants had left they would curse and vilify them.

On the second of June, Ghoncheh and Hamayel went to Qarabagh. Mirza Jalil and I wrote a letter to my cousin Alish that he should come and get us. We had not given up hope to return to our home. But Mirza Ali Akbar was trying to take us to Ahar as soon as possible, but the fighting was still continuing on the road to Ahar.

Khanum Agha advised me: "It is better for you to stay with me and not to go to Ahar or Tabriz until everything has quieted down and then might return to our homeland." Khanum Agha and Agha Khanum had become so intimate with us that at the end they said, let us be soul sisters[97]and we agreed to that. Therefore, the Mulla was called. We hooked each other's pinky finger and the Mulla read a prayer and then we gave everybody presents for the sake of our soul-sisterhood. Then he congratulated us on our sisterhood. From then onwards we were considered to be almost like blood relatives of the Khan's family.

The wife of Samsam Khan's late brother Rustam Khan, Agha Khanum was the daughter of the Khan of Kalibar, Shoja` al-Mamalek. The small town of Kalibar is situated on the east side of the river in a valley. According to tradition, this small town was founded by the Barbar tribe. Nader Shah was born in this place and in childhood he was a goat shepherd.[98]

Agha Khanum with her 3-year old daughter was getting ready to go to Kalibar to see her mother and she invited us there. Her father Shoja` al-Mamalek was also fighting with Amir Arshad.

On 10 June, which was a Saturday, we mounted our horses and started on our way. From our family, I, Munavvar, Muzaffar, and Anvar were going as guests to Kalibar. Agha Khanum was riding a beautiful horse that had a silk horse-blanket, a pretty saddle, and silver reins and it was led by a servant who was well-dressed. On the orders of Khanum Agha one of the servants was leading my

horse by the reins. Among the Kurds this was both a sign of respect and at the same time it was for the sake of safety because of the ups and downs of the road.

We were traveling on a beautiful winding road that went through forests and over mountains. The view of these places that were covered with flowers was beautiful and the air was full of fragrance. My horse was going along with that of Agha Khanum and all the way we were talking. She was saying that nobody could go up so high; at one time only her father knew the road of this mountain. He had come to the peak of Mt. Jegherla and he had a built a house there, dug a well, and had built a windmill so that in the time of war, when there was serious danger he could hide with his family there. She said, "If Amir Arshad comes against us, we will go up there and hide and we will take you with us. We have enough wheat there."

When we were getting near the small town of Kalibar alongside of the mountain we saw walled gardens of the village owner. Agha Khanum told us that the third wife of her father Shoja` al-Mamalek lived there. She was a foreigner, either a Russian or a Jewess.

We arrived at Kalibar in the middle of the day. The town was situated on the right side of the river and on the left side of the river were gardens. The people were mainly working in orchards. They were making grape syrup and dried fruits. The town had one storey-houses made of stone and crooked and narrow lanes. The Khan's house had two storeys. The women's quarter was separated by a wall. Muzaffar was taken the men's quarter. In the Khan's house his eldest wife and cousin Sakineh Khanum was the mistress. She was very beautiful and was constantly smiling. In her arms a 3-year old girl was playing. This was the daughter of the second wife. At that time Parizad had just given birth to a boy and the next day was the naming day and after the Mulla had said prayers the child was given a name. Agha Khanum took us around

97. The term used is *sigheh baji*, meaning to make a pact of sisterhood, see Willem Floor, *A Social History of Sexual Relations in Iran*. Washington DC: Mage Publishers, 2008, p. 334.

98. Nader Shah was born in the fort of Dastgerd in Khorasan and was a member of the Afshar tribe.

in the gardens, where I ran into a lady that I knew. Once her husband was our well-digger and she was amazed that we had left our household and everything and had come to Kalibar.

In the evening Sakineh Khanum's brother, Nasrollah Khan came to see his sister. Instead of smoking a cigarette he was smoking opium. They made me believe that you could not trust Kurdish Khans and also that it was wise to live in Kalibar. They were saying, "Mirza Jalil can teach at the school and life would not be bad for you here." The Khans of Kalibar were not illiterate; they were familiar with the journal *Molla Nasreddin*.

On 13 June after lunch we said goodbye to our wonderful hostess and returned. On the way we tarried and it became dark and with difficulty we managed to reach Aliabad. Near Aliabad Khanum Agha's servant fired a shot and with this he announced that guests were coming. This was their custom.

* * *

Nasrollah Khan with his brother came to Aliabad to get to know Mirza Jalil. He asked Mirza Jalil to come and live in Kalibar. Mirza Ali Akbar was totally against this. With whatever means he wanted to go to Tabriz and continue publishing the journal; this had become the purpose of his life.

When we were talking with Khanum Agha she told us that in the past her mother and father had immigrated from Qarabagh to Iran. They were related to the Javanshir family and her own uncle, Pasha Khan, whose penname was Fateh, now lived near Ahar.

This time I remembered what my late father Ahmad Bey had told me. One time he told me, "if war breaks out and as it was in the past people leave their home and property and flee and you go to Iran, remember that we have family there, they will help you. Among them is one called Pasha Khan

who must be living near Ahar." Therefore, this conversation gladdened our hearts.

One of the singers of the wife's household named Qizqayit Khanum had taken one of the Khan's servants as a wife for her sister's son. For this occasion there was a wedding in the house of Pari, Qizqayit Khanum's sister. The minstrel who was invited to the wedding was singing and playing music, and constantly played dance tunes. Our entire family went there. Mirza Jalil was sitting at head of the gathering and was attentively looking at everything. We made the groom's mother named Pari dance. She was a tall, beautiful, and good-looking woman. Her face and her manner of dancing reminded me of the Cleopatra dancers of the Egyptians. Pari was dancing with a special air. After a long dance she fell down and fainted. They were giving money as a token of appreciation (*shabash*). Accompanied by the music Qiz Khanum was singing, she had a powerful and beautiful voice. The wives of the Khan had not come to the wedding; they were still mourning Rostam Khan's death. The tent was rather small for us, therefore the house of a widow called Ummi was made available for us. She was still young and had two children. Khanum Agha's secretary, Mashdi Memed wanted to marry her. The story of "the Khan's rosary" by Mirza Jalil is alludes to this. As I mentioned above the way to the stable was passing through the house of Ummi. Every morning and evening the herd was passing through our living room.

Abdol-Samad Khan Samsam had returned from the front. Mirza Jalil and Mirza Ali Akbar went to see him and made his acquaintance. He gracefully said that until our relatives came and took us, we should live in his house.

The following day Khanum Agha invited me and introduced me to her husband. When he learnt that we had been robbed near the village of Nugadi he promised that he would find the robbers and return our things. He advised us not hasten our departure, because the roads to Tabriz and Ahar were full of soldiers. The following day the Khan went to war.

Some of our stolen things were found and returned to us. The retrieving of the writings, dictionaries and documents of Mirza Jalil made us so happy that we forgot about the things that were not found.

The ladies gathered and looked attentively at our pictures and those of our friends. Khanum Agha liked them so much that she asked me to give them to her. Among the pictures there was one of Mirza Jalil standing, which was taken in 1907 in Tiflis. I regretted that I gave it to her, because he had signed it for me, but I could not say 'No' to Khanum Agha.

One day, Khanum Agha took us to the mountains to the summerhouse of her sister that was called Gavahan (the Plow). Nature there was much more beautiful than Aliabad and after a few days we returned.

Qizghayit Khanum was with us all the time and she was entertaining us with witticisms and sang beautiful songs, she was an interesting woman and 35 years old. She hated men and that is why she never married. She was a singer and the ladies of the Khan could not do without her. For sure, she was not going to abandon her art for her personal life. Besides, she was living as a steward and manager of the Khan's wife and like a man she would go out all alone on horseback to faraway places and would execute whatever order she had received. She was virtually like an Amazon.

I proposed to her to come to Baku and perform there as a singer in the theater. Khanum Agha was getting ready to come with us to Baku as a guest. She said that "the situation of the Khandom is uncertain. Today we are masters and tomorrow somebody else replaces us. Somebody like Amir Arshad may seize this place and take us captive and make us his slaves. Now that we have known you, it is Good-bye, we will cross the Aras and come and live with you. Don't think that I am hosting you for free." (what Khanum Agha said became

true, because two years later Amir Arshad took the Khandom. Samsam Shoja al-Mamalek somehow was able to cross the Aras and save himself, but his family was captured and taken to Amir Arshad's house. Parizad, Shoja al-Mamalek's wife gave birth to a son in captivity and Amir Arshad called him Asir Khan (Prisoner Khan). Shoja when he heard about this died of grief. All this was told to me by my brother-in-law Mirza Ali Akbar. He, in 1922, was appointed by our government to receive the Iranian refugees and he was an eye-witness to all this.)

Truly, Khanum Agha was very friendly with me and called me 'sister' and whenever I came she stood up and invited me to sit in the place of honor. She would eat with me from the same plate and she would serve the best part of the food with her own hands to me. She never contradicted me. Once she wanted to shoot her servant because of a mistake that he had made. I was there and I took her hands and implored her not to do such a thing. Agha Khanum looked at me and came to herself and told the servant: "Go and be a sacrifice to my sister, because of her I saved you. For her sake I didn't kill you."

In Khanum Agha's tent, behind the fire place, on a carpet there was a rifle, a cartridge case and one Mauser. In spite of her elegant and graceful appearance, she was very brave, and also a wise and polite lady.

Khanum Agha's tent was almost like a government office. All the time, people came from surrounding villages with requests and complaints, or people who wanted to rent a property. Her secretary, Mirza Mohammad, with his documents, papers, ink-holder in his saddle-bag sitting on his knees in front of the fire that was always burning. The Mirza was writing documents and letters on behalf of Khanum Agha all the time; she would read them and put her seal on them. She was able to read.

Samsam sent news with a post-rider to send him provisions and armed men. Khanum Agha gave orders and everybody from the villages brought provisions.

Mirza Ali Akbar was upset with our tarrying so much in Aliabad. He had decided to go with the Khan's people to Ahar to learn how matters stood and if possible to send for us as well. But Mirza Jalil, because of some consideration of his own, did not want his brother go to Ahar. But Mirza Ali Akbar, ignoring his brother's reasoning, took his servant and left Aliabad.

Mirza Jalil exchanged some our animals for two horses, which were used to travel on mountainous roads. He liked horses very much and he looked after them with affection. In accordance with his directions the children would take the horses to the harvested fields and they would cut the grass and bring them home.

At the beginning of my text I said that the Khan's wife and other women wore a long robe over a wide skirt at the bottom of which were silver buttons and on top of the robe they wore a short-sleeved jacket made of *atlas*,[99] velvet or gold-embroidered cloth. The skirts had fringes. Khanum Agha looked extraordinary in this dress. With every movement the silver buttons on her robe and her necklaces would make noise. I had 100 new manat coins, and distributed some of them among the Kurdish women and servants. When they received this valuable gift they were beyond themselves. I treated sick people there with my medicines and as a result they became healthy and the villagers were starting to believe in me.

Agha Khanum had a 3-year old daughter, and Khanum Agha had a 9-year old son called Tarlan Khan, who was considered to be the heir. They were betrothed so as not to divide the property and they would be married when grown up. Khanum

Agha secretly thought that sooner or later Agha Khanum was going to be forced to marry Samsam. Agha Khanum was young and marriageable. If she married somebody else her property would be divided and they would not allow it.

Almost every day a sheep was slaughtered in the Khan's wife's house for lunch. Sometimes, Khanum Agha would herself put the sheep's shoulder on a skewer and roast it in the ever burning fire. She would give the best part of the roasted meat to people around her and she would eat very little herself.

Mirza Mohammad and Qizqayit Khanum always sat by the fire facing Khanum Agha ready to execute her orders. I usually sat there too.

One evening, a very beautifully dressed girl entered the tent and fell at the feet of Khanum Agha. A distinguished woman and two Kurds came in after her. They were interrupting each other, while trying to talk to Khanum Agha. The face of the Khan's wife first showed an expression of agitation and then gradually reddened.

I saw that she was undergoing an internal emotional battle, but she remained silent and let the complainers have their say without interruption. I asked Qizqayit quietly: "Who is this young woman?" She replied: "She is Samsam's wife from Merzili." The young woman had not gotten up from her prostrated position and remained lying at Khanum Agha's feet crying. Finally, Khanum Agha turned to the distinguished woman and the two Kurds, and shouted: "Enough! Be quiet! How dare you humiliate Samsam's wife. You are going to answer for this!"

Khanum Agha ordered the servants to go quickly Merzili and bring some of the animals of the person who has been wronged. She told the young woman: "Bala Khanum! Get up and sit next to the fire! Your place is there!"

Samsam Khan could not find fault with Khanum Agha's decision, therefore, from this moment onwards the Khan was barred from Bala

---

99. *Atlas* is a silken or silken/cotton fabric.

Khanum's presence. Khanum Agha did not allow Bala Khanum to go to the Khan's house. I described this event for Mirza Jalil in detail. Khanum Agha's character interested him greatly. He wanted to personally know this lady, but at this time it was not possible.

At last, a letter came from Ahar from Mirza Ali Akbar. It was opened and read by the wife of the secretary, Mirza Mohammad. Mirza Ali Akbar had written, "the fighting has stopped, the roads are safe, and you should start traveling. It is no longer necessary to stay in that nest of ruffians."

These last words of Mirza Ali Akbar put us in a very awkward situation, because the content of the letter was known to Khanum Agha. Mirza Jalil was very angry because of this rudeness towards our hosts. We were afraid that Khanum Agha would be hurt and would not help us. After all, to go to Ahar we needed experienced guides and mules for our luggage.

I loved Khanum Agha and did not believe he would hurt us. I went to her and talked about everything openly without hiding anything. She listened with respect and I could see from her eyes that she would never abandon us. With much grace she suggested that we stay in her house until her nephew came to take us. But since she knew that we were not giving up the idea of leaving, she called on trustworthy people and recommended that they take us to Ahar. She gave us four mules for our luggage. We were to pay the guides 15 *tumans*.

* * *

Gathering things and starting on the road took a while. Meanwhile, Mirza Ali Akbar could not wait any longer and came himself and he said the people of Ahar will be pleased to see *Molla Nasreddin* in their own town. They had prepared a 2-storey building with an orchard for us there. We were pleased with this news and wanted to leave. As a

gift we sent a milk buffalo to the Khan's wife and since we had lived in her house we gave money to Ummi and we gathered our belongings and went on our way.

Before leaving I went with Munavvar to visit Khanum Agha and Agha Khanum to thank them for their hospitality and we said goodbye with utmost affection. The poor Bala Khanum was watching us with envy. We were going to her native village and we were going to stay the night there.

We left Aliabad on 7 August, which was a Saturday. Flanking the road, which was rising up the mountain, were forests, charcoal heaps, and meadows covered with flowers. By the roadside very often you came across springs that would flow from the rocks. Sometimes you would see nomad tents and herds. We were fourteen people. Apart from Mirza Jalil's horses, my horse and those of Munavvar, Mirza Ali Akbar, all the other horses and mules were loaded with our belongings. The children and Khanum Jan were sitting on top of the luggage and Muzaffar, Sadeq and Shirin were walking and leading the mules and horses.

In the afternoon, we reached the village of Marzeli, situated on an elevated place. We stayed at the house of our guide, Memed Ali, who was the *kadkhoda*. Here we heard unpleasant news. At the front Amir Arshad's forces had won and they were approaching and would reach the village that day. They were saying that they were bringing the bodies of two people killed in the fighting to Marzeli. The village was in mourning. On the road we met a group of weeping women that was going to welcome the bodies. This situation made us think about our own fate.

After talking to the guides we decided to return to Aliabad. When we reached the village I rode ahead and went to see Khanum Agha. She came to me and looked sadly at me and said: "My poor sister, how much suffering do you have to endure?"

They took us to a house with a verandah and a stable. Again we had to settle down. Who knows, what will happen to us tomorrow? Perhaps, even tomorrow Amir Arshad's forces would win and come to Aliabad and make us and the Khan's wives captives. The Khan's wife consoled us saying: "If the enemy forces approach they will notify us very soon. Then we will take you and go and hide in an inaccessible mountain hideout." (I was told by a woman called Pari, who had escaped from Aliabad and had come to Kahrizli that in 1922 that exactly the same thing happened and Amir Arshad captured the wives of the Khans of Kalibar and Aliabad and took them with him.)

The wives of the Khans were hiding their expensive items, carpets and other household goods. All this uproar and excitement was bothering Mirza Jalil. He was pale and was talking very seldom. Sometimes he would go and sit in a corner and think. Of course, he was worried about the fate of his own family, therefore, he could not think.

As it was my habit, I was not dispirited and I believed that matters would end well. I was trying to convince Mirza Jalil that it would be like that. Even the enemies of Amir Arshad were not talking badly about him. They were saying that he wanted to be the king, and that he was a relatively literate person. In the places where he ruled you could put gold on your head and walk and nobody would bother you.

In our new halting place some of our things were stolen. This time Mirza Jalil's oak-colored overcoat and his Bokhara hat were taken.

After a week, news arrived that the Khans had made peace with Amir Arshad and we got ready to depart. When I was saying goodbye to Khanum Agha I wanted to give her a golden brooch and emphatically she did not accept it and said that you have given me too many things and this will be useful to you in Tabriz.

At last, on 17 August 1920 we began our journey and we reached Marzeli village and stayed the night at the house of the *kadkhoda*, Memed Ali. Marzeli was situated on the side of a huge mountain. It had plenty of water, mills, and in the middle of

the village there was an irrigation canal. It was completely covered with boards. The old men of the village said that this channel was built by Harun al-Rashid's wife. The villagers were wheat farmers. They said that Samsam had a large amount of wheat here. On 18 August the harvesting was almost over. The beauty of this village was like that of Bala Khanum, who was an honored prisoner of her rival Khanum Agha.

In the early morning we started; we were trying to get to Ahar before it became dark. We did not want to encounter robbers and smugglers on the road. At Khanum Agha's orders my horse's reins were held by her servant Nasrollah. There were ups and downs in the road. Occasionally we met nomads. Mirza Ali Akbar was attentively looking around and had his arms ready. We could have been attacked by robbers or encountered the horsemen of the warring Khans, which would have cost us dearly. The guides agreed that the roads were dangerous.

On the slope of the mountain they showed us a ruined stone building and said that this was a caravanserai built by Shah Abbas and that once there was a road to Tabriz. In spite of the fact that the road was very steep our horses were going very fast. In one of the mountain passes, a mule with its entire load fell into the ravine. Somehow they managed to pull up the animal. Everything went well. The only thing was that the tea utensils were broken and the samovar was smashed. At noon we reached the top of the mountain. From there we had a beautiful view towards the south. On the other side there was an enormous precipice. It seemed that the mountain tops were ending. From the top of the mountain an endless winding road went down. The guides showed us Ahar in the distance, which was situated in a nice, flat valley and was surrounded by tall mountains. Toward the east, on the left side, the mighty snow-capped Savalan Mountain rose up. On the right side was the border of Amir Arshad's territory, which was called Üzümdil. The guides told us not to go via open sides, because Amir Arshad's border guards would shoot at us. We hurriedly came down from our horses and on foot started coming down the winding road.

When we came down we found a different world. Where we were standing a narrow valley began. There was a stream coming down from the mountain. Here the weather was pleasant and even warm. The guides suggested we stay here and give ourselves and the horses a rest. There were not very many trees here. Our attention was drawn to rocks that were spaced apart and looked like men as if they were carved from stone and had been placed at the road side. One of them looked like the old witches that are described in story books. Mirza Jalil and the children were sitting under "the old witch."

We ate and rested and then continued our way. We came down from the heights and entered more level places. Occasionally we passed villages. After two or three hours we arrived at the village called Ali Reza Chay (Ali Reza Spring), which had huge mulberry trees. We went to a stream, where there were two women and they were looking at us with interest. One of them asked me politely who I was and where we were coming from. I told her that we were coming from Qarabagh, my name, my father's name and that of our village. She was dumbstruck and then suddenly began praising my father. I asked her how she knew him? It became clear that many migrant-workers from this village used to go my father's estate. At the end of the season they would return with much money and provisions. After resting some time we left. Mirza Jalil was very tired and dejected and once he suddenly felt giddy and fell from his horse. I was very scared, but fortunately nothing further happened. Some of our fellow-passengers sat on the horses on top of the baggage, because the road was very level and even suitable for carts. In spite of my insistence, only Muzaffar did not ride on a horse. In accordance with Khanum Agha's instructions, her servant

Landlord and peasants (no. 9, yr. 2, 3 March 1907)

Nasrollah would not let go the reins of my horse, although there was no need for this. But walking in front of me with the horse's reins in his hand was a sign of respect for Khanum Agha.

* * *

One hour before sunset we saw the environs of the town of Ahar appearing; our spirits were lifted, because after so many hardships they were coming to an end and our body and soul would find rest. Eventually, we left the mountains behind and we entered a vast plain with many streams, full of vegetation and crops. Then the walls, the minarets and the houses of the city began to appear. The sun was going down and there was 3 or 4 werst to the city. The guides were anxious and were beating the horses trying to get to the town. They were saying that since the times were unsettled as soon as night fell they would close the gates of the town. Javad Khan's horsemen around the town would plunder anyone that they encountered. You would say that Ahar was neither under the shah nor the khans, it was an independent place. It had its own governor and its own government.

At sunset we arrived at the city; the gates had just been closed. Ali Akbar dismounted and talked with the gate keeper; the gate was opened and we entered the city. Following Mirza Ali Akbar we came to a house that had already been prepared for us. The people in the streets stopped and looked at us with wonder. The house that was assigned to us was big and clean. We immediately opened the luggage and spread the mattresses, blankets and the carpets and we lit the samovar. Mirza Ali Akbar for some reason had left. He returned after less than one hour with a large tray of polow with various stews. This was sent by one of his Ahari friends. After supper we threw ourselves on the beds and slept.

The next day I gave 15 *tuman*s to each of our guides and I gave them about 50 bullets. To the servants, who promised to come to us when we returned to Qarabagh, I gave some presents. On 19 August, Mirza Ali Akbar took Mirza Jalil and the children to the bathhouse, but we stayed at home and began cleaning things and washing the clothes. Mirza Ali Akbar had bought thin *lavash* bread in the bazaar as well as good mutton with fat and other things. For lunch we prepared *bozbash*, which was Mirza Jalil's favorite food and it was fragrant. Since he felt that his family was now out of danger he was no longer and was joking around with the children and had fun.

In the evening people who were the admirers of the journal *Molla Nasreddin* came to see Mirza Jalil. Before their arrival and to give them tea, Mirza Ali Akbar had found and brought glasses that were pear-shaped. The second day the number of people who came to meet him increased. Among them were the notables of the city; they greeted Mirza Jalil with kindness and asked him to remain in Ahar for ever and they invited him to their homes. But as usual, he did not want to become their guest. Mirza Ali Akbar somehow made him change his mind and they went to some of their homes. The famous sayyed, the son of Mir Hashem Aqa, Mir Habib Aqa, who was one of the earliest subscribers of the journal was especially showing incredible hospitality to Mirza Jalil. Mir Habib Aqa had studied in Russia and lived there for a while; he was an intellectual. From his garden he often sent us fruit, vegetables and many sacks of barley for the horses. On 25 August on the Feast of the Sacrifice, Mir Habib Aqa sent us a big white sheep. The sheep's eyes and knees were black. According to tradition, God had sent Abraham such a sheep to sacrifice instead of his son.

The wife of one of the city officials invited me and Munavvar for lunch. We did not know what to do; it was not proper to go in the European manner, unveiled, through the streets, and we did not want to wrap ourselves in a chador. I had a piece of grey colored fabric and I made out of it something like a Moslem chador and we closed the skirts with braids. It looked like as if we had put on a long rain coat with a hood and since we had not covered our faces people thought we were foreigners. Mirza Jalil very much liked our fashion. The woman who had invited us was a middle-aged, beautiful woman and she welcomed us with extreme kindness. She took us to the head of the room and made us sit on cushions. There were other women who had been invited. Like in Tabriz, the women in Ahar were wearing short dresses like a ballerina. This was a fashion introduced by Naser al-Din Shah after having visited Europe. Inside the house, to cover their legs, the women covered themselves with a light chador. They did their housework dressed like this. Except the hostess, the owner of the house, all the women here wore a light chador. When they went out, they wore all-covering chadors of a thick fabric.

As soon as we took our scarves off our shoulders, they put a package in front of us. We looked surprised at the hostess and she told us that in the parcel there were chadors for our use. I thanked her and told her that we wear long dresses and so there is no need to put on chadors. The lady of the house was a bit astonished, but said nothing and they took the packages away. They brought delicious food. The women were asking about our lives and customs and they posed us many questions. Since they had never in their lives left Ahar at all they had no idea of how people lived in different places.

The second time we were invited by Mir Habib Aqa's mother; she was related to the Khan of Kalibar's family. She was a very handsome looking woman and she welcomed us with kindness; in her house they did not offer us chadors. There was a woman, who was an important guest, who was dressed in a very strange manner and she did not wear a chador. On her hair she had put something very delicate and expensive made of *termeh*[100] in the form of beautiful headdress of the princess of One Thousand and One Night. Over her short silk shirt she wore another shirt (*chepkeni*), with a braided hem and a short-sleeved vest. Then, her ballerina-like *atlas* trousers reached to her knees. I asked the woman next to me who she was. Her name was Dilbar and from a very notable family. Since she has visited holy placed she wore this headdress. This "saintly" woman was looking down at our formal, cold, long dress.

The number of people who came visiting Mirza Jalil increased daily. They told us that Javad Khan, who was famous in Qaradagh, was coming to meet with Mirza Jalil. One day he entered the court-yard accompanied by 20 fully-armed horsemen. The Khan was a middle-aged, tall, thick-set man.

Around his back and hanging from his shoulders were broad two-fold Mauser ammunition belts. Two people helped him to dismount and then took his arms and brought him to the house. The Khan's people fastened their horses to trees and walked about in the garden. The arrival of such a honorable warrior to any house was considered a great honor. I wonder what great 'honor' would they have shown us, when these people would have had met us on the way at 4-5 werst from Ahar! I remember that years later there was a caricature of Javad Khan in *Molla Nasreddin*.

I prepared a notebook, and on the basis of what Mirza Ali Akbar was telling us, I wrote down the officials in Ahar, who came to see Mirza Jalil and their name and function.

1. The chief revenue officer (*vazir-e maliyeh*).
2. Eftekhar, the assistant of the chief (no. 1) and his wife, Sakineh Soltan Khanum.
3. Asadollah Khan, commander of the artillerists.
4. Hasan Khan Sadeqi-lashkar and his brother.
5. Mir Habib Agha.
6. Mashhadi Ali Agha (Democrat; merchant).
7. Mirza Mohammad Ali Khan (landowner).
8. Zargham Zeynal Khan (colonel of the troops).
9. The principal of the school.
10. Haji Khalil (first merchant of the guild).

The weather was warm; Mirza Ali Akbar brought us a big bowl of ice every day. In Ahar they give ice to people for free. Some time ago a rich man had made an ice-house that supplied the whole city. After his death he left a large amount of money and, in accordance with the will of this rich man, from the interest of that money the ice-house was filled,

100. *Termeh* is hand-woven cloth made of natural silk and wool. It's a specialty of Yazd in Iran.

so that in the summer people would have ice for free. In this way that person had eternalized himself in the memory of the people of Ahar.

There was a very old mosque in Ahar; its dome was green colored, and therefore, it was called the green mosque. The city had beautiful gardens and orchards and there were small streams running in almost every street. The people liked working and were orderly and clean.

For 15 *tuman*s Mirza Ali Akbar hired a guide and a few mules. On Friday, 3 September, we departed. Many people came to say farewell to Mirza Jalil and accompanied him to the outside of the city. Mir Habib Aqa and some of his friends mounted on their horses and accompanied us until Chayadak, which was the border between the land of Amir Arshad and Ahar. He bade us farewell with much affection and sincerity and said: "Rest assured that nobody in the land of Amir Arshad will harm you." Mir Habib Aqa thought that it was better for us to pay Amir Arshad a visit, and said: "Amir Arshad will be glad to meet with *Molla Nasreddin* and he will be of help to make you reach Tabriz." Later on we learnt that Mir Habib Aqa was engaged to Amir Arshad's daughter.

* * *

The roads were rather good; since our horses had rested they were going very well. We were delighted at the natural scenery. On the land they were harvesting the fall crop; on the green meadows herds of sheep, cows and horses were grazing. We were passing villages that dotted the route to the end. From afar tall plane trees and golden heaps of wheat could be seen. The villagers were threshing the wheat in the manner of our ancestors. The villagers here were dressed much better than the Kurds and they were observing cleanliness. When darkness fell we stayed the night in a villager's house. After talking for a while we found

out that some of men of this village were underground channel (*qanat*) diggers and each season they went to Qarabagh. It became clear that they knew us, because most of them had worked in our *qanat*s. They treated us very kindly as if we were old friends. On 4 September early in the morning we continued our journey. At mid-day we reached the small town of Ovkhara, (in Persian, Abkhvareh), where Amir Arshad, who is the enemy of the Kurdish Khans, had his house. In the town there were big two-storey houses, barracks, and warehouses, surrounded by gardens. Our arrival was reported to Amir Arshad and the men from one door and the women through another door were led into the courtyard. The horses were taken to the stable and the baggage was taken to the storehouse. In the courtyard in the middle of the garden there was a pond with a fountain. All around it were different flowers. The paths between the trees were filled with wet gravel. At two hundred meters on the side there was a two-storey mansion that could be an ornament to any civilized city. Women wrapped in light-colored chadors welcomed us and led us to the guest room in the second storey of the house. It was clean and tastefully decorated in European fashion. We were covered with the dust from the road and we felt somewhat out of place here. Within two minutes a very beautiful woman of medium height in European dress entered. She was Amir Arshad's wife. Later on we found out that her dresses were brought from Paris. She welcomed us kindly and asked about our journey and she thanked Fortune that we had safely crossed the Qaradagh Mountains.

After having lunch we rested and then we went to the bath-house. Later Mirza Jalil told me that Amir Arshad had welcomed them with similar kindness. He had known the journal *Molla Nasreddin* for a long time.

Muzaffar told me that when we entered Amir Arshad's hall there were some 30 guests there. They had just finished having lunch and were washing their hands. After greeting us they asked us to sit down. Immediately they spread a table-cloth and brought various good smelling foods. We, i.e. Mirza Ali Akbar, I, Teymur, and Midhat were waiting for Mirza Jalil to start, so that we could begin. But he was not putting his hand into the food. Then Amir Arshad asked him to eat. Mirza Jalil said: "You have all eaten and finished and you are looking at us; when somebody looks at me I cannot eat."

Then Amir Arshad got up and left and the guests followed him. After everybody had left Mirza Jalil turned to us and said: "Now, we can eat." The next day they brought hunting rifles from Paris for Amir Arshad. He loaded one of the rifles and took us to one of the forests that was full of game. In front of our eyes he shot a number of birds, deer, and he did not miss a single shot.

Amir Arshad suggested to Mirza Jalil to stay in Ovkhara and publish the journal here. He said that he would prepare the printing house, lithography and buy paper and invite the illustrators. To publish the journal every need would be met.

Amir Arshad was living with his guests in another mansion. Only an old eunuch was frequenting the mansion of the women; the rest of the servants were all female.

The name of Amir Arshad's wife was Esmat al-Hajiya, because she had performed the hajj the word of Hajiya was added to her name. While we were talking she learnt that I didn't cover my face, that I manage my farm, that I do everything myself, that I live independently, and that I have my own manager. She talked about this to Amir Arshad and after that , through her, he let me know that he wanted to meet me. The following day he came to meet us and he said that he was sorry that he did not do this before we arrived. If he had known he would have welcomed us in person. Amir Arshad was a middle-aged, tall, handsome, and thin man. His expression was sullen and his eyes were piercing as if he was born to be a ruler. During the conversation Amir Arshad said to me: "Madam,

I don't advise you to go to Tabriz, from reliable sources news has reached me that fairly soon there will be a revolt in Tabriz and it is not known which side will win. It will be dangerous for you there. I have told this to Mirza Jalil and his brother, but they don't give up the idea of going to Tabriz. I have told Mirza Jalil to remain in Ovkhara and publish the journal here."

I thanked Amir Arshad and passed on his suggestion to Mirza Jalil, but our people had decided to go to Tabriz. The lady of the house was very sorry that we were leaving. She wrote a letter for her sister's husband, Haji Ebrahim Aqa, who was living in Tabriz was a wealthy merchant. That same evening some relatives of Hajiya Khanum were her guests. Among them was Amir Arshad's daughter from his first marriage. This girl was the fiancée of Mirza Habib Agha of Ahar.

It was on 6 September that we left for Tabriz. The lady said that her husband was very sorry that we were leaving and he would come to see us off. She gave us provisions and medicines for our journey and she bade us farewell with extreme affection. There was one female servant standing outside the door with a Qur'an in her hand. All of us passed under it, because according to their belief whoever passes under the Qur'an will have a safe journey.

While we were leaving, Ovkhara Amir Arshad with a group of horsemen came and saw us off for a few werst. When he wanted to leave us he told the guides where to rest and where to stay the night. He told Mirza Jalil that he would come to Tabriz and help him publishing the journal.

On the way, we occasionally saw tents of nomads. At noon we dismounted to rest at a house of a Shahseven Khan. He was one of the Khans who was a subject of Amir Arshad and here they received us with great respect. The Khan's wife was very tall and she wore a long dress. She looked more like a man and a warrior. The Khan had six sons and they were also handsome, one looking better than the other. Their household was managed by their four wives. After lunching with them we took our leave. In the town of Ahar we had bought a horse. Now Muzaffar's horse was going alongside Munavvar's horse and they were talking to each other. Mirza Jalil did not like this and he rode his horse to mine and told me: "this friendliness will not have a good result. Tell Muzaffar, don't play around." Although I did not tell Mirza Jalil that these remarks offended me, because Munavvar was married and Muzaffar was engaged. Not to hurt him, I very indirectly told him so.

At 4 in the afternoon we arrived at Kemurchay. This was thus called, because when transporting charcoal to Tabriz on mules and camels they passed this river. From here onwards the road, which was called the Charcoal Road, followed the river bank until Tabriz. At the beginning of the valley there was a small village. The guide stopped and suggested that we spent the night there. Mirza Jalil did not agree. I did not know why, but he was dejected. In spite of the guide's warning that until Tabriz there was no village and we would have to spend the night in the open air, he continued without a word and quietly and we without asking him followed.

After a while we reached the caravan that was carrying charcoal and we joined it. One of the old caravan leaders turned out to be an acquaintance of Mirza Ali Akbar. All the way they were talking together. It became dark. We were all tired. Mirza Ali Akbar told us that we were almost near the halting place Charshanbeh. We remained there until the moon rose and then with the caravan we continued our journey, because going alone was dangerous. Before reaching the bridge we saw a two-storied house on the side of the road somewhat resembling a caravanserai where we spent the night and early in the morning we got up and together with the caravan we went on our way.

When we reached the Aji bridge near Tabriz we had to wait. To get permission to enter the city

Mirza Ali Akbar went to Tabriz. The weather was very warm. As usual, Mirza Jalil could not remain indifferent wherever there was water. He took the children and they went swimming.

Three hours later a rider came with our permit to enter the city. Our people came back from the river, looking pleased with the water of the river. Following the rider we crossed the bridge and I should mention that later Mirza Jalil wrote about this bridge and published cartoons about it.

On the other side of the bridge a nice phaeton, sent by Mirza Ali Akbar, was waiting for us. Mirza Jalil, I, Munavvar, and Anvar sat in the phaeton and pulled the cover, because in Iran it is forbidden that women go in open carriages.

The phaeton went in front and our people followed it. Suddenly we saw that a rider came towards us; he approached us and very respectfully asked Mirza Jalil to come out of the phaeton, because in their country transporting men with women in one phaeton is forbidden. … Mirza Jalil told him: "These are not strangers; one is my wife, the other my daughter." The rider replied: "it does not matter, you cannot travel with them." And pointing to 9-year old Anvar said: "even this child cannot travel with them."

Mirza Jalil was bewildered. He thought that the rider was joking and looked with a piercing glance at him and asked him:

Where can I sit?

He answered:

You ride my horse.

Then where are you going to sit?

Next to the driver.

So, it is better that I sit next to the driver and travel with my own family and you travel on your own horse.

Mirza Jalil managed to put his big body next to the driver with difficulty. Sitting there, he turned his head and said to us:

Put Anvar amidst you and cover him with your shawl. That won't hurt, when the time comes I will tip them.[101]

The rider came with us all the way.

IN TABRIZ

We passed a big cemetery and from there we entered the city. In this place which you could not call a city we passed through crooked winding lanes; there were no windows, only brown-yellow long mud walls. Occasionally we came across small grocery stores (*baqqali*s) and then sometimes there were ordinary gates with knockers. Our phaeton stopped in front of one of these gates. Mirza Ali Akbar welcomed us and took us into a house, which was full of fruit and flowers. This was a two-storey building, like a summer house. The Chinese style wooden ceiling reminded one of the temples of Buddha in China and the halls had a portico and a raised platform. At the top near the porticos there were small rooms. Mirza Ali Akbar had rented this huge house for us for 7 *tuman*s per month. We learnt that that you might say that in most good houses the halls were designed as if they were places of worship and in the months of Moharram and Safar they were used for mourning and funeral gatherings. After a short while, our travel companions arrived as well. The horses and cattle were sent to a caravanserai nearby. Immediately, we unpacked our things and started cleaning. Mirza Jalil with his hands in his pockets was going around looking carefully at everything. I was supervising that things were put in their proper place. I put all the big carpets in one hall, because Mirza Jalil was going to receive his guests there. I designated other rooms for eating and sleeping. I gave the small rooms upstairs to Munavvar and Khanum Jan.

---

101. In *Molla Nasreddin* no, 6, which was published in Tabriz, Mirza Jalil criticized this custom.

Top: "No, no, sitting together is forbidden." "But my Moslem brother, I'm taking my family to see the governor." *Bottom*: Rude phaeton driver, "Madame, do you want me to take you around? I won't charge you!" Lady: "One can't sit with one's own family in the phaeton, but the rude driver is not a problem. How inappropriate!" Drawing by the Tabrizi artist Mussavarzadeh Seyyed Ali Behzad. (no. 6, yr. 16, 23 April 1921)

There was no furniture in the rooms. We had to eat and sleep on the carpet. Mirza Ali Akbar returned from the bazaar and following him there were porters who carried food on platters with cloche covers. There were various stews that were very delicious. Among the fruits, grapes and melons were especially fragrant. The grapes had no seeds and their skins were so tender that they would melt in your mouth. Mirza Ali Akbar was feeling at home here. He had been helping Sattar

Khan[102] and that was why he knew so many people in Tabriz, where he had many friends and admirers.

The same evening, 7 September, admirers of *Molla Nasreddin* came to see Mirza Jalil. His old friend, and the journal's correspondent and representative in Tabriz, Eskandar Khan Ghaffari[103] was the first one to meet him. His coming delighted Mirza Jalil. After this, you could say that almost every day there were people coming to us and they did whatever they could to help us. In general I could say that while we were in Tabriz Ghaffari helped us a lot. We discussed it and decided to sell our cattle and horses. Firstly, we needed money and secondly, feeding them was expensive in the city. Our shepherd and his son wanted to return home. I paid them and sent them off.

The following day, 8 September, the number of people who came to visit us increased. Mirza Ali Akbar was taking care of the food and he had entrusted serving tea to Mashhadi Hasan. On the third day the number was between 50 and 60 and we were afraid that we would not be able to serve them tea. So many people coming and going everyday troubled the local police and from that day they placed a guard in front of our house.

At this time the democratic government led by Sheikh Mohammad Khiyabani[104] was in power. It

Sheikh Mohammad Khiyabani

was thought advisable that Mirza Jalil go and see him and get permission to publish the journal. He and Mirza Ali Akbar went to see him, but it seems that they could not get a definite answer concerning the journal. Actually, at that time the Sheikh did not have time for such matters, because any day now he expected to be attacked. On 13 September around 10 in the morning gunfire was heard in the city. Mirza Ali Akbar told us that the shah's troops had penetrated the city and had begun fighting with the Democrats. Anarchy reigned in the city and the

102. Hasan Agha Haji Agha-oghlu Sattar Khan (1868-1914) was a pivotal figure in the Iranian Constitutional Revolution and is considered by many Iranians to be a national hero.

103. Eskandar Khan Ghaffari used to write under the penname of *Delghir* (vagabond); he was persecuted by the reactionaries. In the journal of 28 April 1908 no 17, there is a cartoon showing Mir Hashem Davachi, one of the anti-constitutionalists, beating him on the floor in a mosque. In this way the people who criticized Eskandar Khan were criticized.

104. Sheikh Mohammad Khiyabani (1886-1920) was the hero of the democratic movement of Azerbaijan and he was actively involved in the constitutionalist movement. Khiyabani was an anti-colonialist dissident, both against Russia and England. After the October revolution of 1917, he re-established the Democrat

Party of Tabriz after being banned for five years, and later, in a protest to the 1919 Treaty between Persia and England, which gave the rights of deciding about all military, financial, and customs affairs of Persia to the British, Khiyabani revolted and took Tabriz and surrounding areas, calling it Azadistan ("land of liberty"); to provide a model of freedom and democratic governance for the rest of Iran. He considered himself not a separatist. In September 1920 the governor-general of Azerbaijan Mehdi Qoli Khan Hedayat, Mokhber al-Saltanah took over control of Tabriz and killed him. Later, Hedayat claimed that Khiyabani had committed suicide.

Eskandar Khan Ghaffari being beaten by Mir Hashem Davachi, one of the anti-constitutionalists.
(no. 17, yr. 3, 28 April 1908)

shops were closed. It was dangerous to go out. He told us: "don't leave the house and be careful," but he himself left.

* * *

Mirza Jalil was anxious, he was smoking non-stop. He was walking back and forth in the courtyard. He did not want Mirza Ali Akbar to go out, but he did not listen.

The sound of gunfire was increasing in the city. A few bullets whizzed past our house and hit the walls and on the second floor one hit Munavvar's window. She ran down with Khanum Jan in a panic. Mirza Jalil gathered the children in a room and told them not to go into the courtyard. That day nobody came to see us and Mashhadi Hasan did not even bring food. Because we did not know what the situation was in the city nor had we news about Mirza Ali Akbar we spent the whole day in great anxiety.

At five in the afternoon Eskandar Khan came. He had wrapped himself in an *aba* and under it he had brought bread and supplies for dinner. This gesture by Eskandar Khan impressed us very much; he told Mirza Jalil what was happening in the city and left. In the evening Mirza Ali Akbar came back safe and sound. It was not known which side was winning; gunfire continued throughout the night. Mirza Jalil was nervous and he could not sleep.

In the morning of 14 September the fight intensified. The whole city was in chaos. Around noon it became known that Sheikh Mohammad had been killed and the government had passed into the hands of the royalists and they were taking revenge on the Democrats.

The building that housed the newspaper of the Democrats was adjacent to our house. That same day they plundered that building and destroyed it completely. Mirza Jalil and his brother were very afraid. The change of government was very dangerous for us and Mirza Ali Akbar, because everybody knew Mirza Ali Akbar to be a devoted revolutionary and Mirza Jalil was famous because of *Molla Nasreddin*, which had been banned by the Shah of Iran. Mirza Jalil's friends advised him to go to the Russian consul and ask for protection. Even under the best circumstances they would imprison us and send us into exile.

What Amir Arshad had said had become true. We should have delayed our coming to Tabriz. *Molla Nasreddin*, which had satirized the clerics and especially Mohammad Ali Shah,[105] had been banned from the very beginning. Now was the time to pay for all those criticisms. Mirza Jalil had to go back immediately, but having to take care of his family prevented him from leaving. After discussing this we decided that I with Muzaffar should see the Russian consul.

On 15 September we went to see the consul. He received us, listened to us and promised that he would protect us. He told me that he wanted to introduce me to his wife and even invited me to a party in his house on Sunday, 19 September. I returned home with the good news. Mirza Jalil very emphatically asked Mirza Ali Akbar to be cautious. He should not behave as before and he told him

---

105. Mohammad Ali Shah (r. 1907-1909) was fiercely opposed to the Constitutional Movement, even when he was still heir apparent and governor of Azerbaijan. Because of his efforts to suppress the constitution and Parliament he was ousted in July 1909 and fled to Russia. He was replaced by his son Ahmad Shah (r. 1909-25).

that we were surrounded by watchers. We should not behave in such a way that something dangerous might happen.

After that Mirza Ali Akbar was going here and there and rented a phaeton to return. We sat in the phaeton and pulled down the top and left. In one of the busiest places in the city a *farrash* raised his baton and stopped us and he asked us of which nationality we were. We replied that we were Turks. Then he said: 'you cannot sit all of you in one phaeton. I pointed at Muzaffar and said this is my son. The *farrash* replied: "In any case he cannot sit with you. Let him take another phaeton or sit with the driver." Then Muzaffar went and sat with the driver. When we went out of the city he returned to his place and sat with me.

The consul was living outside the city in a summer-house surrounded by a garden. His very beautiful wife welcomed us very politely and introduced us to her guests. Among his guests there were some consuls of European countries. Among them was the colonel of the Cossack division Meshedich and his wife. The same lady invited us to the party that she was going to give in her house.

While I was talking to the consul I told him that the *farrash* had forced Muzaffar to sit with the driver and expressed my amazement that such customs still existed in these places and asked: "is it not possible to abolish such things?" The consul answered: "They say that Tabriz has its own god and saints. They preserve it and they don't want to change it. Their traditional habits and old order cannot be changed. Some people have tried to change them, but as a result they have lost their lives."

The day of 15 September coincided with the beginning of *Moharram*, the month of mourning. From that day the Tabrizis went into mourning. Processions started in the streets, day and night there were recitations in the mosques and the houses about the dreadful events that had happened to the descendants of the prophet. The

Moharram procession. "Woe to my master; woe to my father; woe to Ardabil; let us cut our heads; let us take vengeance; woe to my master; woe to my country." *Note at bottom right, the Russian army marching in* (no. 1, yr 5, 3 January 1910)

people were going around reciting these versified stories and then they wept. They poured rosewater into everybody's open hands and put it on their faces. Then tea was served and thereafter the people dispersed. Apart from this, in different parts of the city, wealthy people gave food as alms. The mourners, in groups of 20 to 30, circled around in the courtyard, reciting mournful poems. They were jumping up, right and left, shaking wooden rattles in the rhythm of their chants.[106]

_____

106. Although Vazir's text uses here *çax-çaxlari,* meaning "rattles," it seems that this refers to the custom of *shakhsey-vakhsey* (originally, *shah hoseyn-vah hoseyn*), which is performed by rhythmically moving the hand that holds the wooden stick up and down in harmony with the chant.

These groups, chanting, weeping and jumping up and down, came to our courtyard everyday without asking. They stood in two rows, facing each other, chanting doleful dirges. Under the influence of their words they first started shaking and then gradually they were warming up and then reached ecstacy, then they started suddenly jumping up and down and shaking their rattles and they beat the rattles at each other. As soon as these groups entered the courtyard Mirza Jalil gathered the children, took them inside, and drew the curtains in front of the windows.

We learnt that when Mirza Ali Akbar had rented this house he had agreed with the owner that during the first days of Moharram, in the great hall of the house, mourning ceremonies would take place. This was in accordance with the will of the late father of the owner. When Mirza Jalil learnt about this he became very angry; he vehemently opposed it and did not want to make the hall available. Mirza Ali Akbar somehow managed to pacify him.

On 15 September, from the early morning people began to come. They spread new carpets in the hall and on the big carpets they spread small rugs. On the doors and windows they hung black flags as a sign of mourning. The pulpit that was there was covered with black? They put a big samovar to make tea. The visitors came from morning until evening. The dirge singers and the Mullas were coming every hour. They had lots of work to do; this was the peak-time of their business.

All these activities, comings and goings, mourning, weeping, upset Mirza Jalil. He was nervous, would not leave the house, sat in the room and was tired.

The day of *Ashura*, 10 *Moharram* or 24 September, which was on a Friday, all shops and offices were closed and no business was contracted. Everybody was preparing for the *Shah Hoseyn-Vah Hoseyn* ritual. They were expecting that there would be solemn ceremonies in the city. People were sitting in seats wrapped in black as a sign of mourning. Our children had gone to the roof to look at this spectacle sitting on the chimney. I climbed up to the place where they were; straw and ashes had been scattered onto the streets. The streets were packed with people so that you only saw a sea of heads and if something had been dropped down, it would not have fallen onto the street. At the head of the procession there were half-naked men in shrouds. In their hands they had daggers and swords. They were brandishing them in rhythm with the chants of the dirge singers striking their already bleeding heads. Behind them were a number of people in tattered clothes, who were beating their chests and backs with chains. Then there were people who had pierced their bodies with chains and sharp

objects. The procession continued and people were dressed in the clothes of ancient Arabs. As a sign of mourning among Moslems, young beautiful girls, sitting in the decorated howdahs on the camels of the procession, had unbound their hair and were chanting dirges along with other people for the corpse[107] in a black clothed sedan chair. They were accompanied by servants who held the reins of the horses and camels as well as iron poles with unfurled standards, and then there were others who were carrying banners. This huge procession was surrounded by the population, who were crying and howling, or else they were beating their breasts and knees; some people were going around and scattering straw and ashes from huge bags.

It is a pity that it is impossible to depict whatever you see; it was a touching spectacle. I climbed down and Mirza Jalil saw that I was moved and he chided the children and told them to come down.

They were saying that another procession in the center of the town was much more spectacular. In one of them there was a papier-mache lion. Inside it there was a criminal, who had been sentenced to death and was sitting with a piece of paper in his hand. When the procession passed through the portico of the governor's house, the lion raised his hand and delivered the petition. This was a petition for a pardon. For the sake of the saints, the governor pardoned the criminal. Forty days after this, the city was in mourning again. You could say that in every house they gave alms for the Imams. These charitable acts continued perhaps for three months.

On 26 September the consul and Meshedich came to our house with their wives. Our journal looked very interesting to them and they looked with curiosity at the cartoons. They asked Mirza Jalil many questions and asked him to bring Munavvar as well when he came to their house.

---

107. The 'corpse' was a simulacrum of the killed Ali Akbar, baby-son of Imam Hoseyn, which was placed in the sedan chair.

On 3 October, we were invited to the house Meshedich. As usual Mirza Jalil did not want to go and did not come with us. I had to go with Muzaffar and Munavvar. Meshedich was staying in the winter quarters of the Cossack division, which was outside the city. His wife, Tatyana Petrovna previously had been the wife of prince Shaxovski and after the prince's death she had married Meshedich. She was a member of the elite society of Petersburg. Her manners were very simple, mild and polite. In her house there was a distinguished gathering of officers, consuls, advisors to the governor and many such people.

I came across Consul Blyum.[108] I told him how the mourning ritual had affected me and how I felt so much regret and sorrow that these barbaric customs still persisted in Iran. He told me: "So what, what else can they do. Let them amuse themselves. We even encouraged the leaders of the city quarters to do these rituals."

After Ashura the visits to Mirza Jalil resumed. The number of visitors increased daily. Even two people weren't enough for serving tea to the visitors. Everybody wanted to meet *Molla Nasreddin*. Later we heard that there was a rumor in Tabriz among the common people "that *Molla Nasreddin* is a legendary character, who lives in the sky and he publishes the journal there." Sometimes, lower class women would come to us and wanted to see *Molla Nasreddin*. They would not believe that he did not live in the sky.

For a long time, the reactionaries knew that Mirza Ali Akbar was a devoted revolutionary. They had caught him many times and had given him to the Tsar's government and now we were also afraid of this. The Russians had shackled Mirza Ali Akbar

in Tabriz and had taken him to Nakhchivan. The fact that Mirza Ali Akbar had stayed with us and every day had participated in political discussions made the local authorities uneasy. It was natural that many people participated in these meetings. On 7 October Mirza Ali Akbar suddenly disappeared. In the morning, as usual he went to the bazaar, but he did not return home; we were all frightened. Poor Mirza Jalil did not know what to do. He sent his friends and acquaintances everywhere and asked them whether his brother was in prison or killed or was sent into exile, but he wanted to know. However, nobody was able to give him any news. They searched all over the city; every hotel, every restaurant, and every place of social gathering, but nobody could say that they had seen him. It was as if such a person did not exist.

Mirza Jalil was experiencing dreadful days; he was nervous, he was not eating, he was not sleeping. He thought that the local government, fearing Mirza Ali Akbar, had killed him and had hidden his body. This time Mirza Jalil came with me to visit the consul's office. We related the entire case to him in great detail, and asked him to find out what had happened to Mirza Ali Akbar, and, if possible, to return him to us. The consul promised to do whatever he could, but Mirza Jalil could not rest. In this short time he had aged noticeably and his face looked sunken in. He was sure that Mirza Ali Akbar was not safe.

Meshedichi's wife had many contacts; therefore, I went to see her and told her what had happened to us in every detail and asked her if she could help us to find Mirza Ali Akbar. She listened to me politely until the very end and promised to help. In this way ten days passed. Eventually, the consul told us that Mirza Ali Akbar had been arrested and that he was safe. Given the present political situation, people had complained about his anti-government activities. He had been arrested and the government had exiled him to Maragheh to the house of its governor, Sardar Naser as "an honorary exile"

---

108. Boris Edwardovich Blyum (1884-1937); in 1903 he joined the Diplomatic Service in Astarabad as secretary and dragoman. In 1911, he was dragoman in the political section of Bokhara, and vice-consul in Colombo (1914) and in Ardabil (1915). After he left Tabriz, where he was consul, he went to France where he died.

and that his life was not in danger. He lived and ate there. Sardar Naser was the brother of the police chief of Tabriz. Before long he became friends with Mirza Ali Akbar and allowed us to correspond with him. To get to know Mirza Jalil, Sardar Naser came to our house in Tabriz.

* * *

After the arrest of Mirza Ali Akbar, Mirza Jalil had decided to return home. He first wanted to go himself and then come back to get us. There were many people coming and going from Shusha to Tabriz. Mirza Jalil wanted to join them and return to Qarabagh. Therefore, we decided not to sell our two good horses.

Before being arrested Mirza Ali Akbar had found a suitable house for us. This house belonged to Nosrat al-Saltaneh and it was in the Ustashagerd bazaar near the Dash Hammam. Before returning to northern Azerbaijan we lived in this house. It had eight rooms and two courtyards, one for men and the other for women. It had a big pool with drinking water. In the part for men there was a 24 *arshin* (17 m) long hall. The floor of the house was not made of wood. We did not have enough carpets to cover it. One of Mirza Jalil's admirers, Mashdi Zu'l-Feqar Fayyazov (he was originally from Shusha but a long time ago he had settled in Tabriz, where he was in the carpet business) heard this and sent a beautiful rug and this rug covered the long hall from one end to the other as if it was made for this. This pleased us tremendously and this hall became Mira Jalil's reception room. Apart from this big one we put two small carpets next to it and in this way the problem of the numerous callers was solved.

Next to the hall was a small room where we put a desk and a chair and turned it into an office for Mirza Jalil. The door of the office was opening to the hall that gave equal access to the male (*biruni*)

and female (*anderuni*) side of the building. My room was very bright with three windows. We had separated this room from the dining room and sleeping quarters with a curtain. There was one room opening to the hall, which was the room of Munavvar and Khanum Jan. Above my room there was an attic, which was given to Muzaffar and Shirin. We had rented a stable in the next-door neighbor's house for the horses. The horses were used by the children.

Now the time had come to see from what sources we would be able make ends meet for this large family; after all we were 10 people. I had neither gold coins nor jewelry or anything that could be exchanged for money, because I was never interested in wearing jewelry. Only the gold brooch of my late mother and the golden watch of my late father were with me and I had kept them as mementos of parents. The day that my father died the watch had stopped and never had worked again thereafter. I sold my mother's brooch for 28 *tumans* and paid for the rent of the house and bought firewood for the winter and whatever little was left I spent on necessities.

Mirza Jalil's friends arranged a job for Muzaffar and Shirin.[109] At least they could pay their own expenses. Sometimes it was very hard for us. In this way we were forced to sell our silver items as well.

We put our sons Anvar and Midhat and also Mirza Jalil's nephew, Teymur in the American school of Tabriz. They studied there for free and they gave them school supplies. In the school they were teaching English, French and Persian. The children were the whole day in school and they ate breakfast there.

* * *

---

109. Shirin Javanshiri was a relative of Hamideh Khanum and at that time she was living with Mirza Jalil's family in Tabriz.

Some respectable people who had come to visit Mirza Jalil were expecting that he would pay them a counter-visit. But he did not want to. He said, "I have no time to go visiting nor do I want to go anywhere." Of course, people resented this trait of character.

Apart from Eskandar Khan, there was another friend whom people had given the nickname of "Armenian" and this was Mehdi Khan.[110] I would say that he would come almost every day to us and ask about our situation and gave us financial help and sometimes he would bring provisions like Eskandar Khan under his *aba*. Mirza Jalil had gone to their house with me; the women did not veil themselves when he came in.

The young engineer Hedayat Khan had come to our house. He had been educated in Moscow and his brother Enayat Khan was the head of the municipality in Tabriz. In no. 5 of the journal, there was a caricature of him on the last page, and he was hurt by this.

Towards the Bagh-mesha quarter they had a very nice-looking house with gardens. They were living in prosperity and wealth. Their mother was a respectable Westernized-woman. This woman with her daughter came to see us and she invited us to her house. We became friends. She wanted to start a girl school in Tabriz under my direction. They were influential people and they had many friends. For this purpose they were holding meetings in the homes of important people in Tabriz with my participation.

In the middle of October, Amir Arshad came to Tabriz for a while. He came to our house with a phaeton accompanied by 20 armed horsemen. He also came in the Qaradagh style to lunch gatherings accompanied by his armed guards. On 18 October

Enayat Khan, head of the Tabriz Municipality: "God be praised. Our city is so clean due to the efforts of the officials of the Municipality (no. 5, yr. 16, 10 April 1921)

his wife invited us for lunch. In this party, the wives of the consul and of Meshedich were also present.

Mokhber al-Saltaneh[111] was appointed governor of Tabriz. He had completed his higher studies in Berlin and during Reza Shah Pahlavi's reign (r. 1925-41) he was a member of parliament. One of his friends, Abu'l-Fath Alavi[112] had completed law studies in Istanbul and knew several foreign languages. He liked Mirza Jalil very much and was reading *Molla Nasreddin* very avidly. He was from a family of sayyeds and originally from Darband. Such a learned person, in Tabriz, per force wore a green turban and an *aba*. When I was surprised by his dress I asked him: "Why are you dressed like this?" and he said: "You cannot dress otherwise in Tabriz." In the picture that he had taken outside Iran he wore a European dress and a top hat.

Alavi was cajoling Mirza Jalil not to go anywhere and that he would get permission from

---

110. Mehdi Khan Sharifzadeh was a progressive intellectual and after Mirza Jalil returned to Baku he became the Tabriz representative of the journal *Molla Nasreddin*.

111. Mehdiquli Khan Hedayat Mokhber al-Saltaneh (1881-1954) was one of the reactionary officials of Iran; he became three times prime-minister. In 1920 he suppressed the democratic movement of Sheikh Mohammad Khiyabani and persecuted his supporters.

112. Abu'l-Fath Alavi was one of the progressive intellectuals of Azerbaijan in the early 20th century. He founded the Alavi School.

the governor to publish the journal in Tabriz and continue its publication. He even took it upon himself to get permission from the governor. Since Mirza Jalil had it in his mind to return home he did not consent to this. Alavi came very often to our house and carried on very long conversations. Eventually he became friends with Mirza Jalil and persuaded him to continue the publication of the journal and obtained permission from Mokhber al-Saltaneh on condition that he would write it in Persian. Mirza Jalil refused. The discussion about the continuation of the journal continued. The winter was very cold.

On 3 and 4 November the first snow fell in Tabriz. Our house was very cold. We could only manage to heat one stove in the house and therefore, the entire family would gather in my room. Mirza Jalil would receive his close friends in my room as well. In the receiving hall and his office guests would sit with their overcoats on. In Tabriz firewood was sold per *pud* and it was expensive. Mirza Jalil did not like to sit idle. He himself cut the wood and put it in the stove.

Mirza Jalil's daughter Munavvar had fallen seriously ill. To make her room warm he decided that half of the window should be closed with bricks. Therefore, the children prepared mortar and very nicely they closed up half of the window. Munavvar's illness lasted long and gradually became worse. Our friends advised us to call the best doctor in the city Fakhr al-Atebba.[113] He had been educated in Europe and for some time he used to be court physician in Tehran.

Doctor Fakhr al-Atebba was a noble and graceful man. He greatly admired Mirza Jalil's talent. He even kept the letters that he received from Mirza Jalil as precious souvenirs. Fakhr al-Atebba treated us for free and furthermore, he

brought the medicine that was needed for free from his clinic. He said that Munavvar should have chicken soup and brought three chickens under his *aba*. Anvar very much liked one of the chickens and so he kept it. Therefore, the doctor, in addition sent us two more chickens and one rooster. The doctor asked Mirza Jalil's permission to bring a photographer and take picture of him while standing, but Mirza Jalil did not allow it and the doctor was disappointed.

I had a portrait of this physician and a copy of a manuscript of an English, French, Russian and Persian dictionary that he had prepared. He had given this copy to Mirza Jalil for publication in Baku.

* * *

One of the leaders of the Kurdish tribes, known as Sardar Mokri, was living in Tabriz at that time. He was a young man and educated in the Moscow cadet corps. He became very close to Mirza Jalil and occasionally he came to visit us. Twice he invited us to his house. In these parties people of several nationalities were gathered. We became friendly with two Armenian families and started to visit each other's houses. Most of the Armenians spoke Persian and Azeri.

The Armenian quarter of the city had a better appearance than the Moslem quarter. The Armenian quarter was different from the Turkish quarter in that the Armenian houses had windows that opened onto the streets. They had beautifully decorated shops, pharmacies, clubs, schools and clean bathhouses. In the whole of Tabriz there was only one theater and that was in the Armenian quarter. (On 20 May 1921, we staged the play of 'The Dead' in this theater. Mirza Jalil was the play's director and the actors who played the roles had guns in their pocket).

---

113. Fakhr al-Atebba was one of the famous intellectuals of Tabriz. At that time he was very active in the social life of Tabriz.

Moslem intellectual and his wife in Paris and in the Caucasus (no. 4, yr. 4, 25 January 1909)

The condition of the Armenian quarter was totally different. In the streets well-dressed people were walking; the face of some Armenian women was visible in spite of the fact that they wore a *chador*. There was a club with a big garden.

First they did not want to allow our young men from the Caucasus to the club, but then, after they knew who they were, they allowed them. Apparently, the Iranians had behaved badly several times there. They had bothered women but not only that they had pinched them. In the journal there is a story about this.

On 24 and 25 November again heavy snow fell and it was minus 10 degrees centigrade. The frozen windows were covered with snow. Mirza Jalil with the children went onto the roof and cleaned it. The iron stove did not give enough heat; therefore, our room was cold. Munavvar's illness lasted long. I brought her behind the curtain to my side of the hall. Apart from Fakhr al-Atibba, the female Armenian doctor Kalipso Kechimovna Tarakanova was treating her. This lady had studied in Geneva. The girl's sickness and our lack of money was very much troubling Mirza Jalil. We had sold and spent everything. Only we could not sell our carpets, because they were paying very little for them. Mehdi Khan was keeping our two horses in the village with his brother. We had kept them in case we went back. Muzaffar was giving most of his wages to us. We managed somehow.

On 1 December the cold became severe and reached minus 20 degrees Celsius and when our children were coming from school they were trembling because of the cold. They did not have tall boots; over their socks they wore loafers. Mirza Jalil felt sorry for them. He would change his youngest son's clothes and warm his ice cold feet and hands and consoled him.

Abu'l-Fath Alavi talked with the governor and his advisors about the publication of the journal. To the suggestion that the journal should be published in Persian only Mirza Jalil replied: "I have published *Molla Nasreddin* for 15 years in (Azeri) Turkish. Like in Azerbaijan of the Caucasus in Iranian Azerbaijan also only Azerbaijanis live and talk Turkish. Here only the educated and a few other people speak Persian, but I don't publish *Molla Nasreddin* for them, I publish it to educate the majority of the people. The thing is that even the Russian government permitted me to do what you are not allowing me to do. In the city of Tabriz there are four Armenian journals, but of course, there is not a single Iranian who knows Armenian. I know some Armenian; so, allow me to publish the journal in Armenian."

This proposal put the governor's advisors in a bind. They asked Mirza Jalil to be patient. After a time, Abu'l-Fath Alavi came and said, "The governor has agreed to allow the journal to be published in Azeri, but with this condition that the editorial should be in Persian in each issue." Mirza Jalil did not agree to this, but Alavi somehow persuaded him and promised that in each issue he would write the editorial himself. After having come to an agreement about this problem we started thinking and discussing about lithograpy, how to prepare the printing-shop, finding good artists, suitable paper and other things. Furthermore, how would we get money for all this? At their daily meetings, which took place in the evening, they discussed this.

They were saying that *farrash*es had been placed at our gate and all the time they were taking note of who were coming and going, what the topic of discussion was and other things. Of course, there were informers among the visitors.

In Tabriz only a government journal was published in 100 copies. Lithography and printing-presses were in a terrible bad condition. To put the publication affairs in order, Mirza Jalil started working. Mashdi Zu'l-Feqar Fayyazov promised to lend us paper. In the past, he also had given money to meet the expenditures of the journal; a good artist was found as well, viz. Sayyed Mohammad Ali Behzad.[114] Mirza Jalil was pleased; they had lots of things to do. Every day he was on his feet to make the journal a success and his friends were helping him in every manner.

I forgot to say that the permission to publish the journal was given on this condition that it should not criticize religion and the religious class. Mirza Jalil did not agree with this for a long time. Alavi persuaded him to agree for the time being to this and then to see what happened later.

In the beginning of February 1921 they were saying that the Bolsheviks had taken Tiflis and Yerevan. Quite a number of Armenian refugees came from Yerevan to Tabriz. The local Armenians had formed a committee to receive and organize the refugees. They welcomed the refugees and they took them into the city in phaetons. The first thing they did was to take them to the bathhouse and give them clothes. In every house two refugees were placed. One could say that all the refugees were educated people.

The occupation of Yerevan upset the foreigners who were then comfortably living in Tabriz. The British closed their bank and the consulate was

---

114. Sayyed Mohammad Ali Behzad (Mossavarzadeh) also drew cartoons for the newspaper *Azerbaijan*. He had studied in Tabriz, Tiflis, Moscow, Paris and Rome and for a while he held the function of royal painter under Mohammad Ali Shah.

"O my brothers, I have not been created without a tongue that you are trusting these tongues into my mouth!"
(No. 38, yr. 1, 22 Dec 1906)

ready to be closed. Such events scared the people. The Russian consul Blyum was finishing his work and was getting ready to leave for Paris. Col. Meshedich and his friends were getting ready to leave as well. There were different rumors in the city. There was fear that the Bolsheviks might come to Tabriz.

Mirza Jalil became acquainted with the painter Sayyed Ali Behzad. He invited him to the house and asked him to draw the cartoons of the first issue. In this cartoon, there is an Englishman who is fleeing

Tabriz out of fear for the Bolsheviks and behind him a barefoot Iranian youth, who is imploring him not to go. The censor did not allow the caption that explained this to be published. Mirza Jalil did not want to approve a variant of this drawing. In this way the picture was left without caption.

Mirza Jalil had asked Behzad to draw the picture of the office that dealt with the foreign consuls (*kargozarkhaneh*) on the backcover. Under it Mirza Jalil wrote *Bikarkhaneh* (house of the jobless), which rhymes with it. Mirza Jalil asked the cartoonist if he knew the head of this office, because the man in the cartoon looked very much like him. After explaining the rest of the pictures that he had to draw he talked about his remuneration. The cartoonist drew some sketches and promised to deliver the pictures in one week.

On 26 January about one meter of snow fell. The price of firewood increased again. Therefore, Mirza Jalil was working in my room. I gave Abu'l-Fath Alavi the manuscript copies of *Ölular* (The Dead) and *My Mother's Book* and he was reading them. He said, "*The Dead* is excellent, but I like *My Mother's Book* more." Alavi was convinced the Mirza Jalil was a despot and he told him so. Mirza Jalil argued with Alavi. Alavi was familiar with European literature and he had read the works L.N. Tolstoy in French; he liked Anna Karenina very much.

On 10 and 11 February it snowed heavily and on 12 and 13 it was very cold. Because of the cold Mirza Jalil wrapped a cloth around his head and was running to the lithographer and then to the press. They were getting ready to publish the journal. Mashdi Zu'l-Feqar Fayyazov had kept his promise and had given three month's supply of paper. Mirza Jalil had ordered a special cliché for the journal's cover. He had prepared the cliché in the same manner as the one printed in Tiflis.

Abu'l-Fath Alavi and other friends of Mirza Jalil were coming very often and asked when the journal would come out. On 16 February the weather became better. One day later it became even milder.

* * *

On 19 February 1921, in the morning, the porters came and brought the journal *Molla Nasreddin*, which had just been printed and put them in the room. We all gathered and started folding the journal. Mirza Jalil was writing the addresses. Mehdi Khan recommended us to ask Asgar Khan Qasemzadeh[115] (who later came with us to Baku) to distribute the journal to the subscribers and he found and brought a number of young boys to sell the journal in the streets. It was about noon that we finished folding. Some of the journals would go to Asgar Khan to be distributed to subscribers in the city and the rest were given to the young boys. The shouts "Who wants *Molla Nasreddin*?" filled the streets and the covered bazaar of Tabriz. Two hours later they gave me the money received from the sale. It was one *tuman* and 8 *qrans*. Then they were given some more journals and they hurried away. That was a big event for us. The publication of the journal was considered to be a major happening in the city.

The first print run was 1,000 copies and on the first day 600 copies were sold; the rest were with me.

On 20 February, in the morning, after tea, Mirza Jalil hurriedly left for some business. As usual, he had 7 or 8 visitors; they were sitting in the office and waiting for him. I don't know why I came to the hallway but I noticed that outside there were two policemen. I asked the reason for their presence. They told me: "The governor has ordered the seizure of *Molla Nasreddin*. We have been sent to collect all remaining copies and take them to the office."

An Englishman fleeing Tabriz fearing an invasion by the Bolsheviks "
(Cover page, no. 1, yr. 16, 20 February 1921)

I was very angered by these words and blasted them. Mirza Jalil's guests had gathered at the door, while I continued shouting at the policemen. I continued: "How could he order the seizure of the journal when he has read and approved this issue. This is not possible. This is a misunderstanding!" The policemen said that the governor himself had ordered this. I could not control myself and told him: "So why did he allow its publication. Why did he make us spend so much money? We are refugees; we have sold our last possessions and spent it on the journal to educate our people. In Tabriz, we have a small Armenian population and they publish four newspapers, but we don't even

---

115. Asgar Khan Qasemzadeh was one of the intellectuals who helped the publication of the journal in Tabriz and he went to Baku with Mirza Jalil in 1921 and lived there until 1928. He returned to Tabriz.

have one newspaper in Turkish. Wait! Sooner or later you will fall into foreigners' hands and become their slaves! Even the Russian government, for the last 15 years, has permitted us to write and educate our people. But here from the first number it has been suspended. Go and tell all what I have said to the governor. I won't give the journal." I said all this and went to my room. After a while, one of the visitors knocked on my door and entered. He introduced himself as one of Mirza Jalil's great admirers and said that he wanted to help us. He said: "the best way to make the police leave is to give them a few copies of the journal." He said that he himself would take the remaining copies via the other door of the house to avoid any possible search. I gave four copies of the journal to him to give to the policemen and the about 400 remaining copies were taken from the house by this friend.

I was afraid that Mirza Jalil might be arrested and I was waiting for him impatiently. Eventually he came. I welcomed him in front of the door and told him about what had happened. He was very astonished and with equanimity said: "Why are you upset? Let them collect the journal, let them close it, what is wrong with it?!" After saying this he went to the visitors, who, full of emotion, had gathered at the door and answered them with the same equanimity he had shown me.

In the evening Abu'l-Fath Alavi came and he talked about the reason why the journal was closed. It became clear that it was because of the cartoon and the article about the office of the *kargozar*[116], which was in this issue. The man in charge of this office, who had more than 30 properties and many friends in Tehran, felt insulted. After seeing his cartoon and reading the article he had become very angry and had gone to the governor and while weeping said that he had been humiliated

and scandalized in the eyes of the whole world. He had asked the journal to be seized and closed and its editor to be punished; otherwise he would go to Tehran himself and complain to Ahmad Shah.[117] Mokhber al-Saltaneh had tried to pacify him and told him that a few years earlier he himself had been depicted in a cartoon in the form of a monkey, who had a leash around his neck, held by the Mullas, and whatever they wanted he would do. But this had not appeased the man. Therefore, the governor had ordered the journal to be seized. What angered His Excellency to this degree was the following article:

THE JOBLESS QUARTER

One day, I was walking in the bazaar in Tabriz and saw people sitting left and right, watching. I asked: "Why are they sitting here?" And was told: "They are jobless."

Some of those sitting there were women and children with open hands asking for money to buy bread. Of the rest, some were picking lice off their bodies while others were dozing off.

Then one of the Treasury's servants came with a sack containing 4,000 *tumans* under his arm and entered a magnificent, large building. I wanted to know what that big building was. I entered and saw several rooms with people sitting: one was smoking a water pipe while another was dozing off. "What is this place?" I asked. I was told, "This is the *kargozar-khane*."

"Is this the same office, which if it did not exist, the affairs of Azerbaijan would come to a halt and nothing would be done?" I asked. "And, well, what- is this place's function?"

---

116. The *kargozar* was the agent of the Ministry of Foreign Affairs charged to resolve disputes between foreigners and Iranian subjects; he also was in charge of the issuing of passports.

117. Ahmad Shah, born in 1897 and died in 1930; he reigned from 1909 to 1925 and was the last king of the Qajar dynasty.

Kargozar office (office that dealt with foreign consuls, back page, no. 1, yr. 16, 20 Feb 1921)

I was told: "This is the same office that foreign consulates use to contact the government of Azerbaijan."

I said: "Very well then, in that case, it doesn't need to be so large and grand to answer the questions of two or three consuls—one official will do. For example, in a large town like Tiflis, one official answers 14 consuls' questions. And their office is in one room with only one secretary in the governor's building. What's more, the wages of these two together would only be 100 *tuman*s per month."

While I was thinking about this, I saw the Treasury's servant opened the bag and start to distribute the money to the idle ones.

"Well," I said, "Good. If the purpose is to distribute the money among the idle ones, why not to those in the alley? There are so many of them. Why is the money legitimate (halal) for the ones in the office and not for those outside?"

One of the gentlemen, who was smoking a water pipe, said: "My dear *Molla*, there's a reason for this. It is true that the *kargozar-khane* doesn't have any work at the moment and that even when there's no work, it gets 4,000 *tuman*s in wages. But our office has rendered many services to our country in the past. If you remember the events of the Aji Bridge[118], you will agree that this money is legitimate for us. My dear *Molla*, if you speak without ill-will you should mention that. In total, there are 14 *kargozar-khanes* in Azerbaijan, why is it that you only pick on us? Why don't you say anything about them?"

I could not say anything to answer this gentleman. ...

Signed, Gadfly.

Later we were told that the article that Mirza Jalil wrote about the brothels, which were situated in the middle of the city and came under the fire of Mirza Jalil's satire had such an effect among the people and government officials that they ordered the closure of these brothels and the owners were ordered to abandon this activity and take the women beyond Iran's borders within two days. The text of the article about the brothels is given here:

Before coming to Tabriz, I thought that brothels were a bad thing. For instance I saw that in Tiflis, the Armenians, Georgians and Russians would not allow them in their quarters. The Moslems allowed them at first, but after seeing that the Christians did not allow them, they thought and thought and after divination with the Qur'an, they decided to keep them away from their quarters. But in Tabriz, I saw that Moslems had brothels in their quarters in four places. And shameless girls are inviting Moslem children who are going to school. To tell the truth, I am bewildered, I don't know whether the brothels are a good or a bad thing. If I say that it is a good thing, after all between ourselves, if we speak truthfully, we saw that it was not a good thing. Because, first of all, a brothel destroys people's morals. Secondly, young men get suddenly afflicted with incurable diseases. Thirdly, in our *shari'at* such things are considered as great sins.

If this is the case, now I am again bewildered. Sometimes I tell myself, if it is such a bad thing, why am I the only one talking about it. Is there no one except me who is wise, pure of heart, and chaste? You see that every day several thousand good and honorable Moslems pass in front of those brothels and they don't protest. Am I the only person in this city who gets this?

This is not the case. Also, in Tiflis and in other cities, Russians, Armenians, Georgians, Jews are they also mistaken? Are they oblivious? Perhaps the brothels are a good thing. In truth, I am absolutely bewildered. Please. Make me understand if I am going crazy or whether the people are crazy? May I be your sacrifice, please, make me understand; else I am really going crazy. Oh, oh. The Crazy One.[119]

This article caused a tremendous uproar. Especially, it upset the men of the city and the women came in groups to our house and expressed their gratitude to *Molla Amu* (uncle *Molla*) for this beautiful article. They told us that as a rule, in the evening, their husbands would take the money that they had earned with their business and go to the

---

118. This may be a sarcastic reference to a 1911 incident on the Aji Chai bridge outside Tabriz, where Russian troops disarmed and imprisoned the nationalist Mirza Aqa Bala Khan and his men fighting the notorious tyrant Samad Khan.

119. For further information about brothels in Iran at that time, see Willem Floor, *A Social History of Sexual Relations in Iran*. Washington DC: Mage Publishers, 2008, chapter 4.

brothels. They would return home drunk close to daybreak and the families often would go hungry.[120]

In the city and the bazaars when the news of the closure of the journal was circulating people began to protest. Many people shouted and said: "Since *Molla Amu* is telling the truth, they have closed his newspaper. If this is the case we will close our shops and we will refuse to do business."

After a few days following the closure of the journal one of the commanders of the regiment, which was stationed in the *Sharafkhaneh*, sent a telegram to the governor and asked the journal to be published again. A number of our acquaintances came in a state of agitation and told us that there was discontent among people and something might happen because of the closure of the journal. After that they did not come and search our house and they did not punish Mirza Jalil. Mirza Jalil was very quiet as if he was pleased with this incident. Our house was like a beehive. People were coming very quickly, bringing news, and leaving soon thereafter. It was as if the owners of the brothels, who were women, had become terrified. Because the establishments were so spread out over the city they could not close down their activities in two days. They went to the mayor of the city and begged him that at least the time for their departure would be extended to six days. The governor accepted this and ordered Treskinski, the head of the Tabriz-Jolfa train to prepare the wagons and take the women out of Iran on that day.

Later we were told of six of the city's young notables, who were very much in love with some of the women. Two of them had poisoned themselves and two others could not bear the separation and had gone with the women, and two others, after the women had become Moslem, married them. After

six days, to be exact on 27 February 1921, the train from Tabriz to Jolfa carried 600 women and most of them crossed the river Aji and were left in Jolfa. Among the women who were exiled there was not even a single Moslem woman.[121] It was said that when these women were leaving there were heart-breaking scenes at the station. On the same day, the governor once again allowed *Molla Nasreddin* to be published.

* * *

At this time the people of Iran were under the influence of Mullas and sayyeds and they were standing before the Khans and Beys like slaves. The authorities of Tabriz considered us as Bolsheviks. Every step we made was watched. The spies were in front of our house and were watching us all the time. Skillfully, they had stolen my Mauser and my pistol from the house. Sikkat al-Islam, the head of Tabriz's religious leadership wanted to get acquainted with Mirza Jalil. This astonished us, because Mirza Jalil in 1908 in the journal (20 January no. 3) had published a cartoon criticizing the *mojtaheds* (juris-consults) of Tabriz and because of that they had issued a *fatva* that said that the man who kills Mirza Jalil would go to heaven. Of course, Mirza Jalil did not want to go and visit him. It was not his custom to frequent high dignitaries. But later his friends persuaded him and took him to visit the *mojtahed*. I don't remember the conversation between them, but I know his friends made him take off his shoes before going into the *mojtahed*'s house.

Mirza Jalil was preparing to issue the second number of the journal and he was very busy. The people who were coming to visit him took much of his time. Mirza Jalil was working mostly at night. On 10 March the second issue was published.

---

120. For a similar and earlier criticism of the behavior of husbands and their licentious way of life, see *The Education of Women & The Vices of Men. Two Qajar Tracts*, translated by Hasan Javadi and Willem Floor. Syracuse: Syracuse UP, 2010, pp. 95, 99, 110-13.

121. This seems very unlikely, because other data shows that most of the prostitutes were Moslems, see Floor, *A Social History*, ch. 4.

Three lines of the text from page five were ordered to be deleted.[122] To blacken out these lines Mirza Jalil helped us. Again the young kids went to the bazaars and streets to sell the journal. In three days the entire issue was sold.

On 20 March no. 3 appeared. That was sold very quickly. The publication of the journal coincided with *Nowruz*, which was on 21 March. Mirza Jalil liked this festival very much and because of that he gave gifts to the children as well as to the servants and the poor. He bought a lot of sweets, hazelnuts and fruit and asked everybody to join in. The highly intellectual physician Dr. Fakhr al-Atebba sent us a big pot of polow and roasted lamb; we had gone to visit his wife. She recommended that I should go and see the wife of the former governor of Tabriz, the late Sheikh Khiyabani. I accepted this with great pleasure. The late Sheikh's wife was young and beautiful; she had large and penetrating eyes and she was very well educated. She was a very nice eastern beauty and she had two little children, who were beautiful too.

Of course, we had some income from the journal, but our expenses were increasing rapidly. The Iranians were not yet used to paying for the newspaper. Sometimes, we were absolutely penniless. At these times Mirza Jalil smoked an awful lot of cigarettes. Once we did not have money for tobacco. Mirza Jalil was nervous and was pacing up and down the room. Little Anvar was sitting and was attentively looking at his father. He suddenly said: "Father, the shopkeeper from whom I buy things likes you very much. I will go and ask him to give some tobacco on credit." The child went and brought some tobacco for his father. Mirza Jalil was moved by this and embraced his son and patted his head.

* * *

Mirza Jalil was hard at work trying to have his brother's exile revoked, but his endeavors were fruitless. I don't remember who, but somebody suggested that it would be better to submit a petition under my name and that I would agree to stand security for him. I agreed to this. Mirza Jalil wrote a petition under my name that I would be his guarantor and I sent it to the governor. After a few days we received the news that Mirza Ali Akbar had been pardoned and that he would return shortly.

On Thursday 21 March 1921, the fourth issue of the journal was published. On its first page was the picture of a man with a donkey that was heavily loaded. At its side was a teacher who had put his hands to his chest and was bowing to the donkey and said: "I am bowing to you, O animal of god, because of the transportation tax our wages have not come for the last six months. I am begging that you and your comrades honor us by coming more frequently to our city."

It seems that in Tabriz they had imposed this regulation that they would collect a tax from the owners of the donkeys who entered the city and this tax was called *topraq basdi* or stamped earth.[123] This tax paid for the wages of the teachers. The same

122. The deleted text was an alleged letter in Persian from Sanduq al-Molk to *Molla Nasreddin*, to wit: An announcement, signed by Sanduq al-Molk has reached our office; as follows: First, whoever wants to lodge a complaint to the Justice Department has to sell his property beforehand so as to have enough money for bribes. Secondly, to appoint an attorney or an heir, so that if the trial does not finish in his lifetime they can pursue the matter afterwards. The attorney should be one of those attorneys who is well-connected and a go-between with the higher-ups in the Justice Department. For information on the functioning of the judicial system in Iran at that time, see Willem Floor, *Changes and Developments in the judicial system of Qajar Iran,"* in: *Qajar Iran*, E. Bosworth & C. Hillenbrand eds. (Edinburgh, 1983), pp. 113-147.

123. This *navaqel* or transportation tax was levied all over Iran, see Willem Floor, *The Fiscal History of Safavid and Qajar Period*. New York, 1999, pp. 412–19..

cartoon had an impact on the Office of Education and the teachers' wages, which all of a sudden were paid. This issue was very soon sold out.

Eventually on 6 April, after 7 months of exile, Mirza Ali Akbar came home. We were all happy. Mirza Jalil's happiness had no bounds. The children did not leave their lovable uncle alone. As usual, he had brought many gifts. He also had brought a *pud* of honey and more than one *pud* of sweets. Mirza Ali Akbar gave me a leather purse, which contained one hundred silver *tuman*s, as a gift. While he was living in exile, each day he received 2 *tuman*s for his expenditures, but he was living and eating in the house of Sardar Naser. Consul Blyum[124] had stopped working for the Tsarist government and was getting ready to go to Paris. Before leaving he came to meet us and he said en passant: "Nothing new ever interests the religious people of Tabriz. I am amazed that your journal *Molla Nasreddin* has gained so much success in the city and that it has so many admirers." In Tabriz a society had been created by some enlightened women to establish a girls' boarding school with a dormitory. The location of the society was in the house of one of the women. One of the organizers of the society was the wife of an engineer who had been educated in Russia and she had come to take me with her to the society. On the way, while we were talking, it became apparent that she and her husband were not Moslems, but were Zoroastrians. In the gathering there were quite a number of women; most of them wore European dress. We became acquainted and talked about the preparation for the girls' school. After deciding on the date for the next meeting, we left. Later I heard from Abu'l-Fath Alavi that they wanted to appoint me as the mistress of the school.

In Tabriz there were many refugees from the Caucasus. Most of the refugee women wrapped

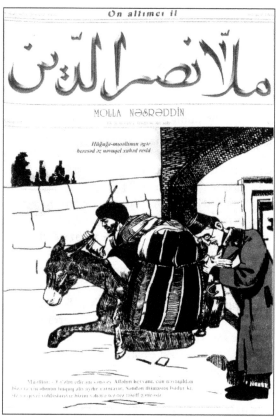

The donkey tax (no. 4, yr. 16, 30 March 1921)

themselves in their Caucasian chador. But some Caucasians who had come earlier to Tabriz wore the traditional black chador of Tabriz and put on a face veil (*picheh*), which was black and made of horsehair and covered their entire face; it was like a sun-shade. Tarlan Khanum Kengerli who had come with her husband from Nakhchivan and had settled in Tabriz was wearing such a face veil and black chador. She was a tall, stout and beautiful woman. One day Tarlan Khanum went with her female servant to the Amir bazaar. In the bazaar she was pinched by a man. She turned, grabbed him and beat him twice hard on the head. He became dizzy and fell down and she began kicking him. The servant started helping her. The two women gave him a proper trashing. While she was kicking him, Tarlan Khanum, in a loud voice

124. After the October Revolution many of the Tsarist officials who were against the Revolution did not return home and Blyum was one those diplomats. See note TK.

from under her veil, berated Iranian men, about their pinching in the bazaars and the streets and their stupid behavior. She scandalized them. People gathered and a *farrash* came, but nobody dared to come close to her to protect this insolent man. As she kicked the scoundrel, she was shouting: 'Your Iranian women are oppressed, helpless, and terrified. You men use this to pinch them everywhere, in the bazaar and streets. The women are ashamed and don't dare to voice their anger. Is this why you men have become out-of-control? Do you think that the women from the Caucasus will be silent and not say anything? Next time I will come with a pistol to this bazaar. Let anyone dare and touch me. I will trash him.'

This became the talk of the town. The influence of the Caucasian women in Tabriz increased. After that they knew us and did not touch us. From that day Tarlan Khanum no longer wore the Tabriz chador, but one in the Caucasian fashion. Mirza Jalil wrote an article about this event titled "Pinching."

On Wednesday 12 April, the new issue of the journal came out. In this issue Mirza Jalil satirized the bathhouses of Tabriz, especially the pools, and their uncleanliness. After this issue, the city authorities immediately started doing something about this, so that the bathhouses were repaired and basic measures to keep them clean were imposed.

In the last page of this issue there was a cartoon of the mayor of Tabriz with his officials, going around in the filthy streets of Tabriz that were full of garbage up to the knees. The mayor, his mother and brother were our very close acquaintances and definitely they were not offended by this cartoon and even after this they invited all of us to their house.

* * *

Abu'l-Fath Alavi received permission for the performance of 'The Dead."[125] On this occasion there was a large gathering of the actors and volunteers in our house. Mirza Jalil himself was in charge of the selection of the players and the staging of the play. The role of Eskandar was played by the great actor Boyk Khan.[126] The role of Sheikh Nasrollah was played by Mirza Ali,[127] who was from southern Azerbaijan (later he came with us to Baku and Mirza Jalil found a job for him), the role of Karbala' Fateme was played by the Armenian actress Liza and the role of Nazli was played by Mirza Jalil's thirteen-year-old nephew Teymur. The role of Jalal was played by our late son Midhat. For three weeks the actors would gather in our house and practice. In Tabriz there was only one theater building that was in the Armenian quarter. We rented the building for 1 May. We sent a number of tickets, according to a list, with Asgar Khan to institutes and notable officials. The actors were practicing their role with great passion, but they were afraid of the people. Therefore, it was decided that until they went to the stage they should carry a pistol in their pockets.

On 28 April another issue of the journal came out. In this issue there was a cartoon that criticized the American missionary school. Our children were going there and this subject was suggested by them. In the school, at fixed hours, the children

---

125. This comedy in four acts is about the credulity of people, who are hoodwinked by a dervish who claims that he can resurrect the dead.

126. Boyk Khan Nakhchivani was one of the active members of the drama society of Nakhchivan and for a long time he played the main roles in the plays. Later he moved to Tabriz and there he was working in the Red Sun-Lion society (Red Cross counterpart of Iran) and was participating in the city's dramatic life.

127. Ali Azari (1900-66) was a literature candidate Ph. D. In 1921 he came with Mirza Jalil to Baku where he lived until the end of his life. He taught for many years at the state university of Azerbaijan in the Oriental faculty, where he prepared some Persian text books. In 1966 he published some of his memoirs about Mirza Jalil as *Birjeh Yarpaq*.

Public bathhouse (no. 32, yr. 2, 28 August 1907)

would be taken to church where they were forced to recite prayers according to Catholic rites.[128] Mirza Jalil wrote an article, and with great humor satirized the missionaries. The Americans bought 30 copies to send to America, after that they did not force the children to go to prayer sessions. The text of this article I present herewith.

In Iran there are still signs of old colonialism and the missionaries is one of them. In Russia missionary work was created by the father of despotism, Paul I (r. 1796-1801) and although as a result of liberalism of Alexander II (r. 1855-81) the missionaries lost their respect somewhat, yet at the end the reign of the last tsar Nicholas II (1894-1917), the missionaries again gained influence. So much so that the famous Radloff[129] among the Moslems of Kazan, in Turkestan Ostrumoff[130] and in Trans-Caucasus people like the Miropivs,[131]

128. All American missionaries in Iran at that time belonged to Protestant denominations.

129. Vasily Radlov or Friedrich Wilhelm Radloff (1837-1918), German-born Russian founder of Russian Turcology. He published ethnographic studies on Turkic ethnic groups and a four volume dictionary of Turkic languages.

130. N.V. Ostrumoff, *A Geography of the Turkestan Country; with a short Account of the Khanates of Bokhara and Khiva.* Translated by Lt. E. Peach, Samarkand, 1891.

131. Michael Alexeyevich Mieropiev (1852-?) was a Russian Orthodox missionary, who worked in the Caucasus. He was the director of the Caucasus teachers Seminary and it is probably to the graduates of this seminary that Mamadqulizadeh refers.

oppressed Moslems for years. In the recent Revolution they ceded their place to the missionaries in Iran and vanished.

For one hour we considered ourselves freedom lovers and we agreed that Moslems should have rights as well, so that in America or Japan they also could propagate their own religion as the Christians are free to disseminate their religion in our countries. But the point is this that Christian missionaries have been established by the force of capitulations and this is why the Iranian government grudgingly suffers and says nothing about the problems created by the missionaries and has not been able to find a solution for their problems. For example, let us take the case of Esma`il Aqa [Simqu] – those who are aware of the political events at the Western borders of Iran may remember some of the troubling subjects to which we are referring. We are a weak nation and we may expect much spiritual and material help from a great nation like America and for each of them we should express our gratitude. Recently, in the time of need, America has extended a helping hand towards us, we praise the existence of such a great and courageous nation in the world, but there is a time for a thousand regrets that America, which is the center of many sciences and industries instead of sending us professors and masters sends us missionaries with long beards and long skirts as gifts and instead of technical schools and technical colleges they open parsonages.[132]

On account of hospitality and freedom for all we welcome all those Christians who live in our country, including the missionaries. But because of the same principle of freedom they should take into account the demands of modern times and give up the imposition of their religious ideas and forgo all religious propaganda. They are not forced to accept non-Christian children in the schools that they have established with their own money, but when they pity the needy and they don't want to leave them deprived of education then they should not put such a heavy burden on a seven or eight-year-old child so that the children are forced to learn the customs and lessons of the Christians.

How can it be that young Moslem children are forcibly taken away from the religion of their parents, and have the lessons of the Evangel and Christianity instilled in them. They are brain-washed and forced to go to Christian prayer houses. I wonder whether the civilized American nation can see this point. Even in the past ages of despotism the imposition of missionary activities was not as much as they are nowadays in Iran.

I wonder whether our office of education will not be offended by this article.

Molla Nasreddin

On 30 April the last rehearsal of "The Dead" was performed in our house. Mirza Jalil was very pleased with the performance of the actors. Our sons were performing their roles not badly either. The role of Eskandar that was played by Boyk Khan was exceptional. Munavvar and I also wanted to go to the performance on the first day, but it became obvious that up to then no women's feet had reached a theater in Tabriz[133]. Mirza Jalil was

---

132. This is not entirely correct. In 1883, the American missionaries had opened a medical college in Urmiyeh and in 1915, in Tabriz, had started the first training program for nurses, see Willem Floor, "The history of hospitals in Safavid and Qajar Iran, an enquiry into their number, growth and importance" in Fabrizio Speziale ed. *Hospitals in Iran and India 1500-1950s* (Leiden: Brill, 2012), pp. 37-116.

133. This is incorrect. Already, since 1881, Armenian women occasionally played in and attended theatrical

the director of the play and therefore, he came home after the third act because he did not want to appear on stage at the end when the audience called for it. Eventually, Mirza Ali Akbar came with the children; the play had been a great success. The performance was without much ado and no incident had occurred.[134] The money collected from the play was considerable; the performance was on 1 May 1921. The next morning Mokhber al-Saltaneh sent 100 *tumans* to Mirza Jalil to distribute among the actors. The people who had received complimentary tickets each sent 10 to 15 *tumans*. Abu'l-Fath Alavi was very pleased with the performance and congratulated Mirza Jalil on this occasion. He wanted to have the play "My Mother's Book" performed in Tabriz.

* * *

On 2 May there was a telegram from Baku from the Soviet of the Azerbaijan People's Commissariat inviting Mirza Jalil and his family to Baku.

At that time, to be precise on 25 April, Alish Bey, my cousin from Qarabagh, whom we had been expecting for a long time, came to Tabriz. He told us that the local government and the villagers were asking us to return. The local commander had approved this and had issued an authorization. Apart from this, I had received a letter from

Education by missionaries (no. 6, yr. 16, 23 April 1921)

our dear Dr. Karim Bey Mehmandarov[135] in which he asked us to return home as soon as possible; he was siding with the Soviet regime. Abu'l-Fath Alavi was trying to persuade Mirza Jalil not to leave Iran; he was saying that Mirza Jalil was awakening the people here and that this was very useful. Later he told us that they had received news from Tehran that they wanted to give him a major function in the field of education.

I talked to Alavi and said that I have received a letter from our dear friend Dr. Mehmandarov in which he chided us for having left without

---

performances in Tabriz. After 1891 this became a normal occurrence, see Willem Floor, *The History of Theater in Iran*. Washington DC: Mage Publishers, 2005, p. 240

134. According to Ali Azari and Samad Mowlavi, the performance of 'The Dead' had not been all that very peaceful in Tabriz. The police had first wanted to stop the performance and after the play the actors were forced to leave via the backdoor to escape the anger of the reactionaries. Ali Azari, *Birjah Yapraq, Memories of Jalil Mamadqulizadeh*. Baku: Azarnash, 1966 and Gholam Mamadli, *Molla Nasreddin: The Life of Jalil Mamadqulizadeh and his works*. Baku: Azarnash, 1966.

---

135. The letter from Karim Bey Mehmandarov sent to Hamideh Khanum from Shusha is now in the Institute of Manuscripts of the Republic of Azerbaijan. Archive no. 6, file no 2.

considering the consequences and he praised the activities of the Soviet regime. He asked us to return as soon as possible. Alavi received the letter from me and left; after a few days he returned it.

I want to quote a few lines from one of the letters of Dr. Mehmandarov:

Mirza in his journal always goes after the colonialists, the powerful, the Beys and the Khans. In all the time that the journal was published he has satirized them in a very bold fashion and published cartoons about them. In this way he has created many enemies for himself. Of course, the Bolsheviks will accept him in their ranks and will give him their journal. I attach great importance to this Revolution; it will give the East great benefits, while bringing freedom to the colonized, oppressed and trampled people. Great works are being done. You will say that there are many mistakes, but there are many exaggerations and distortions. Suddenly the Revolution happened to us; we were not prepared. Provocateurs make use of this. They are saying many stupid and nonsensical things and we pay heavily for such things. Now things have quieted down.

Alavi came, once more, to our house to see what we had. Mirza Jalil was undecided, because he had advertised that the first subscription would be for one year. "If we return, what do we tell the subscribers?"

I told Alavi that if Mirza Jalil had to stay I would take the children and return to my homeland. My cousin had been sent by the executive committee and the local people to invite us back. Alavi tried to persuade me to stay. He thought that if I would remain on this side of the [Aras] river it would be more beneficial for me than to go back to the other side. I could send my children abroad for higher education. Other friends advised us to return.

This time, several people had gathered around Mirza Jalil. Everybody was discussing this matter and most of them regretted our decision to leave. Mirza Ali Akbar was feeling ill most of the time; he was a man whose health had deteriorated. Seven years of prison under [Tsar] Nicholas had left indelible marks on his health. His active revolutionary life had also affected his health. He was getting sick very frequently and could not follow the physician's advice and was getting nervous.

There was another telegram for Mirza Jalil from the office of Commissar in Baku. It asked whether or not he wanted to return to Baku. He replied that he wanted to return.

On 6 May the seventh issue of *Molla Nasreddin* came out. In this issue Mirza Jalil announced that he had been called to Baku and asked the subscribers to only pay for three months. In this issue an article titled "O Nikolai" was printed. For a long time this article was not allowed to be printed, but then the shortened version was allowed to go into print. There was another article that ridiculed the Tabrizis, who fasted in the day time, but became drunk like a Templar at night.

The first of Ramadan was on 9 May; everybody had to fast. Nobody dared to smoke in the street or at home. His friends told Mirza Jalil, "don't smoke the water pipe." The shops that were closed in the afternoon would open at night until daybreak and people would eat, drink, and have parties and some would even drink wine and spent time having fun. In number eight of the journal Mirza Jalil criticized such people.

At that time Mirza Jalil told me: "The Baku revolutionary committee wants to appoint me as commissar of education, but I don't consider myself worthy of such a position. I will ask them to allow me to continue the publication of *Molla Nasreddin* in the old fashion way. It is my duty to represent whatever is worthy of criticism and satirize it in a humorous way. I hope that there is absolute freedom of speech there, in essence, that is what attracts me."

Mirza Jalil made a list of all subscribers in Iran and promised that he would send them the journal from Baku. Dr. Fakhr al-Atebba gave a part of the English-French-Russian dictionary that he had prepared to Mirza Jalil and asked him to publish it in Baku.[136] Somebody who had made a globe brought it to Mirza Jalil and asked him to manufacture it in [Russian] Azerbaijan and distribute it among the students. The head of the central committee of Nakhchivan, Valibekov,[137] sent, at Baku's recommendation, a telegram to Mirza Jalil. In the telegram he asked him to come as soon as possible and said that his family would be sent to Baku in safety, and when they arrive in Baku, all travel expenses would be paid.

Mirza Jalil began finishing all his activities. On account of the journal's paper we were 71 *tumans* in debt to Mashdi Zu'l-Feqar Fayyazof and for this we gave him our big carpet. We sold the remaining small carpets and the two horses that we had and paid our small debts. We bought a very good quality piece of broad-cloth to be tailor-made into a costume for Mirza Jalil. With the remaining money we bought provisions.

Mirza Ali Akbar was sick and he was nervous. The illness of his brother worried Mirza Jalil. In our house the situation was not good. Mirza Ali Akbar wanted to stay in Tabriz and wanted to become the representative of *Molla Nasreddin* in that city, but the governor did not allow him. The old representative of the journal in Tabriz was Eskandar Khan, but Mirza Jalil had given it to Mehdi Khan and Eskandar Khan was annoyed.

On 17 May the last and eighth issue of the journal was published in Tabriz. The chief of the Tabriz-Jolfa railway, Terskinski lived in Tabriz.

We had come to get to know him in the house of Engineer Hedayat Khan Kalantari. In one of these meetings, Terskinski criticized the owners of the railway who were not paying his, Hedayat Khan Kalantari's and other workers' wages. Only when there was a need to send troops to a certain place or an important person wanted to travel did they send money and they asked the train to be ready at the specified hour. Mirza Jalil had promised him to criticize this irregular situation. In number 8 of the journal he devoted an article called "Calamity" to this subject and here is that article.

In the Tabriz-Jolfa railway we have encountered an incredible calamity. It is true, as they say, Nikolai has created many problems for us and one of them is this railway. In the old days the camel caravans would leave and take merchandise and load it on camels and in one week or 10 days they would get safely to Jolfa. Yes, they made the railway as if to make transportation easy and speedy. It was as if we were pursued by a rider on a horse. As if with this railway our young men would go to Germany and America and study in their universities. Now, look. This is the railway. When it works it bends like a snake and moos like a cow and frightens both the camels and the village women. When it does not work some jobless people criticize the government and the merchants: "look at the wisdom of these Iranians." Nikolai has spent 12 million and has created the railroad, but such a magnificent government and such great merchants cannot keep this little railway in working condition.

For God's sake, see what they are talking about. My brother, we are not incapable. Why are we unable? First of all we are the wisest of all and the smartest of all. One example of our cleverness is that when you see the Georgian people they spent money from their own pockets to repair the Kakhti railway. But

---

136. This dictionary was published in Tehran in 1995 as *Dictionary of Four Languages*.

137. Bahador Qasem-oghlu Valibekov (1894-1938) since 1918 he was a member of the Soviet Communist Party of Azerbaijan and had many official functions.

we have made it so that we own the railway for free. Secondly, the railway of other people for no obvious reason works day and night and consumes a lot of fuel and they pay quite a lot of money to quite a number of workers and officials that are loafing. But whenever there is a need for our railway we only spend 16 *tuman*s to buy wood so that we can burn it and take our troops or merchandise to their destination. But after the necessity of sending troops or merchandise has past there is no need for the railway; then we let it sleep and send the workers to their villages. It is true, when the railway is not running some people come and take the iron tracks. To hell with them, let them steal it, as long as our camels are all right, why should I give 3,000 *tuman*s every month so that the railway is in working condition? Let our caravans of donkeys and mules be safe. You mind your own business.

Signed, Gadfly.

This article had such great impact on the directors that they paid all the back wages and promised that after that all the monthly wages would be paid regularly. In this connection Terskinski wrote a "Thank you" letter to Mirza Jalil and in it he said: "I express my deepest gratitude for having shown concern for my disastrous situation and you as a servant of the public and as a writer you have instantly understood the situation. You are the only light of hope for me here. Once more I express my sincere gratitude. Tabriz, 1921/9/5.

We prepared to start our journey. I bought provisions for one month. Mirza Ali, who had played the role of Sheikh Nasrollah in the play "The Dead" as well as one of the staffers of the journal, Asgar Qasemzadeh and a refugee from Yerevan, Zahra Khanum Aghayeva with her 5 children were coming with us to Baku. She was a widow who was joining her brothers in Baku.

They assigned an entire train car to us. For Mirza Jalil and his family they had reserved a place in the first class compartment. We had many things. Half of the car was occupied by Zahra Khanum and in the other half Mirza Ali Akbar and other men were sitting. During the last days our acquaintances were coming in groups to say good bye. The part for the men was always filled with people. There were almost 400 people in our house on the day of our departure and speeches were given and they spoke touching words. In front of the door of the courtyard policemen were standing. Mirza Jalil's fans wanted to come to the train station to see him off, but the police authorities fearing fiery speeches did not allow this. Ing. Terskinski was instructed to prepare a train for 24 May. That day, apart from us, there were 200 Armenian refugees who were returning to Yerevan. The American charitable organization had informed us that since we were refugees they would give 19 *tuman*s to each family. Mirza Jalil did not want to accept it, but since we did not have money for our journey at Mirza Ali Akbar's recommendation one of the children went and received the money. Mirza Jalil never knew about this.

Dr. Fakhr al-Atebba had sent his own *kareta*[138] to take us to railway station and at mid-day of 24 May we were there. In spite of the ban on assembly 20 people had come to the station to say good-bye and they said a very warm farewell to us. They carried Mirza Jalil on their hands to the car. The Armenian refugees were coming with us in the same train. The track was not good and the train was moving slowly. The head of the railway was accompanying the train in his own automobile. In some places the passengers left the train so that it could easily pass a bridge.

In Marand the train stopped for a long while. There Mirza Jalil's friends brought us bread and

---

138. A *kareta* is a four-wheel horse driven carriage of which all four sides are closed.

provisions. The next day we reached Jolfa. There we learnt that a train had arrived from Moscow with 12 commissars and the newly appointed chief of the railway, Mironov. Mirza Jalil went to him and showed him the telegram that he had received from Baku. Mironov showed him great respect and assigned a first-class compartment in his own wagon for us. The car that had transported us from Tabriz was linked to this wagon. As a result of this fortunate coincidence we were very comfortably seated.

OUR COUNTRY WELCOMES US WITH A SMILING FACE

There was not enough room for the Armenian refugees in this train. Quite a number of them gave us letters so that we could give them to their families in Baku or Tiflis. From Mironov's restaurant car, we were sent tea, breakfast, lunch and dinner every day. In the Customs they did not look at our things. In Russian Jolfa we noticed that the passengers were getting big pieces of salt rock and they were hiding them under the seats. We got some of those and took them with us to Baku.

Mirza Jalil was very happy since he was returning to his homeland. If he would have had wings he would have flown. He wanted to go to Nakhchivan to the house of his son-in-law, Askar Aqa Kengerli and take his niece Aziza and his nephew Jalil to Baku to send them to school there. But the train stopped for a short while in Nakhchivan so he could not go there. We arrived on 26 May 1921 at Yerevan. Mirza Jalil sent a telegram from there and announced his arrival.

On 29 May 1921 we arrived at Tiflis and we went to the house of my son-in-law, Davud Khan, who was the Iranian consul there; my daughter Mina was also living there. But a few days prior to our arrival she and her husband had gone to Baku. In Tiflis, Mirza Jalil went to the People's Commissar of Culture and discussed matters about his printing

press and his various typesetting scripts and other things. In the press of the journal *Molla Nasreddin* Mirza Jalil had various supplies. These consisted of the allotment of paper bought for the 1916 issue of *Molla Nasreddin* in Baku, which had remained there. But in his absence all of these had passed through many hands and were lost. Similarly, the equipment and furniture of the house that we had bought in 1917 had gone. Only a clock on the wall and a stool were left.

We left Tiflis on the third of June and arrived in Baku on the fourth. There was no phaeton at the train station. Mirza Jalil had to transport our things on the backs of porters. We and the children were worn out and tired and we walked behind the porters to watch that they would not disappear into the alleys and walked to no. 18 Guberniya Street. Our son-in-law Mamedbeyov had rented this place. Our wagon from Tabriz arrived at the same time. Mirza Ali Akbar and our other co-travelers had arrived.

Like a horde of gypsies we managed to accommodate ourselves in this big hall of mirrors. The new occupants were allowed to settle everywhere in the house except one small room that was left for our son-in-law and his family. There was not enough room. Comrade Bonyadzadeh[139] and Aliheydar Qarayev[140] came to see Mirza Jalil. They promised us better accommodation and other

---

139. Dadash Khoja-oghlu Bonyadzadeh (1886-1938) was a member of the Communist party of Azerbaijan and a government official. In the early period of the Azerbaijan Republic in the Soviet period he was a member of the Revolutionary Commissariat of Azerbaijan and at the same time member of the cultural committee and inspector of the farms and village commitees. In 1938 he was called 'enemy of the people' and executed.

140. Aliheydar Qarayev (1896-1938) was a notable party member and government official and from 1926 to 1929 he was first secretary of the central committee, but in 1937 he was imprisoned as 'enemy of the people' and he was executed in Moscow.

things and then they left. In this way one week passed and nothing happened.

Mirza Ali Akbar was sick, he was ashamed and getting nervous. Mirza Jalil was also really getting nervous because of this situation. Eventually he decided to go and see Nariman Narimanov.[141] Narimanov as soon as he found out about the situation we very hurriedly were transferred to a house in the Old Post street no. 64. (Now it is no. 56). On the third floor we had a 5-room apartment, which had a separate servant's room and a kitchen.[142]

On Tuesday 14 June we moved into this house. Apart from beds, a table, chairs and a bench, which were made of cheap wood, there was nothing in the house. Mirza Jalil and I went to the Education Commission and they asked for a list of the things that we needed. I sat down and began writing the list and Mirza Jalil was standing and looked at it. While watching he told me: "write only the necessary things, don't write anything extra. Write the things that you cannot do without and don't write anything else." He did not allow me to ask for one carpet and floor covering, whereas we needed them and in Tabriz we had sold our carpets to pay our

debts. They gave us a piece of paper and send us to a store-house located in Boslshoy Morskoy.[143] In the store-house there was nothing, but we received a few things such as a commode, a table, chairs, a bench, which needed serious repair. We also received a varied assortment of cutlery, which had been left by people. But we had to take some of these things. In the center of Baku a group of hungry and poor porters gathered around us like locusts. Mirza Jalil was attentively listening to the conversation of the porters and later he wrote about this event in the story called "The Porters."

Mirza Jalil could not reach a definite agreement about the journal *Molla Nasreddin* with the authorities. He was getting angry and furthermore his brother Ali Akbar was ill; blood was coming from his lungs. To care for him he had to give him good food and at the same time he had to provide for this big family. It was a good thing that I had brought provisions from Tabriz.

I RETURN TO QARABAGH

After a while, the People's Soviet made me the director of the weaving factory in Shusha and it also returned to us the mill and the property that we owned in the village of Kahrizli. Because of lack of repair in one of our underground water channels there was absolutely no water and in another one it had decreased and therefore, the mill was not working properly. Mirza Jalil advised me to go to the village. He had not yet put his affairs in order and our life was hard. Munavvar was divorced and her husband Idris had remarried and therefore, she was living with us and wanted to take a midwifery course.

Eventually, I got ready with my two sons and with our former Armenian weaver, Natalya, and the people who had come from the village; we decided to go back. Qarayev gave Mirza Jalil a document

---

141. Nariman Narimanov Najaf-oghlu (1870-1925) was an Azerbaijani revolutionary, writer, publicist, politician and statesman. In 1920, Narimanov headed the Soviet government of Azerbaijan, the Provisional Military-Revolutionary Committee (16 May 1920 - 19 May 1921), replacing Mirza Davud Hoseynov, then he was the Chairman of the Council of People's Commissars (May 1921 - 1922). In 1922, he was elected chairman of the Union Council of the Transcaucasian SFSR. He was also Party Chairman of the Central Executive Committee of the Soviet Union from December 30, 1922, until the day of his death. Narimanov translated into Turkic Nikolai Gogol's *The Government Inspector* into Azeri and wrote many plays, stories, and novels, such as *Bahadur and Sona* (1896). He was also the author of the historical trilogy *Nadir-Shah* (1899).

142. Later this street was called Soleyman Taqizadeh Street, now the museum of Mirza Jalil Museum is in this house.

143. To-day it is called Nightingale Street.

in a sealed envelop. According to this document a car was going to be given to us in Yevlakh to go to Kahrizli. On 24 August, we left by train to Yevlakh. During three hot days the mosquitos were tormenting us; eventually we got a private phaeton and arrived in the village on 30 August. Since our house was not in spic-and-span condition we stayed in my nephew's house. The news went around that we had arrived. The women hugged and welcomed me dearly. They were kissing me and were weeping from joy; even some men were weeping. After all, we had grown up together in one place and we were extremely close to one another. I had not harmed any of them and whatever I could do that was in my power I had done for them. I had tried to make their life easier and to make it possible for them to get an education.

The next day they gave us our mill. I saw that it needed much money for repairs. We started to clean the house and put it in order. After a few days all of us were stricken with fever. This was the result of spending some time in Yevlakh. After a few days of regaining our health, on 17 September, we moved into our own house. Some of the furniture and things of the house had been taken by our family who had kept it for us. Among the things that they returned were stools, a commode, crockery, kitchen utensils, even the big wall mirror, a sewing machine, carpets and some clothes. In this way a nice homey atmosphere was created inside the house. My nephew, Alish, sent us a milk cow and I should mention here that this cow became the subject of Mirza Jalil's short story "The thieving cow" (ogru inek).

Again, a few days later, all of us were stricken by fever and we were bedridden. Our family members were coming in turns and looked after us. I wrote a letter about our condition to Mirza Jalil. Bandits started plundering the area around the village and they even broke into our courtyard. A big tragedy happened. In bright daylight they beat up our groom Habib Hamid-oghlu and killed him. Out of

necessity we took in my old aunt Sa'adat and her son Jamil for their safety; they stayed with us and helped us around the house.

Mirza Jalil enjoyed talking with my aunt Sa'adat and he listened to her advice. By nature she was a very wise and warm woman. Also, she always took part in the meetings of the men in the village of Efatli as well as those of the village elders; she was very poor.

On 9 October I received a letter from Mirza Jalil saying that he was not going to publish the journal. He was trying to get the road money that they had promised us when we were in Tabriz and with this money he would do the necessary things and come and help me putting the village's affairs in order. The children were getting sick very often; the village was stricken with typhoid fever and our miller and our faithful friend Qasem became sick and died. Mirza Jalil was saddened when he heard the news of Qasem's death and that was one of the reasons that he wanted to come home as soon as possible. Meanwhile I had entrusted my old school teacher Soleyman with the task to manage the mill.

* * *

On 8 December 1921 Mirza Jalil arrived at the village. He brought a young and well-educated man to tutor our sons for school. His nephew Teymur had come as well. Mirza Jalil had received permission from Narimanov to get a phaeton for me and he brought it as a present from Baku. At the same time he had 10 million manat in Russian money to buy two horses.

After Mirza Jalil came home we gradually recovered from the sickness. After getting somewhat better the children started school and Mirza Jalil also began to work very hard. From here and there we bought cattle. We repaired the mill and we raised the fallen fences of the yard and the orchards and cleaned the *qanats*. Gradually our lives found its normal rhythm.

Mirza Jalil's brother, Mirza Ali Akbar regained his health and obtained a government job. They sent him to various districts. In connection with his job he had gone among the Kurds in the area above Shusha, who stole his overcoat. As a result, he got a bad cold and when he returned he fell ill and became bedridden in Aghdam. We learnt about this on 22 March 1922. Later it became known that Mirza Ali Akbar had serious pneumonia. Mirza Jalil went to Aghdam and brought his brother back. To treat him we brought physicians to the house, but nothing helped. He was just melting away like a candle in front of our eyes. The inflammation had reached his intestines; he was getting restless and nervous. Mirza Jalil was becoming nervous as well. Mirza Ali Akbar was so ill that he could not get up. Seeing no hope he was losing his temper and as a result he was so angry that when you even only touched him he lashed out. A terrible situation prevailed in our house.

At the same time, the scarcity of bread was making itself felt and people were going hungry. Typhus had broken out in the village. Mirza Jalil was spending the whole day in the mill and was distributing flour to the hungry villagers. He was able to bring just enough flour to the house that sufficed for our family. Sometimes there was no wheat flour and we were forced to eat barley and millet bread. There were even villages that did not have any bread and would eat only meat. It was at the end of April that the plants started growing again in the forests and gardens. The village women gathered grass, which they boiled and ate and thus, they survived in this way. Sometimes, villagers would come to our door begging for one meal or a handful of flour. I started helping those afflicted by the epidemic. In general, when there was an epidemic in the village I would provide medical help to the sick and to other people who came to me and I was never afraid of getting infected. But

this time I was infected in the beginning of May and became bedridden. The doctors decided that I had typhus. Mirza Jalil did not know what to do. In one room his brother was spending his last days in the grips of relentless tuberculosis. In the other room his wife was abed stricken with typhus. The children were without supervision and everybody was asking for "bread, bread, bread!" Sometimes there was something to eat and at other times they had to go hungry. Aunt Sa'adat and her son Jamal were looking after Mirza Ali Akbar. My cousin's widow, Fakhri Khanum was looking after me.

On 22 May Mirza Ali Akbar died. At that time I was unconscious and I did not know that he had passed away. Only one week later I regained consciousness, when I recognized the children. Anvar hugged me and began to cry and told me that uncle had died. Mirza Jalil became angry with him, because he had told me this terrible news. He himself was burning with grief and could not be consoled. Every day he would go to the cemetery and would sit there for hours wrapped in dark thoughts.

Mirza Ali Akbar's death was a great loss for us. In him we lost the closest of our relatives. They said that in the last minutes of his life he said: "O God, instead of Hamideh Khanum let me die, so that these children will not be left without a mother."

Mirza Ali Akbar loved our children very much. Mirza Jalil prepared a big headstone for the grave of his brother and on it he had inscribed "Mirza Ali Akbar Mamadqulizadeh Nakhchivanli."

When I recovered and left my bed, it was the middle of June. They had started threshing. It was the peak period of the wheat harvest. They brought the new harvest to the mill; there was no longer a famine. In these days the poor Hilal, son of Ibish died of the same illness.

Mirza Jalil was in a hurry to take us to Shusha to go to the summer quarters, but he was going to stay for a while in Kahrizli. At the end of August he wanted to take the children to Baku and devote his time to writing there. Also, he wanted to continue his literary activities.

In Shusha we rented a place in Qara Zeynal's house. I submitted a petition to get back my weaving machines, because I wanted to start a factory in Kahrizli and teach the girls how to weave. The machines were returned. Our old weaving mistress Leyli Alieva asked me to take her to Kahrizli so that she could train weavers and work. They were saying that it was possible to get silk from the Lenin weaving factory. Mirza Jalil promised us that he would look into the problem of yarns. But he only could come to see us at the end of summer. After resting a while he took the children to Baku. Leyli and I took the machines and returned to Kahrizli and I started working.

From the share of cotton that was allotted to me in 1912, I still had some in my warehouse. They had returned this to me as well, but nobody wanted to buy it as yet. I had a part of this cotton cleaned and gave it to the women of the village who were spinning yarn. From this yarn we made fabrics. We placed four weaving machines in the old school building. For the time being, until we could get silk from the Baku factory, we were slowly teaching the girls here how to weave.

Mirza Jalil received permission to restart publishing *Molla Nasreddin* in the fall of 1922 and he started working on it. At the same time he was visiting government offices to take care of the affairs of the villagers of Kahrizli and help them with their problems. Our *qanat*s had not been repaired for the last 3 years. Because of this they were blocked and the water was lost. The *qanat* that passed through the village was in complete disrepair and its water had diminished. To get water people had to travel one werst. Infectious diseases were everywhere.

The government authorities in Baku allowed me, under certain conditions, to rent my own *qanat*. To do this engineer Petrov came to Kahrizli and suggested to me that we should document this. We called a meeting of the villagers of Kahrizli as well

as those of neighboring villages who were using the *qanat*s and they all agreed that it was necessary to restore the *qanat*s, because there was nobody, except their original owner, who knew how to have them cleaned and make them work and how to use them. If there were no *qanat*s it would be impossible to live in this area. I was forced to accept this, because if the *qanat*s were not cleaned and their water would not flow then the mill would not work. If it was not done I could not live in this area.

My relative Alish Bey became my partner, on condition that he would take one-third of the profit. He had a small mill that was located below mine on the big *qanat*. Also, there was somebody who wanted to buy the old and spoiled cotton. I sold half of the cotton and the other half I bartered for coarse cotton fabric. Because fabric in general and broadcloth in particular was very scarce our clothes had become very old. The poor, you could say, were left naked.

With Alish Bey we hired four digging teams (*charkhah*), or 12 workers, who started to work. They needed lodgings and food.

To provide drinking water for the villagers we first cleaned the *qanat* that passed through the village. The diggers who were cleaning the *qanat* found a rotten corpse in it. That was the reason why the epidemic had afflicted the village for many years. Later we watered the half-parched gardens and the plane trees. Then we cleaned the big *qanat*, which made the mill work.

* * *

It was 1923; the ill-wishers were not pleased with what I was doing on my own property that had been returned to me by the government. They were spreading all kinds of rumors about me everywhere. Officials from the Education Department of Aghdam came and asked me to vacate my house and turn it into a school. When I said that it had been returned to me by the government they replied: "Government is local. Here we decide ourselves what to do!"

Of course, they could not evict me by force, but they made me nervous and frustrated. On 22 January 1923, I wrote a letter to Mirza Jalil and complained about the situation. He answered me with the following letter.

1 February 1923.

Hamideh. I received your letter of 22 January 1923. The children became worried when they heard about the epidemic in Kahrizli. Since I promised them, I remind you once again that the day when you have almost completed the affairs of Kahrizli and the Kahrizli villagers come to Baku. Unlike you, here all is quiet and the affairs are in their normal way. The children and I are living without conflicts and fighting. If the mill stops working, we once and for all will go to Baku permanently and occupy ourselves with our children. As long as god gives me life, I will work in the field of literature. If it happens that I am old and incapable of work then my countless friends will not deny me their grateful attention. On the other hand our children will grow up and help us. Don't think that we have to only depend on the mill and the farm to live on. Even I think that the publication of my works will earn something for our children and might provide them with some income. If you are afraid of the cold now you should come at least at *Nowruz*.

In one word, I want to say that if one day you come here it will be a great feast for our children. While I will see my children happy you will make me incredibly grateful. Anyway, write me in detail about the weaving machines and how much more yarn you still need. Write me the size of your rubber boots so that I'll buy them for you. Mina and the children are doing well, they are all healthy,

they go to school, and in the evening they prepare their lessons with the tutor Suvorov.

Of course, I very much like to help putting in school at least one of the children of Alish Bey and you should talk to him about this. I cannot forget the kindness he has shown to us in recent years. Therefore, I want to do him a favor, especially in the area of educating his children. You yourself write to me about your own decision and let me see what we can do.

Also, I want to help the son of Jalal.

Give my regards to Aunt Sa'adat, Alish Bey, Soleyman and Jalal. What is Muzaffar doing? Did he get all the packages? Did he bring them home? The brigands might have taken them from him en route and therefore, I am worried.

Our journal is coming out. Have Muzaffar settle the accounts with Soleyman. From the first to the 11th of the month I have sent him ten copies. He had to sell them according to the price given on the paper. He would take 20% for himself, i.e. out of 100 million he has to take 20 million for himself; he has to give us 80 million."

* * *

To accept Mirza Jalil's invitation to leave the village for the city was impossible. The contract with the engineers for the repair of the *qanat*s, the payment to the workers, the weaving plant, and the operation of the mill – all of these required my being there. I could say that my hands were tied. My enemies would not let me have one moment of peace. I was a big big problem for them.

By chance my letter to Mirza Jalil of 22 March 1923 was preserved among his papers.

22 March 1923.
From Kahrizli

Jalil. I cannot drop everything and leave here. Remaining here is also not possible. It is unbearable. There are several offices here. One contradicts the other. They set people against each other. There is absolute chaos. You don't know what kind of spectacle they create. I did not want to rent the *qanat*s for one year. After all, they were in disrepair. Water was brought. The epidemic caused illness, typhoid fever and others have spread it everywhere. The villagers openly confessed that they cannot use the *qanat*s. Therefore, with the local executive committee they came to the decision that the *qanat*s be returned to the old owners.

Hydro-technical engineer Petrov leased the *qanat*s to me and Alish for five years, basing himself on this as well as on the Center's directive that said: "unless the villagers of Kahrizli clean the *qanat*s by the first of February, they may rent the *qanat*s to trustworthy persons." In spite of finding the condition difficult, we accepted it, because at this age leaving our birth place is hard. I could say that for two months we exhausted ourselves, we found the means that we needed, we talked with the workers, and we repaired the ruined *qanat*s. When the work was about to finish the head of the Political Bureau, Islam Hajiyev[144] with his colleague Mokhtar Esgerov made their appearance. They called me in great haste for questioning otherwise I would be taken to court. I immediately went with them to the house of Jamil Agalarov. There they criticized me for renting the *qanat* of the villagers. Why had I expelled Isa Qahraman- oghlu

from my own garden? I showed them the last directive of the Land Committee's head Hajibeyli and the surveyor Jukov's document dated 16 November 1922. According to these documents, the garden had to be vacated and returned to its former owner. They did not care for this document and said that he could not be expelled from the garden. In the same manner they questioned me why the engineer had allowed me to rent the Kahrizli *qanat*s. They wrote the report of the interrogation and made me sign it. Then they said that we should return the *qanat*s to the villagers of Kahrizli. To my question: "Am I supposed to let the workers go and stop the work?" They answered: "No. You should continue to clean the *qanat*s and we will pay you." Then they said that I could leave.

You know me and you understand how much I suffer and in what situation I am! In this remote place, faraway from the center, I don't know what to do and whom I should believe – Ing. Petrov or the head of the Political Bureau! I don't know whether to continue or to stop the work?

I have to finish the work else I will be taken to court. What shall I do, advise me. You talk to Bagirov[145] and Aqamali-oghlu and Qarayev. Answer me by telegraph. Poor Alish and I have spent all we had on the *qanat*s and we have many debts. It is not a joke to give the workers every day 8 to 10 *pud* of cereals! I feel greatly humiliated and betrayed. The envious and freeloading bullies are delighted at my plight. They are throwing their hats into the air. They are rubbing their hands and saying we are getting the *qanat*s clean for

---

144. Islam Abdollah-oghlu Hajiyev (1889-1938). At the end of 1919 the Communist Party sent him from Astrakhan to Baku to work against the Republic of Azerbaijan. After the fall of the Republic he became chief of the militia of Shusha and later he held several position in the local administration. In 1938 he was executed as an enemy of the people.

145. Mir Jafar Mir Abbas-oghlu Bagirov (1896-1956) was the head of the secret police (Tcheka) of Azerbaijan from 1921-22; the head of the Azerbaijan Polit Bureau (1922-30), first secretary of the Azerbaijan Communist Party (1933-53). He was Stalin's henchman in Azerbaijan.

Hamideh Khanum's house in Kahrizli

free. I cannot write more. I am awaiting your answer impatiently.

Hamideh

A letter came from Mirza Jalil: "we are celebrating the 18th anniversary of *Molla Nasreddin* and for the first time they are going to stage the play "The School of the village of Danabash." Therefore, he and the children asked me to come to Baku. On 20 April I gathered everything and went to Baku. In the newspapers, articles were published about the journal *Molla Nasreddin*. The play was going to be staged at the Mailov Theater. In connection with this event they had invited me and Mina twice to the house of Samad Aqamali-oghlu. The performance if I am not mistaken must have been on 10 May. On 5 May, in the newspaper "Workers [of Baku]" somebody under the name of Shaduntsa had written "the charitable lady of the past," Hamideh Khanum, had taken the *qanat*s of the villagers and was selling its water, and similar nonsense. The charitable lady of the past was written with quotation marks. Of course, those who knew me did not believe such rumors and knew better.

Mirza Jalil was very angry about these slanderous remarks in the press. He wrote, under my name, three petitions to the People's Commissar and other organizations and complained of these slanderous articles. In these petitions Mirza Jalil had asked that my activities be investigated to refute these strange accusations. He wanted them to be sent to the Commissar of the Hindarx district.

The first day of the performance arrived. We were all sitting in the grand-stand box. Mirza Jalil was getting nervous. In those days, during the interlude, music was played, but today they were not playing. After the second act the play was stopped and people were wondering why. It became clear that after the second act the actors were promised to be paid their wages, but they were not paid and that is why they did not play.

It was a big scandal. Mirza Jalil had lost himself and was very dejected and he wanted us to return home. On the way he told me, "after this, I will never consent to celebrate an anniversary."

Mirza Jalil did not believe in dreams, but on 18 May in the morning he got up from bed very despondent because he had had a terrible dream and he was very saddened. In his dream he had seen many people dying and much blood.

The same day I wanted to go and see my daughter Mina. Recently she had been very dejected, because she suffered from kidney pain and was worried about this. She was afraid and did not want to have an operation. I somehow got delayed and suddenly the door was opened and Mina's fifteen-year-old Rashid entered in a very agitated state and said: "My mother killed herself with a gun." Mirza Jalil was in shock. It seems that he had seen my daughter in his dream, who was bloodied and was dying. With all his heart he shared my tragedy and he was consoling as much as he could.

He took Mina's children under his protection. She had written a letter before her suicide that she was fed up with life and she was asking me to forgive her and to protect her children. Mirza Jalil was looking all the time after our son-in-law and was trying to console him.

* * *

The days were hot. I took my children and grand-children and on 6 June we arrived in Kahrizli. Munavvar had just completed the midwifery course. She came with us and she wanted to find a job in this area.

In Kahrizli a big head-ache was awaiting me. The son of Sa'adat Khanum, Jamil had died of tuberculosis. According to our tradition, the women embraced the tragedy stricken families and were weeping and when I came face to face with Aunt Sa'adat she did not weep and wail at all. She looked at me and said: "Gather yourself. Don't despair. Don't weep. You have many enemies. Be prepared to hear bad news. The Political Bureau has jailed Soleyman, our manager of the mill and they have arrested our guard Jalal and his brother."

As they say, I was showered with bad news every day. They were right when saying that when pain comes it comes in loads. A few days after returning to the village, as a result of the petition that we had submitted about my activities, a commission came from Baku. There were two Comrades whose names were Vayner and Shikhian. Vayner said that he had talked to everyone in the district and gathered information and nobody had said anything but good things about me.

Vayner summoned the executive of the village committee Jamil Aghalarov and asked about me. He said that he was very positive and that he had received his education thanks to Hamideh Khanum and that he was grateful to me. In fact, he had been educated in the school that I had started for the children of the poor. Furthermore, I had sent him to the agricultural school of Tiflis.

Comrade Vayner said: "I have written a report about you that in my view, taking into consideration the views of the people, the Soviet government will village was very hot we could not return to our house. We rented a room in Shusha and I lived there with the children until the hot season passed and also to see what I could do to release my people who were unjustly in prison. I did my best and it did not take long before they were released and before we all returned to the village a letter came from Mirza Jalil.

26 June 1923

Dear Hamideh,

I have only received from you a letter dated 10 June which is about the arrest of the people and the confiscation of the horses. When you were in Baku I advised you not to return to the village. I mean that the terrible situation there will make you suffer tremendously. After your departure, the Central Committee here issued a decree that the land of the former landlords should be confiscated. Although I don't understand which lands they are talking about, because after all nobody owns any land anymore, I just want to remind you that to be free of trouble and discord stay away from the branch of the Land Office and don't rent land from them. It makes no difference; your good intentions will eventually be vilified. I am sincerely begging you once and for all consider coming to Baku. Here you will be occupied with the education of the children and if you want you can help me with my work.

If you want to get a job Agha Mali-oghlu has told me that whatever kind of job you want he will be able to get one for you.

I have talked with the people in charge about those in prison, the horses, and the guns. Hamideh, by God, to tell the truth I am fed up with all these village affairs. You have not even finished one task when another one pops up. Therefore, there is only one way out, once and for all we have to settle permanently in the city. We should either sell the phaeton

Mina Davatdarova

value your activities and will not allow having you unjustly accused."

When my relatives saw my situation – misery, sickness coming at me from all sides, descending on me like a flock of crows - they consoled me saying that I should get a big tent from someone and take my children and grandchildren and go to Turshsu, in Kechaldagh, a place with good air. Living in Kechaldagh was cheap, because it was not necessary to pay for the summer house. A few families got together with servants, both male and female, and cattle, with horse carts, and like a migration of nomads we went to Turshsu.

In the beginning of August rains start in the mountains. Because of this we had to come down from the mountains, but since at that time the or bring it to the city and we should rent the mill. After all, do you want to live in peace or not?

Recently, I have sent Munavvar's equipment by mail to Muzaffar's address in Aghdam. I have forgotten to include the bandages, which are in the cupboard. The measuring cup and the mirror I have not yet been able to obtain, but I will get them and send them.

Lida did not want to come, because changing my mind and not sending Jalal to Kahrizli did not please her. I understood why this has upset her, because now I don't have any contact with her. Let Muzaffar invite her.

How is your health? Why have you stayed so long in the village? Why are not you writing me more often? Do you need anything? I live with this hope that at the end of the summer you will come with the children and we will live together.

I am finishing the play that I started writing in the winter. I am busy with the publication of my works and other matters. Let us see what will happen later. For the time being fare well and give my regards to Alish Bey.

Your Jalil.

* * *

12 August 1923

Dear Hamideh!

I have received letters from you and the package that I sent to Muzaffar contained 10 *funt* of sugar, one *funt* tea, coffee, and three pairs of socks. I did not buy the most expensive socks, because you are to wear them after all in the province. The *Baku Reporter* and *Molla Nasreddin* have been sent to you; have you received them? It was very difficult in Baku for a while, but now it has cooled down. Bahador (Rahim Bey's son) has

come. He has met Muzaffar and Alish Bey in Aghdam.

You write life is hard for you there. I had foreseen this and did not think that going to Qarabagh was the right thing. I told you not to go there. After this the situation will be even worse in autonomous Qarabagh. It is obvious that for some time there will be disturbances, etc. A number of people will be hurt for no reason. I think it is best for you that, at the end of August you take the children and come to Baku and stay here. Did not you see how innocent Jalal and his brother were kept jailed all summer? This was a great injustice. After all nobody asked what was the crime of these people who had worked faithfully all their lives. I see no other way than distancing yourself from the Political Bureau of Shusha. It is as if you are purposely trying to be near them. If you are not able to eat your bread comfortably at the top of the mountains why are you living there?

I have made a chicken coop for Anvar with one rooster and three hens. You can lock it and every day I feed them. I am going to buy a bicycle for Midhat. Give my regards to everyone.

Jalil.

* * *

I sent four grown up sons to school in Baku; my six year old grandson Murad stayed with me. Mirza Jalil was writing letters frequently and said "abandon everything and come to Baku," but in spite of that I did not want to leave because with incredible difficulty I had put the weaving factory together and was hoping that very soon everything would be all right. I did not consider it right to leave the village girls who with quite a lot patience wanted to learn how to weave and were hoping to become skilled workers and get good wages. This was such an interesting and rewarding job that I could not abandon.

Mirza Jalil had gone everywhere, had tried everything, but could not find yarn. We were making shawls, table cloths and handkerchiefs from the yarn that we spun by hand. From silk yarn we had made a very nice fabric. Mirza Jalil liked it very much and he had given it to be made into a summer jacket for himself. Our children and our close relatives were wearing jackets of the same fabric. The village women were bringing yarn and we were making materials for them. This craft was liked by everybody and we thought that it was going to be spread throughout the village. I had read that in Holland, Belgium and other countries, having these kinds of machines, the villagers were doing quite well and living nicely. It is obvious that there is a big difference between handmade and machine-made fabrics. Our girls and women were very skillful in making beautiful patterns.

In the spring of 1924, Mirjafar Bagirov came to our district on an official mission. He came to see me. He came and saw our weaving factory and he liked it very much. He promised to do everything to send 100 *pud* of silk in the most economical way from Baku.

* * *

In the summer of 1924, Mirza Jalil and the children came to the village. We went to Shusha and rented two rooms in Mashdi Ali's house in the Haji Yusofli Street. This simple house pleased Mirza Jalil tremendously.

In the hottest part of the summer we went for three weeks to Turshsu and lived there in a big tent. The wonderful climate of Turshsu and its cool, delicious water pleased Mirza Jalil very much. It was so cold that we had to light the hearth. We did not have any servant to bring firewood from the forest. After deliberation, Mirza Jalil took a sack and a rope and told the children, "let us go to the forest to gather wood." The children fastened the firewood rope and quickly went with him. They were all barefoot. After a short while, we saw that Mirza Jalil was returning with a sack of firewood on his shoulder. The children, too, had sacks of firewood on their backs. Our neighbors were looking at them with surprise and later they did not consider it beneath their dignity and went to the forest to get wood.

On 20 August we returned to Shusha. A few days later, on 26 August, only Mirza Jalil went to Baku. Again my health was bad. I was coughing badly, my chest was hurting. The physicians were thinking that there was an inflammation in my throat and lungs. They considered it necessary that I go to a sanatorium on the Black Sea. I wrote about this to Mirza Jalil. This news worried him greatly. About this he wrote me letters nos. 952 and 955. These letters have been transferred to the national archives.

* * *

As I mentioned before Mirza Jalil's daughter from his first wife, Munavvar, had finished the midwifery course in 1923 in Baku and had obtained a job in the hospital of Aghdam. My son of my first husband, Muzaffar Davatdarov was working in a credit company that was located in Kahrizli village. This office was located in our big hall. Muzaffar was helping me with my village work.

In September 1924 I went to Baku with the children. When I wanted to go to Baku Muzaffar told me that he wanted to marry Munavvar. Munavvar left the hospital of Aghdam and got a job in Hindarx, which was at a distance of 5 werst from Kahrizli. I entrusted my affairs to them and went to Baku for treatment. Our dear friend Ebrahim Bey Mehmandarov began my treatment.

I did not find Mirza Jalil at home. He had gone on a business trip in relation with the creation of a new alphabet and a press at the invitation of Aghamali-oghlu.

Having the office of the journal *Molla Nasreddin* in our house (Post Street 56) had made our space very tight. In our house there were five children and teenagers. At the same time they were going to school. Furthermore, our cook Olya Razina and her daughter were living with us. When we were not here, the years 1921-22, Munavvar had given one of the big rooms to her school friend, Nina Abramova, who was living there with her mother. As a result, all these people were forced to live in two rooms. We made the room in the middle, which did not have much light, into the dining room. Some of the children slept there.

* * *

Mirza Jalil and Aghamali-oghlu returned from their trip in November. Mirza Jalil was satisfied with his trip. They had travelled to Moscow, Leningrad, Samara, Orenburg, Samarkand, and other cities. Mirza Jalil was full of descriptions of his journey and things that had happened. He had brought many books with him.

On the "Health" book that he had bought for me from Moscow he had written: "To Hamideh Khanum who has spent her life treating villagers." Apart from these he had bought a light spring overcoat for himself. In the following years he had to wear this light coat in very cold winters until the end of his life.

On this trip, Mirza Jalil, did not buy many gifts for us because money was tight, and therefore, he apologized profusely.

It was 1925. The first issue of *Molla Nasreddin*, which had 6 pages, was ready for sale on 3 January. In issue no. 2, Mirza Jalil had written a short article with the title: "The Funeral Messenger." Of course,

he had made up this name. But in spite of this everybody knew whom he was alluding to. Therefore, many humorous conversations and allusions were made and many rumors circulated. Many women would come in person to the office to get the journal.

* * *

It was the end of January. Mirza Jalil was ill and complaining of terrible headaches. In fact, there was no incident or conversation that would have affected his health. That same evening Mirza Jalil did not write anything and went to bed before his usual time. It seemed that he was in pain, but he did not want to talk about it. It was in the middle of the night that I was woken up by a cry. I saw that Mirza Jalil was moaning as if he was being suffocated. With difficulty I woke him up. He was in a deep sleep; he did not want to awake up. After he roused himself somewhat, I asked him: "what has happened, why are you moaning?" He was silent and was looking around in despair. After a while, he came to himself and said: "I had a very bad dream." I said: "Please, tell me." He said: "I saw in the dream that they are trying me and that they find me guilty and want to wall me up in the basement. First, they take me to the basement and then they wall up the door and then they cover the only hole in the ceiling as well. I was shouting and begging, please, at least let the small window open! At least, let me breathe! Don't deprive me of air!" After this Mirza Jalil confessed that there were serious problems with the publication of the journal. After issue no. 6 he had removed his name from the journal as the author.[146]

146. After no. 6 Mirza Jalil instead of his name signed as "the editorial board." Although Hamideh Khanum does not say it openly the journal was going into a direction that was contrary to Mirza Jalil's philosophy and became a vehicle for anti-religious sentiments

In January 1925, I went to the village to look after my property. Because of certain reasons I could not stay in the city. In Baku the office of the journal was in our house. That is why our house was very crowded so that I did not even have a corner for myself. Wherever I went there would be somebody. I was feeling that I was cornered and did not know what to do. I wrote a detailed letter to Mirza Jalil about this. He wrote back and politely insisted that I come to Baku. He did not wait for my coming. Before long he came himself and took me to Baku. In June, I took the children and for a few days we went to the village and from there to Shusha. We rented two rooms in the house of Soleyman Amirov. In the middle of July Mirza Jalil also came and we went for two weeks to Turshsu. As always, he was feeling happy here. Every day he was swimming in the cold water and was drinking mineral water. He was joking with everybody.

One of those days, Mirza Jalil was summoned suddenly to Baku in connection with the journal's work. He was very upset and gathered his things and went to Baku. After three days he returned again to Turshsu. This coming and going was so sudden that I thought he had made a U-turn halfway. It seemed that the heat of Baku had bothered him so much that he had done some necessary work and after that he had obtained tickets that same day and had come to Yevlakh and from there to Turshsu.

For many years a family that had fled from Iran had worked on our farm and the man was doing the farm work. In the past, his wife Telpari was spinning very good silk in the weaving factory and later she was baking very good *lavash* and *yukha* bread, which Mirza Jalil liked very much. Telpari was a hardworking woman, whatever you asked her she would throw herself into the work. She was witty, always ready with an answer, and reliable.

With her daughter Golpari she was working in our weaving factory.

One day in summer in the same Turshsu next to our tent Telpari made a fire and baked *yuxa* bread. The bread she had baked was paper thin and fragrant, we were all hungry and we ate the *yuxa*. We talked with Telpari. At this time Mirza Jalil came to us, he rolled the *yuxa* and ate it with considerable appetite. When he started on the second *yuxa*, he said: "Telpari, come and let me take you to Baku and I will have your teeth fixed." Her two front teeth had fallen out. When Telpari was turning the *yuxa* on the baking plate and flattening it she said in a very nice voice: "O Mirza, may I be your sacrifice. I am afraid that in Baku you won't fix my teeth but create a head ache for me."[147]

Very unwillingly, we departed from Turshsu. The weather was very hot. We took our luggage and sent it ahead by cart. Once again, we went to the spring with the children and then we drank from the water to our heart's desire and we got into the phaeton and departed. Mirza Jalil was in a good mood. He kept looking constantly at Mt. Kechaldagh and he was happy. The road was winding and turning and going down through a very green valley. At the end of the valley there was a crystal clear spring. Half-way down he asked the driver to stop. He got out and went to the spring and we followed him. Behind a rock, Mirza Jalil took off his clothes and jumped into the water and then he tried to persuade me to join him saying that the water is not cold.

Since my heart was troubling me I was afraid of swimming in cold water, but he managed to persuade me to get in. When I got into the water I suddenly felt very bad and somehow I managed to get out and dress and then I fainted. Mirza Jalil was very scared. With difficulty he managed to take

[Mehrban Vazir].

147. Telpari makes a wordplay between 'dish' (tooth) and 'ish' (an affaire), which is difficult to render in English.

me to Shusha and call a doctor. Only the next day I came to myself. Jalil was very sorry and since he had made me to go into the water he was apologizing many many times. When he saw a pool he was not able to resist and therefore, to get into it, he very often took the children and went to Dashalti. At the end of August Mirza Jalil took Midhat and went to Baku. In the beginning of September, I first sent Anvar and Teymur to school in Baku. A few days later I followed them.

* * *

It was 1926.

Mirza Jalil loved our late son Midhat more than his own life. Midhat was a very serious boy who was reading books and scientific journals and he loved handicrafts. He was always busy with something. He was making airplanes and was flying them. These contraptions rose into the air with much noise. After a few meters they came down. One time, he asked me for silk fabric for the wings of the airplane. I gave it. After many trials he made an airplane that was about one meter in length. It rose up and after 40 meters it came down. These strange inventions of his interested his father tremendously. In spite of this, Mirza Jalil was telling him all the time: "don't waste too much time on these things, concentrate on your studies."

Midhat was seriously interested in radio and was reading the journals and managed to build a radio receiver. He spent a lot of time on it and built some of the parts himself. He saved his pocket-money and used it to buy necessary parts for this radio receiver. When he was away from his studies, he was not idle and was busy with all these things. Unlike other children he did not go for walks, but was sitting at home busy with the radio.

Eventually, he was so involved with this activity that he began to neglect his studies. A chronic head cold prevented him from studying. As a result,

in the end he did not get good grades for some courses. But eventually he managed to build a four-lamp receiver, with an antenna on our roof, and we could easily listen to the broadcasts from Moscow and foreign stations. The neighbors would come and look at it and wonder at the child's invention. Mirza Jalil who was sensing that Midhat would have to stay in the same grade was very angry. Out of anger he took a brick and wanted to destroy the radio. He became ashen-faced and trembling he shouted at his father, and said: "Throw it." He was shouting in such a way as if his life depended on this contraption. I immediately grabbed Mirza Jalil's hand and took the brick and led him into the other room. To quieten Mirza Jalil I promised that I would go with my friend Blaqovidova to meet with the school director to ask him for some time to make up his studies. Then I went to poor Midhat; I was afraid that he would have done something to himself. I consoled him somewhat and asked him to go with me and Varvara Nikolevnaya Blaqovidova, who knew the director. Midhat agreed.

We went. Blaqovidova was eating. She saw that I was very agitated and she became worried. When she heard of the situation she left her food and immediately she took me to director Kireyev. We explained to him exactly what the problem was. He considered the situation of the poor boy with sympathy. He told us not to worry and he would resolve the problem. Director Kireyev sent the prefect of the class with us to our house to look at the radio and bring it to the school.

In those days the radio was a rarity. In the school they showed great interest in the contraption; they tried it and they liked it and told Midhat not to worry. They gave him time to prepare for another chance at the exam. After this the director promised that he would see to it that he could attend a special technical school with a specialty in electronics.

The chronic and severe head cold created problems for Midhat to study well. We tried very hard with the help of Blaqovidova to persuade Midhat to go and visit a specialist professor. Eventually he agreed and we took him to the specialist. The physician immediately operated on him. After this, we went to Shusha and Turshsu in the summer and his health improved and he was studying quite well.

In the fall Midhat was sent to the school for electronic technology. Midhat became one of the best students. The principal Popov said that he would have a brilliant career ahead of him.

* * *

In 1926 my late daughter's sister-in-law, Sara Khanum invited me to Tiflis. We had not seen her for a long time. Also, I needed to take the sulfur waters. I wanted to go. First Mirza Jalil did not allow me, but then somehow I changed his mind. I went to Tiflis on 31 May 1926. On 10 June he wrote me a letter in which he said:

> Yesterday evening the children left. I wrote that they should send a phaeton from Yevlakh to meet them. To take care of every possibility I gave Midhat money, so that if the phaeton did not come they would get an automobile to go there. I have prepared everything for the road; they had obtained a sleeper seat in the train, which was very comfortable. Of course, Anvar was crying and 5 manat dried his tearfilled eyes. Aska, the son of Engineer Rustambeyov[148] went with them. A few days

earlier I had sent Allahyar. Alesh (the son of the Soleyman in whose house we were staying in Shusha who had lived with us for 2 years and was studying pharmacology and now he is a doctor) and his friends had gone the day before.

I am thinking of going to Shusha on 5 July.

Is it not strange that Esma'il Haqqi (the office manager of *Molla Nasreddin* in Tiflis) has not visited you? I have written to him asking about the health of the children (my grandchildren) and also of Sara Khanum and Yusif Khan.

For the time being, until we meet, greetings to all.

Jalil

June 10, 1926

* * *

In the middle of June I took two of my grandchildren and we went to the village and from there to Shusha. In Shusha we again had to stay in the house of Soleyman Amirov. In the early days of July Mirza Jalil came. This summer, in Isa Spring and Dashalti he organized walks and we took a group photograph. We went to Turshsu as well. Our picture was taken by Alish Amirov. He played the *tar* beautifully. Sometimes he played the *tar*, while Mirza Jalil played the *kamancha*. This performance was very much to the liking of Mirza Jalil.

I gave a copy of the picture that Alish took with my sons and grandchildren to the EAAzF.[149]

While we were in Shusha Mirza Jalil rested well. His headaches ceased and he became very relaxed. He was promising that after this he would work very well. At that time he had a lot of unfinished work. Apart from his Memoirs, for the last two years he was working on the play "The Gathering

---

148. Fathollah Bey Asad Bey-oghlu Rustambeyov (1867–1946) was one of the first Azerbaijani engineers educated in Europe and a famous intellectual. He also graduated from the St. Petersburg Technological Institute and from 1893-1908 he worked in the oil industry of Baku, where he was in charge of the M. Naghiyev Oil Institute and was one of the members of the High Commission of the Oil Board of Azerbaijan, chief technical director and teacher. His children were also successful.

149. *Elmlar Akademiiasy Azerbaijan Filialy* or the Azerbaijan Section of the Academy of Sciences.

of the Fools." Therefore, he had read many books about crazy people. One day he told me laughingly, "I am reading and writing about the life of the crazy so much that I am afraid that one day I will become crazy as well."

In mid-August Mirza Jalil went to Baku. On the first day of September 1926 he wrote a letter to me from there.

In 1926 after Midhat had gone to the school of electronic technology, where he was doing well. Anvar was also trying hard. Their father was pleased and relieved with their situation and devoted himself completely to work. During the day *Molla Nasreddin* was taking up all his time. Apart from this, he was working at night as well; after everybody slept he was writing plays, Memoirs, and short stories. Mirza Jalil could only do creative work in the quiet of the night. The slightest things such as the tick-tack of the clock would disturb him. Therefore, he would stop the clock.

In these years the journal was coming out regularly, each year 52 issues. Mirza Jalil was a person who was so engaged in his work that he could not tolerate anyone coming and disturbing his work. Even when my guests came he would get angry, because they would make much noise. If there was too much noise he could not write and stopped working, because then his mind would be disturbed. Because he had a very sensitive ear, he would hear the slightest noise, and this would make him nervous and stop the train of thought and made him lose his patience. Therefore, he did not want to go to people's homes or have somebody as a guest. And he hated to attend conferences and parties. This standoffishness and misanthropy seemed very strange to many people and very often this was not very good for him. People did not like him and were calling him arrogant. In reality, his brain was working all the time and it was full of thoughts and ideas. He was afraid that he would forget the thoughts that were in his mind and he wanted to write them down as soon as possible.

* * *

In the summer of 1927 we went to Shusha again in the Hammamqabaghi quarter we rented a house next to R. Taqiyev's big mosque. Midhat had taken the antenna of his 4-lamp radio to the top of the minaret of the mosque. This was for us, for our acquaintances and neighbors a great pleasure. The same summer, a friend of Midhat, Igor and his mother Varvara Nikolayevna Blaqovidova came to Shusha as our guest. With them we went to Turshsu for a few days. Igor and Midhat wanted to walk to Turshsu. They were taking shortcuts in some places. They were running on narrow trails. In this way they were not behind us, who were traveling in phaetons. After two days in Turshsu we returned.

That summer I fell ill. The doctor advised me to go to Tiflis to take the sulfur waters. Therefore, on this occasion Mirza Jalil promised to write to Dr. A. Eritsya, our old friend.

In the beginning of August Mirza Jalil went to Baku. Before going and prior to his departure he was very nervous. Since I did not know the reason for this I was very astonished. Later, from Baku, Mirza Jalil wrote the reason for this:

> Thank you for creating a good atmosphere for me. Unfortunately, when I was leaving you I was nervous. This was the result of sleepless nights and this is not your fault. It does not matter, it passes. I am sending you money and some small cash for the children.
>
> Jalil

This summer Asgar Khan also came to Shusha and he was thinking of getting married. This was the same Asgar Khan who in Tabriz was working in the office of *Molla Nasreddin* and had come to Baku with us. Since coming to Baku he was living with us and was working as a tailor. Our servant

Hamideh Khanum and Mirza Jalil with their loved ones in Shusha, 1926

Sakineh had found a very good girl for him and they became engaged. She was the daughter of one of our neighbors. He wanted to have a quiet wedding and, of course, I and Muzaffar were very much involved in this good affair. He had nobody besides ourselves here. I don't know why Mirza Jalil was against this marriage.

After Mirza Jalil went away Munavvar came from Baku and we all got together and prepared the wedding for Asgar. His wife Rubabe was brought as a bride to our house. Her parents said that we won't give our daughter to a man whom we don't know and it is only because of you that we consent to this marriage and we entrust our daughter to you.

I took the bride to Baku. Since the children were going to school we send them ahead of us. I knew that Mirza Jalil would not be happy with me for doing this and this was the case. He did not

welcome us with a smile. But later when he got to know Rubabe better he liked her character. Mirza Jalil respected Rubabe and he thought Asgar Khan had found a good wife for himself.

* * *

In the fall and winter of 1927-28 the children, especially Midhat, were doing very well in school. Mirza Jalil was very pleased and he was working all nights. He finished his memoirs and a play that he was working on. The same winter he wrote an interesting play called 'The Wedding of Qamar' and he read some parts to me. Later he did not like the play and despite my protests did not listen to me and tore it up and burnt in the stove.

Baby bride carried by her brother (no. 24, yr. 8, 24 October 1913)

In December 1931 the weather was very cold. We did not have firewood. In spite of my profuse protests Mirza Jalil burnt quite a lot of his manuscripts to keep us warm.

In the spring of 1928 Mirza Jalil took me to see the performance of 'The Book of My Mother' in the Naberejnideki Theater.[150] They put us in a loge. Mirza Jalil did not like the performance of the actors. A young writer came to Mirza Jalil and asked: "Did you like the performance of the actors?" He answered laughingly: "If I tell the truth (pointing with his head to the actors), they won't like it."

In the spring of the same year I received a summons from the office of the chief of the militia for 10 in the morning. Mirza Jalil indicated that he wanted to come with me. We went there together. The chief asked about my property in Qarabagh and when did I leave it and to whom had I entrusted my property and other things. I answered all the questions. Then Mirza Jalil asked the chief to find and read the proceedings of the conference of the year 1921 or 1922. The chief found these proceedings and read them and then he very politely apologized to me and said: "I have bothered you unnecessarily. You are free to go."

A few days later Mirza Jalil received a document in my name assigning me title to the property. It

---

150. This is the Taghiev Theater. According to Zamanov, this was the Theater at the Coast (Saheldaki Teater). It was the theater for the Turkish workers. At that time, this theater was located in the same building where the Puppet Theater is now.

read: "Hamideh Khanum Javanshiri's property in Kahrizli is not going to be confiscated. She has the right of living in Qarabagh and wherever in Azerbaijan where she wants to live."

In the same year the Qarabagh Beys and well-known noble families were forced to move to other districts.

* * *

Mirza Jalil was complaining about bad headaches and too much palpitation of the heart. The physicians forbade him to smoke cigarettes and to eat meat and recommended a serious diet. For treatment they wanted him to go to Borzhoma. Midhat had passed his exams and graduated from his school. It was summer. I took my youngest son and my grandchildren and for a few days we went to Kahrizli and from there to Shusha. To help me with the housework I asked my relative in the village, Qamar and her 9-year old son to come to Shusha. (Qamar later married Mirza Jalil's nephew, Teymur).

Qamar and her son were seriously afflicted with malaria. This mother and her son very much needed treatment and a change of air.

Munavvar and Muzaffar were living all the time in the village. In Shusha near the bazaar we rented two rooms in the house of Reza Ibrahimov who was a confectioner. Midhat passed his exams in the middle of summer and came to Shusha. After only 3 weeks of rest he returned to be accepted in the Oil Institute of Azerbaijan.

* * *

Having Jalil's *Molla Nasreddin* office in our house caused a space problem. This was really bothering all of us and was creating all kinds of arguments. This is quite obvious in Mirza Jalil's letters. I was

thinking seriously about this and did not know whether to go to Baku or to stay in the village. For me to be living away from my children and not participating in their upbringing and education and not looking after their health was difficult. But in the present situation being with them and not having my own room was making the problem of space even worse.

I had to stay for a while in Shusha and the air was very good for me. Qamar and her son were also staying with me. It was necessary to have them treated for a long a period and also to get them an education. Every day Qamar with her son went to the Pushkin hospital in Shusha to have injections. The hospital's dentist, our close friend Rahil Lvovna Leven-Berlin liked her very much. With the help of Leven-Berlin, Qamar got a job in the hospital. Then she finished a course in nursing and in her spare time she was helping me with my daily work. In the evenings I was teaching her to write and read Russian and Turkish.

Gradually Qamar started to recall what she had learnt in the village school. Due to my encouragement she did away with her *chador*. Being a nurse and under the orders of the doctors she would go to the homes of the patients and give them injections.

Qamar's parents were illiterate. To show me respect they had allowed her to attend the school that I had established when she was very young. Later they did not allow her to continue school and when she was 13 years old they married her off and caused her unhappiness.

Qamar and her son both became healthy and they were even getting better. They were both depending on me. I did not want to leave them here. I wanted to take her and her son to Baku and put her in a school. For this purpose I wrote a letter to Mirza Jalil so that he might rent a room for them. He promised but he could not find a room. Whether we wanted it or not we had to stay in Shusha. Mirza Jalil was sending me 50 to 60 manat every month for my expenses. Sometimes,

Muzaffar was sending some supplies from Kahrizli. The children were often writing letters and I was very much missing them. At that time, there was an intellectual group composed of physicians, nurses, the head pharmacist and others working in the Shusha hospital.

In the winter holidays Anvar came to visit me. A very strange thing happened here to the poor child. It was like this. Qamar and Firuzeh, the wife of our landlord, were throwing snowballs at each other. Anvar joined them. The landlord was drunk. When he saw that his wife was throwing snowballs he got angry and beat his wife. Anvar swore at him profusely and they almost started fighting and the neighbors separated them. Mirza Jalil wrote about this incident when he with our writers went to Yerevan to meet Armenian authors.

In the same year of 1929, Muzaffar and Munavvar had to give up their work in the village. They went to stay with Mirza Jalil in Baku. He wrote about this to me in his letter dated 17 April 1929.

On 14 July 1929, Mirza Jalil went to Borzhoma for treatment. At that time he wrote this letter to his daughter Munavvar.

Munavvar,

Now, I am going to Borzhoma. Slowly I am becoming better. I am giving my address in Borzhoma. The gist of my letter is this. Earlier, you were not getting along well with Hamideh Khanum. I am writing you to try not to displease her and listen to her. If you do what I am saying I will be very pleased with you. I will very much love you like I used to do. Don't forget what I am saying. Remember this. This is your duty.

Before this, I have written one or two lines to Hamideh Khanum. Therefore, there is no need to write to her about this now. I will write from Borzhoma. For the time being, your father Jalil.

Baku 14 July.

The same summer all our children and grand-children came to us in Shusha. We spent our holidays very nicely with our friends. Often we went to Isa Spring and Dashalti and other places for picnics. In the evenings, every time we gathered in somebody's house. We would make music, dance and perform plays. The Commander's wife, Anna Vasilyevna's reading of some parts of *Mitskevich* by Zoshchenko[151] was beautiful and particularly impressive.

In August Mirza Jalil came from Borzhoma to Shusha. He was not feeling well. He stayed a few days with us and then because of the work of the journal he went to Baku.

In these days my very dear and old aunt Sa`adat was our guest. Mirza Jalil liked her very much and respected her greatly and whenever he came home he brought her gifts. The following year she died.

When returning to Baku, Mirza Jalil promised me that I would get a room so that I could take Qamar and come to Baku. Mirza Jalil's nephew Teymur was serving in the military in Stepanakert. He came to visit us. At the end of the summer the children left. With Qamar we rented a comfortable and warm house and went there.

* * *

In the beginning of February 1930 Mirza Jalil sent me the letter that he had received from Ali Azhdar Sayyedzadeh[152] in Moscow. Sayyedzadeh was requesting that I should provide information about documents that I had of my late father, Ahmad Bey Javanshir. He wrote that he was putting the finishing touch to his work 'The poetry of Ahmad Bey Javanshir' and very soon he would send it to

---

151. Mikhail Mikhailovich Zoshchenko (1894-1958) was a Soviet author.

152. Ali Azhdar Sayyedzadeh (1899-1970) was a famous literature scholar and professor.

Baku to be published. I sent a short biography of my father to this author together with his poems that we had published with Mirza Jalil's help in Tiflis in 1906.

It was around this time that I started writing my 'Memoirs' about my late father.

In his second letter, dated 19 May 1930, Sayyedzadeh again asked many questions. At the same time he said that he would come to Baku to gather information about our poets Vaqif and Zakir. I should mention that he had written from Moscow to me, saying that he had found my father's book entitled "The political situation of the Qarabagh Khanate."[153] He wrote that he was sending the book about my father for publication to Baku and he promised that he was going to send a copy to me. I wrote an answer to this letter and gave necessary information.

In September of the same year I received the last letter from Sayyedzadeh. He thanked me for writing my 'Memoirs' and he wished that I wrote it in greater detail. Then he asked me whatever material I had to send him to Baku by certified mail.

* * *

In the spring Mirza Jalil wrote: "I have rented a room in the house of one of my employees, Haji Akhundov (Tatarski Street no. 12).[154] If you want to be treated in Surakhan you can come to Baku."

In June I went to Baku. I put my things in the house of Akhundov and then I went to see our people. Mirza Jalil had aged. He was not well. It seemed that he was not attending properly to the journal's work. We had quite a few people in our house and our expenditures exceeded our income.

All this was affecting Mirza Jalil's health and he was suffering from rheumatism.

I took my lodgings in Tatarski Street. Every day Mirza Jalil and the children would come and see me after doing their homework. Sometimes he would lunch with me and until 9 o'clock he would stay with me. He was very troubled and nervous. He was often complaining of heart and headaches.

My friend Dr. Ebrahim Bey Mehmandarov was often coming to my house. He was treating Jalil. One day he told me that Mirza Jalil had started suffering from serious sclerosis, because he did not keep a diet and did not listen to the advice of his doctor.

According to our neighbor, Yelizaveta Nikolayevna Abramovan, one time, in the summer of 1930 (when I had gone to Shusha), Mirza Jalil together with all our neighbors sat in the communal mirrored hall and had tea with sour-cherry jam. She was with her daughter Nina and they saw that suddenly Mirza Jalil's face became very pale, he was trembling, he opened his mouth but could not speak, he wanted to get up, but could not. They asked him: "what has happened to you?" With great difficulty he said: "I don't know; I have trouble speaking. My feet have become heavy." After a while, Mirza Jalil came to himself. According to them, Mirza Jalil talked about his condition to the doctor (this was in July 1930).

* * *

Muzaffar and Anvar wanted to get the booklet of the Workers Association. To get this, their friends had advised them to go to the Buta Station and work there as laborers. And they did so. After exactly 2 weeks of working as laborers they came for one day to rest at home. The hands of both of them were full of blisters and scratches.

* * *

153. This same book was published in 1901 in Shusha.
154. Today Tatarski Street is Ali Mardan Bey Topchibashiov Street.

The hot weather had started. In Surakhani, after getting a bathtub treatment 20 times, I was getting ready to return to Shusha. Midhat with his friends was sent from the Azerbaijan Oil Institute to work in the Don River area. On 10 June, Mirza Jalil bought tickets and sent me, Munavvar and Anvar to Shusha. He promised that he would come in a few days. But he just managed to come at the end of July. He was very depressed. When he saw me the first question he asked was: "Have you received a letter from Midhat?" When I said I had not received any letter he started weeping profusely. I was afraid. "Why are you crying?" I asked. He said that he had not received a letter from Midhat for a long time. He said that he was afraid that he might suddenly get a telegram about his death. I consoled and chided him and took him for a walk in a place that he liked. On our way we visited the grave of Mulla Vaqefpanah.

After a few days Mirza Jalil very hurriedly got his things together and left for Baku. He was thinking that in Baku he might receive a letter from Midhat. On 27 August I received the following letter from Mirza Jalil.

Hamideh,

This trip of Midhat has greatly disturbed me. Despite the terrible heat and mugginess of Baku I have to stay and every day I drink about 100 *pud* of water. On 19 August Midhat asked for 25 manat from Leningrad. The same day I sent him 45 manat. I think I have written to you about this. The second telegram dated 24 August totally baffled me. It said, "Quickly send money." From this telegram I understood that my 45 manat had not reached him. I explained this to myself in this way, that the first time I sent the money from the October Railway Station, because this was mentioned in Midhat's telegram. Therefore, I once again sent 50 manat to him by telegraph and also gave information about the first telegram. In this way I was certain

that this time he would get the money, because I had sent it express to his Leningrad address. Can you guess what happened next? On 27 [August] he sent a telegram: "Father, sent another 25. I don't have enough money to return."

Now, imagine my situation. He did not tell me whether or not he received the money that I had sent first. If he had received it why did he need this 25 manat for? If he had not received it, why did not he? Just now, I sent 25 manat by telegraph to him and I gave information about my earlier remittances. And I asked him to tell me about the receipt of these amounts and when he would come? Up to now I have not received a reply from him.

I guess he is returning and is under way. If he has not received what I have sent recently it is a very strange thing, because one week ago, I sent 30 manat to Midhat via Samara municipality. He answered yesterday that he has not received the money.

In the end, I should say that this trip of Midhat has kept me in Baku. In this heat I have to remain in Baku. After all I cannot leave my child faraway without help. He can ask me every day. I could neither go to the Borzhoma nor to Kislovodska baths, which is really necessary for my health. I am sitting in the house day and night, waiting for his arrival. At the middle of the night from every sound of the street, of a phaeton, I jump up. I want him to come soon. I will push him into a phaeton and bring him to you. Until I do this I am not going to leave for the bathhouses of Kislovodsk.

My greetings to you and the children. Embrace my other son Anvar for me.

Jalil

Mirza Jalil added that if Midhat had not received this 120 manat he would have to sell his gold watch and other little things in Leningrad to come to Baku.

Later, I received a letter from Mirza Jalil that Midhat had come to Baku safe and sound and eventually he had calmed down. But these worries that he had to suffer had worn him down as was clear from his writing for his hand was trembling.

At this time I received a letter from Muzaffar that he had obtained a job in the village of Alvand in the region of Kurdemir. He had rented a beautiful two-room house. He had nicely decorated it. He and Munavvar invited me there.

On 20 November our relative Samad came in our phaeton to Shusha. He suggested to me that we would go to Muzaffar's place via the road of Aghch-abadi. He told me that "the old Gavurarkh (infidel stream) now had been extended to Aghchabadi. The old dead lands have been developed, now they have started beautiful cotton farms." This interested me greatly. I decided to go. I got ready and left. I thought I would come back in two weeks.

On the way we stopped at Kahrizli and we stayed the night at the house of one of our relatives. The next day we left and at mid-day we arrived at Aghchabadi village. There had been great changes. This village that was known for ages for its aridity now, you could say, had become a watery place. Everywhere there were canals rushing with murky water. There was a new spirit in the village. One was carrying cotton, the other equipment, etc. Everywhere the Turkmen with their special hat and their veiled wives could be seen, and everywhere it was green. It was the time of the cotton harvest.

We wanted to hurry up; we had to cross the plain and reach the village of Alvand, which was on the other side of the river Kur before sunset, before the bandits that occasionally were active in the area started marauding. From Kahrizli we had taken Ali Akbar the Turkman, who was very familiar with the area.

Muzaffar and Munavvar would have expected that I would come via Kurdemir station, but they could not imagine that I would come via the empty and dangerous Mil plain and crossed it. At sunset we stopped and looked at the river Kur and then we continued on our way towards the Ponton Bridge. The old bridge guard was looking with interest at us. When he found out that I was the mother of Muzaffar he greeted me with respect and gave his son as our guide. We put the phaeton on the bridge. In exactly 5 minutes our phaeton reached Muzaffar's house. When Muzaffar saw us he was very astonished. He did not move from where was sitting and raised his arms and showed his amazement. He was staring at us and could not believe his eyes that we had crossed the arid Mil plain where nobody, neither man nor jinn, lived. Munavvar was also astonished and could not come to herself for a while. Our arrival in the small village of Alvand was a big event.

Muzaffar sent the news of our arrival to Baku. After one week we received a letter from Anvar. He wrote that his father was ill.

On 18 November 1930 Mirza Jalil became paralyzed. The movement of his left hand and foot had become very slow. Professor Amosov diagnosed that because of sclerosis and too much work his veins had become clogged. He advised that he should be treated in a sanatorium for a long time. He had to be taken to Kislovodsk. The People's Soviet had given 200 manat for his trip and a travel order. Midhat took his father to Kislovodsk.

The physicians forbade Mirza Jalil all intellectual activity for good. His illness had worried us all. This was the end of the journal. I, Munavvar and Muzaffar wrote to Mirza Jalil in Kislovodsk compassionate letters. We gave him hope. Mirza Jalil kept my letter. He wrote a reply.

20 December [1930] - Kislovodvsk

My dear ones, Hamideh, Munavvar, and Muzaffar,

I received your letter. My dear ones, thank you. On 18 November, my blood vessels in my brain were damaged. The movements of my left hand and foot are impaired.

For my treatment Midhat brought a few physicians, among them professor Amosov. Midhat brought me here in his arms. I am now resting. Later I am going to be treated. In the house Midhat, Anvar and Paulina[155] took turns in taking care of me. Write me often and let me know the latest news. But don't write about politics, life has become very strange. My health is really bad.

Hamideh, let Midhat find you a room in Baku, and go there. After the journal closes you should come with the children and live with us. Write to Teymur, let the management of the place where he works write a letter to the Buildings Union so that the space that has been allocated to him is not given away to somebody else.

You don't know how much I wish to be with you. I will be expecting my father Midhat at the end of December.[156] I am begging you not to write me such disturbing letters such as what has upset Munavvar. It affects me too much. I should avoid being agitated. I beg you to forget the irritation about Pauline. Inform the children as well. Until you came she was living with her sister in our house.

Hamideh, write me long letters. Write about all new things. I got tired. I cannot write. I kiss you all.

Jalil

A second letter from Mirza Jalil dated 5 February 1931.

---

155. Paulina Afanasievna Dobrobinko (1883-1943) for many years worked in the office of *Molla Nasreddin* and was very close to Mirza Jalil's family.

156. Mirza Jalil used to call his oldest son 'my father', because he had named his oldest son after his own father.

Hamideh Khanum, Munavvar and Muzaffar I am sending you greetings. The chickens that you sent by mail we received. We relished eating them. The fate of the journal is going to be decided in the coming days. You will know the result. By that time we will resolve the coming of Hamideh Khanum to Baku. For the time being, all the best.

5 February 1931, the city of Baku.

The third letter was received. He had written it on 17 February 1931.

Greetings to Hamideh Khanum, Munavvar and Muzaffar. The sickness in Karyaqin is not dangerous [he is talking of the plague]. They have it under control. The fate of the journal has not been decided yet. It will be resolved shortly. I am slowly getting better. Anvar says that he is writing very often, but you are complaining that he is not writing enough. All the best, Jalil.

17 February 1931.

In February 1931 Anvar wrote to us that the 25th anniversary of the journal of *Molla Nasreddin* would be celebrated shortly. Much later I asked Mirza Jalil why they did not celebrate this date. His answer to this question was this: "I told them it is too early to celebrate the 25th year. God willing, we will celebrate its 75th year." Of course, he said these words with sarcasm, because he had not forgotten the 1923 fiasco of *Molla Nasreddin*'s celebration. He could not forget it.

When in December 1930 Mirza Jalil returned from Kislovodvsk he brought a sealed envelope from his doctor that he had to give to the doctor that was going to treat him in Baku. Later Mirza Jalil told me that when he arrived in Baku he could not wait and he opened the enveloppe and read it. The letter said: "The book of the patient is closed. He will not live more than 2 months."

These words had frightened him. Mirza Jalil was very afraid of dying. After this date Mirza Jalil lived another year and he told me in December 1931 that the doctor had made a mistake. "I have lived 10 more months than he predicted."

* * *

In March 1931 Muzaffar got a job as an accountant in the cotton factory in Kurdemir. We all went there to his 2-room house that was given to him. At this time I received letters from Mirza Jalil and Midhat. They were asking me to come hurriedly, because Midhat with his friends was sent for training to Severstroy, which was a big construction work in the north of the country. For this Midhat needed bedding and warm clothes.

I came to Baku in early April. Mirza Jalil had changed quite a lot; he had become thinner and older. He was talking very little. He was feeling depressed. Apart from his own illness, the departure of his beloved son for a long time to a cold and northern place grieved him greatly. His weak health and the likelihood of getting ill saddened him greatly. On the other hand he did not have money to buy a warm overcoat for Midhat. This was bothering him. Also, in my turn, I tried to console him. I suggested that we should put cotton inside the linen lining of Midhat's old coat. I did it this way. I prepared warm eiderdown and other things. Then, I turned the outside of his trousers into the inside and then I lined it with another fabric.

In mid-April Midhat and his friends first went to Leningrad and from there to Severstroy. Mirza Jalil was humiliated. He could not write. He could not stay idle. He could not find a place for himself and the whole day he was trying to kill time somehow. Impatiently, he was waiting for a letter from his son. This worry of the poor father was not without reason. His very sensitive heart was sensing the calamity.

Exactly one year later, on 4 July 1932, Midhat died of a swelling that was growing very rapidly.[157] His weak southern constitution could not endure the northern cold climate. Midhat had apparently fallen ill there, but he had not told us. He did not want to frighten his father. After getting better, unlike his friends, instead of returning he had continued with his work. The leadership of the construction had given him a very good recommendation. Only towards the end of the fall, he had returned from the north. He was buried near the grave of his father.

* * *

Towards the end, Mirza Jalil was abiding by the instructions of the physicians and was seriously keeping a diet; he was walking a lot, and took the tramway. Several times he sent me to the Surakhani baths. He was thinking of coming with us to Shusha in the summer. The scenery of Shusha pleased him greatly. Doctor Balayan had given him permission on condition that he first spent three weeks in the outskirts of Shusha and then he could go to the city. Muzaffar and Munavvar were getting ready to join us. They had written a letter to Mirza Jalil, saying: "first come to our house in Kurdemir and then we all go to Shusha."

Finally, on 7 July 1931 we got together and began the trip. Muzaffar and Munavvar welcomed us at the station of Kurdemir. For the time being, Mirza Jalil stayed with them and I went on to Shusha to rent a suitable place and put it in order. In Shusha I went to the house of the butcher Shamil. My relatives were also there and they had rented the big hall for me. With the help of Qamar, we found a very pleasant place on the outskirts of Shusha. This was near the river, down from the Isa

---

157. This part is out of place, because it creates the impression that Midhat died before Mirza Jalil, who, however, died before Midhat, viz. in January 1932.

Spring in a place called the Alexan Bey garden. I sent a telegram to Mirza Jalil and he came with Munavvar.

Mirza Jalil was pale and looked tired, but he was smiling and kind. He was treating everyone with respect and kindness. At night he was restless. Mirza Jalil and Munavvar spent that same summer in a tent and we stayed in Shusha. In the early morning we loaded the things that we had bought and our provisions that we had on horses. Mirza Jalil was riding on a separate horse. Munavvar and the other children were walking. It seems that in the early days they were living very comfortably. In his first letter he wrote:

Hamideh, I received the medicine. We lost your teapot, but I promise that when I come to Baku I will get one that is exactly the same. We are not settled properly yet. Tomorrow our landlord Rahim will go to Shusha and will get from Shirin Khanum, your landlady, the felt that she has promised to give for the tent. (Asadzadeh knows this). I think I am getting accustomed to live in a place at a higher altitude. As soon as we get settled you can come and join us. It is a beautiful place and its water is like that of the Isa Spring. There are many good berries and this is good for me. Send Qamar and let her buy 5 *girvanka* of rice and send it to us with Rahim. Let Alish, the son of Soleyman Kishi send me the iodine that I have left in his house and also the one that they have prepared (both of them are white). Do you have any news from Anvar and Midhat? I miss them. When I was leaving I was so nervous that I forgot to say good-bye to you. This was unintentional. Please, don't be hurt, forgive me.

It would not be a bad idea that you talk to Rahim so that we know how much rent he will ask if we stay in the garden until the end of the season. Also, how much we have to pay for the tent. (Of course, the bringing and

removing of the tent has its own cost). We have to talk about these things beforehand so that there will not be any argument later and no problem.

Ten *girvanka* of potatoes, send us some coal. Cheers. Munavvar sends greetings. And send about 5 *pfund* of fresh beans.

I sent 20 manat with Qamar.

One day later I sent provisions to Mirza Jalil and wrote a letter and asked how he was doing. In general he was very pleased. Munavvar after knowing her father's needs served him very well. For one month they stayed in that isolated place. Eventually, news came from Midhat. One of his friends, who had fallen ill had come to Shusha to rest and he brought us a letter from him and a box of chocolate. Mirza Jalil was delighted like a child and his heart was at peace. He had become so well that he wanted to come and live with us in Shusha. He stayed exactly two weeks with us in Shusha. All of us, children and adults, were serving him and we were fulfilling his smallest request. Every day I went for walks with him. It looked as if he was completely recovered.

In one of those days, Stepanekert and Isa Spring could be seen from the western part of the city, and Mirza Jalil smilingly pointed at the garden of Alexan Bey, which was down at the bank of the river and said: "I have spent a good time in this garden and I have rested there. That garden has wonderful water and tasty fruit and its owner is a kind man." Mirza Jalil said these words and paused a little while, he then turned and looked to his left side. He saw the Jidir plain, sighed very deeply and said, "When I die bury me in one of these hills."[158]

---

158. Hamideh Khanum wrote down these words as soon as they were spoken by Mirza Jalil. [Mehraban Vazir].

At that time I tried to slowly change the subject and we went home. The following day, the two of us, for the last time, went for a walk. We had hardly gone about 300 paces when there was a flash of lightning and the roar of thunder and heavy rain started. We had to return home. It was in the last days of August.

Muzaffar came; with difficulty he had obtained a ticket for the bus. Mirza Jalil went to Kurdemir and stayed for a while with them. Munavvar was taking care of him as if a mother was taking care of her child. She was bathing him herself and because of this Mirza Jalil was very much touched and moved. In spite of this he was not giving up having himself pampered and with his insisting demands would exhaust Munavvar.

I saw him off with a heavy heart. I felt that this was going to be his last visit to Shusha. Before leaving our farewell was very emotional and he asked me to come to Baku. Mirza Jalil stayed a short while in Kurdemir because he was impatiently waiting for Midhat's return to Baku.

On 20 September I took my grandson Murad and went to Kurdemir to Muzaffar's house. In early October I left there to go to Baku. When I arrived Midhat, who had come from Leningrad, was already there. After arriving at Baku, Murad became ill three days later. The physician suspected that he had contracted typhus. Later it became clear that he was suffering from malaria. His severe illness wore me down. Mirza Jalil was very unhappy. I regretted that I had come. After an injection with quinine the child started getting better.

Anvar had finished the tenth grade and entered the Azerbaijan Oil Institute. Midhat had finished the Institute and was working. Teymur had returned from military service and had married Qamar. Both of them were working in a cooperative.

Midhat took an apartment in the office of the journal *Molla Nasreddin*. Anvar was living in a small room and at night I slept there. Mirza Jalil was sleeping in a dark room of the house, because the noise from the streets did not reach there and it was warm. Murad was sleeping in the dining room. Mirza Jalil was getting tired from going up the stairs every day to the third floor. Therefore, he wanted to move to one of the rooms on the first floor, but the children did not agree to this. Doing this was not very easy. In this situation he wanted to go to any room on the first floor and live there alone, so that he did not have to go up and down these stairs. Very slowly and with long pauses he would climb the stairs despite his heart was beating hard.

Our son Midhat was taking the intermediate examination and at the same time he was working as scientific secretary to State Planning Commission in Mingechevir. His salary was 200 manat.

Mirza Jalil was only getting a pension of 180 manat. I was getting from my son-in-law, because of my grandchildren, 100 manat per month. By selling the old phaeton I had 600 manat. This money we gradually put into a common pot for general expenses and to buy provisions. I had Liliyan as servant and we were managing somehow.

* * *

FOR THE LAST TIME
HE LOADED THE STOVE

Mirza Jalil always said that it is better to feed the children properly otherwise they would get sick and die. But his money was not sufficient to buy good food. Therefore, he was getting nervous and worried. He could not speak about it to anyone and he felt ashamed. All the time he was thinking what to do. He was very much hurt since he was not appreciated.

We could not get firewood. Except for the room where Mirza Jalil was sleeping, all the windows were opening to the north. It was very cold, especially the wind from the Caspian. Our house was becoming ice cold. Two or three times Mirza

Jalil with the help of Anvar gathered old broken furniture, boards and cupboards from the storage space and took it to the small room where I slept and stacked it. But poor Midhat was sleeping in the small and unheated room and worked there.

One of the evenings in December, when there was uninterrupted cold and snow and when the Caspian was stormy and the wind was blowing from there, Anvar and his friends were preparing their lessons in the small room. Mirza Jalil carefully went to his room and looked at the situation and came and told me: "It is very cold. They cannot remember anything. Whatever happens we have to load the stove." He went to his room and opened the cupboard where he kept his manuscripts and he looked at the papers and began to throw them down to the floor. I looked at what he was doing and became worried. I went to him and said: "What do you want to do?" He answered that he wanted to load the stove. I begged him not to burn these writings, these might be needed later. "Let's find some boards and wood and burn them." He said: "Whatever could be burnt, I have burnt." He threw big packages of paper and various writings into the stove. He was very agitated and I could not tell him anything. I was standing next to him and with heavy heart I looked at this. Then slowly he began to throw whatever was left of the manuscripts into the stove. I felt that this was a great loss. But I could not stop him. He was very dejected. Eventually, he closed the door of the stove and went to Anvar's room. When he came back from there he said: "The stove is warm," and he was pleased and quiet and went to sleep. This was the last time that he loaded the stove. He would often tell Anvar that: "My son, study well. Study is the key to your future." Midhat was working day and night and there was no need to tell him to study. Midhat was sacrificing his health to work. He did not have time to eat. He had an endless love for work. The pleasure that he had from work he could not get from anything else. Mirza Jalil had an endless love for him and he would never tire from watching him and praised him to the skies.

In December 1931, an article appeared in the newspaper 'Workers of Baku' signed by Rezazadeh[159] and Mamadqulizadeh about the problems of Mongechevir. Mirza Jalil read the article with extreme pleasure and was impatiently waiting for Midhat from work. When Midhat came he embraced him hard and kissed him and with a voice that came from the depth of his heart he whispered, "You are my father." My poor son loved his father very much and he was treating him with fondness.

One time Midhat asked for a loan of 6 manat from his father. A few days later he returned it and kissed him on his head several times and then he went to his room to work. His father was staring after him with affection and fondness.

* * *

In the evening of one day at the end of December, I was sitting with Mirza Jalil having tea. I was talking about the life and death of my late father Ahmad Bey; that he fell ill of bronchitis and how he died with great difficulty. Also, I read to him my Memoirs of my father, which I had written in a notebook. This interested Mirza Jalil very much. He asked me to continue writing it and got the

159. Eskandar Mirza Jabbar-oghlu Rezazadeh (1897–1938) was one of the students that the Republic of Azerbaijan sent to Europe. He studied energy engineering in Paris, Nancy and Darmstadt. He played an important role in establishing the first hydro-electric station in Azerbaijan. He was the head of the SSR State Energy Planning Commission and a member of the High Commission (1931-33). He was deputy head of the Azerbaijan People's Commission for Heavy Industry as well as of that for hydro-electricity. Later he taught at the Azerbaijan Polytechnic Institute and became chairman of the electricity department (1925-37). He wrote some of his articles in collaboration with Midhat.

notebook from me and looked at the end of the notes and said: "Why have not you written your name at the end of the notebook?" Then he heaved a heavy sigh and said: "I will die easily. I will not bother anyone." Then Mirza Jalil added: "When I die, never ask for a Mulla." It was the end of December. It was snowing and it was very cold. In spite of this, every morning at 11 o'clock Mirza Jalil would go for a walk. His overcoat was heavy; when he went down the stairs he complained and walking was not easy for him.

Once he read in the newspaper that they were going to distribute sugar cubes in the cooperatives. Mirza Jalil was overjoyed and said: "I have to get money and buy a lot of sugar cubes. The children like sugared tea and this is very useful."

On 31 December the children were not at home and Mirza Jalil was resting in his own room. I was sewing something in the dining room. At that time he got up and washed his face and hands and went to Midhat's room and took his *kamancheh* and went to his room (Midhat also played the *kamancheh*). He sat down and started playing on it. He was playing so beautifully and full of emotion that automatically I left my work and listened to him. The last melodies that he played were so moving and emotional that one's heart was touched. I could not help but cry listening to the lamentations of the *kamancheh*. After playing Mirza Jalil hung the *kamancheh* on the wall in its place. This was the last time he played.

* * *

On 31 December, Mirza Jalil's nephew Jalal came from Kengerli district. He had long talks with his uncle. Later Mirza Jalil told that Jalal finally had come to his senses. "He wants to go to college. I am very glad. We have to keep him in our house and let him study and become a man."

On New Year's Eve the young ones had gathered in Midhat's room and they were playing and singing. Teymur was playing *tar*, Midhat *kamancheh*, and Jalal was playing on a tray as if it were a tambourine and he was singing. Every now and then they made him get up and dance. Mirza Jalil undressed as he wanted to sleep. Half undressed and laughing he passed me and then he stopped at the door of Midhat's room and looked at them with pride. Then he left and retired for the night.

* * *

On the first of January 1932 when it was very cold and the ground was frozen and slippery, Mirza Jalil was getting ready to go for a walk. I tried to persuade him not to go, saying you may fall down. He told me that he had some business and with that excuse he left. As he went out I sent our relative Ali (Qamar's brother) after him and asked him to accompany Mirza Jalil to the place where he wanted to go. But Mirza Jalil sent him back.

After a while Mirza Jalil returned home tired and dejected. On the slope in front of Tarayevski's home he had slipped and fallen down on his face. Passers-by helped him to get up and had accompanied him home.

He slept very badly that night. He felt like as if being suffocated and was getting agitated. He left the light on the whole night. In the morning he was alright, but he looked very pensive and silent. He said that he wanted to take a bath. Since none of the children were home he did not want to go alone. The same night of 2 January and the next one of 3 January he did not sleep well.

On 3 January, Mirza Jalil to buy sugar cubes went to get money from the credit office in Filotrov Street, where he had 150 manat in savings. After 2 hours he returned in order to give me the money that he had received and said: "Today I came across

Midhat, Anvar, Teymur and Jalal's musical ensemble

quite a few funeral processions. Too many people are dying."

In the evening he was complaining that he could not go to the bathhouse. He was uncomfortable that his hair and feet were not clean. I told him: "Let me heat water to wash your hair and feet at home." I begged him, but he did not want it. I said: "Let me pour the water and Lisa will wash you." Again he declined. (It was not his habit to bother anyone).

Finally, I brought warm water in a basin and put it in front of him and he somehow washed his head and feet, changed his clothes and lay down. At night I saw that there was light in Mirza Jalil's room. Again he was short of breath and he could

not sleep. In the morning he told me: "It was as if a hand was pressing me on the neck and was suffocating me. I slept very badly."

On 4 January, when Mirza Jalil got up, he was not very bad and he came to the balcony. He put his feet on a stool and was brushing his boots and then he washed his hands and face. Thereafter, he had tea with milk and ate his breakfast. He asked me whether Midhat was at home. Then he went to look at his room. When he did not find Midhat he sighed sadly and returned to his room.

Teymur, Anvar and Jalal were going to the bathhouse. Jalal told his uncle to come with them, but he did not want to. He went to the dining room and asked me to bring a hammer, pliers and other tools and put them next to the window.

It was about 12.30; he brought a lock and a key from his room and was busy repairing it. At that time I was sitting with my son Muzaffar at the table and was writing a letter to Kurdemir. Mirza Jalil was beating hard on the key with the hammer. He stopped suddenly, turned to me and said: "Am I bothering you?" I said: "No," and continued writing. When I finished writing he put down his hammer and asked to wash his hands. The fingers of his right hand began to tremble and I began rubbing them. After five minutes his left hand began trembling. When I saw this fear came over me. I asked him let me call Qamar[160] and hurriedly went to find her. Suddenly his color changed. He was telling himself, 'my sight is getting dark' and then after a short while he vomited. When he came to himself he said: "call Midhat. Tell him to come immediately. There is no need to call a physician."

At that time, our neighbor Abramova hurriedly came and wanted to see what was happening in our house. I whispered to her that Mirza Jalil was ill and he heard this and very seriously told me: "Please, don't whisper over there." I and Qamar were agitatedly rubbing his hands, Yelizaveta Nikolayevna hurriedly left to call Midhat by telephone. She asked: "Where can I call?" Mirza Jalil answered: "The State's Planning Committee 90-91."

In a few minutes Mirza Jalil became very weak. Qamar and I put a matrass and a blanket on the floor and with difficulty transferred him from the chair to the matrass. We put a hot water bag on his feet. We began rubbing his hands with warm water and we wetted a handkerchief with cold water and put it on his forehead. Abramova had found Midhat

and asked him to bring a doctor. There was nobody except us in the house.

About 15 minutes later Mirza Jalil asked: "Did Midhat come?" (These were his last words). I replied: "He will come soon." He then vomited. We again rubbed his hands and feet with warm water. Quickly Qamar injected him with camphor. He was breathing very heavily.

It was about 2 o'clock poor Midhat pale faced and very frightened arrived. He sat next to his father while saying: "Father, father" and began kissing his face and eyes. Of course, it was too late. The father did not recognize his son. The sign of life had left his face. The light of his eyes had gone. His breathing was getting heavier.

Midhat jumped from his place and rushed to telephone and called the doctor. Soon a doctor came, looked at the patient and said: "He had a brain stroke. He has lost consciousness and there is no more hope."

We raised the patient and put him on his bed. We continued rubbing his hands and feet with lukewarm water. Again they injected him. Anvar and Teymur came. Fayeq Efendi, his old collaborator in the journal came.

I could not believe that he was dead. I continued rubbing his hands and feet and I was wiping the perspiration from his forehead. Qamar was rubbing his left hand. It was around 3 o'clock that the doctor occasionally felt his pulse, who told me in a whisper: "His heart is all right, another person in his situation would have died long ago."

Suddenly, Mirza Jalil's face became very pale. He sighed his last breath and rested eternally. It was 3 o'clock, 4 January 1932.

The End

---

160. Qamar Alieva (1903-?) was a granddaughter of Hamideh Khanum's uncle. She had grown up in the family of Mamadqulizadeh. Later she married Teymur Kengerli (1907-44), who was Mirza Jalil's nephew. She published her Memoir in 1966 about Mirza Jalil, see 'Baki' of 29 January, no. 24.

Hamideh Khanum and children at Mirza Jalil's coffin

Hamideh Khanum

Hamideh Khanum with family and musicians circa 1907

APPENDIX 1

STOPPING THE LOCUST INVASION

By Hamideh Khanum Javanshir

The main problem of the cotton farmers is locusts. From 1902 to 1912, except for 1910, our fields have suffered from locusts. In all these years our fields were totally or partially destroyed. To destroy locusts normal methods are of no use. As much as possible you have to cover the plain of Mil over an area of an estimated 500,000 ha with water. The soil of this area has not been plowed for ages and it is very fertile. At the same time there are many indications that this area has been a nest for locusts, and locusts appear in areas that have not been plowed. To irrigate the plain of Mil you have to dig canals from the Aras and you have to join them with the stream of Gavur and extend it to the village of Lambaran. Here I should also mention that this stream was made in 1866 by my late father. Thanks to this stream we harvested good and plentiful crops. My father also wanted to get the permission of the respective offices to extend this stream to Lambaran village, but the local organizations did not give their consent. I still have the correspondence about this affair.

The soil around this stream has a special quality and if it is watered there is no limit to cotton production and at the same time one can stop the damage of the locusts that destroys the work of millions of people.

"Suppose I stopped these locusts, how shall I deal with the turbaned locusts?" (no. 19, yr 2, 25 May 1907)

In our existing cotton fields there is a shortage of water. The water from Kahrizli is not sufficient and in spring, we use the water of the canal that comes from the Gargar River. The people who are above us, especially the landowners, have started planting cotton on a large scale and they use the water from the Gargar and don't let it go downstream. The irrigation official (*mirab*) of Aghdam should be given instructions to divide the Gargar water in an equitable way.

The cotton traders don't play a small role in the field of cotton production. But sometimes, for their own benefit, they don't sell good quality seed to farmers. Also, they bring down the price of cotton and fix the price as they like. They divide the districts among themselves and do whatever they want. In this way, the cotton traders get more than those who produce it. To get out of this situation it is necessary to create small credit unions in the regions so that the cotton farmers can get loans to acquire seed and equipment.

In our district there are many fields that don't have water. On these fields cattle and sheep herds that graze them cause damage to their crops. The cattle owners must be fined so that they will not do this. In our parts, stealing of cotton is very prevalent. It is necessary to seriously punish these thieves and those who trade in stolen cotton so that we put an end to this.

To create a culture for cotton production in the villages you have to establish agricultural schools. Apart from this, one should create model farms and attract talented farmers to work there. In this way, if the villagers understand the scientific way of cotton farming they will adopt these methods themselves, as a result both quality and quantity of cotton production will improve. One of the things that creates problems for us is that not only we don't have paved roads, but also we don't even have proper roads between the villages. Therefore, coming and going between villages is difficult, and carts and carriages break down. People sometimes stay for hours on the road and they are late for work. It should also be mentioned that because of this there are no factories for cleaning cotton, while we need those factories.

Our region has two main roads; one is from Khonashen to the plains of Kecherli, which is 50 werst long. The other one from Aghdam to Aghchabadi is also 50 werst long, but unfortunately both of them are in a terrible condition and the people want good roads.

In our parts, people don't have access to proper medical care. There is neither a medical assistant nor a physician. The people, especially children, die of contagious diseases and fever in large numbers. Therefore, neither literate workers nor managers want to come to our region.

In our district there is neither a post office nor a telegraph office. Whoever's in need of them has to go the Aghdam region which is very far. Between the railway station in Yevlakh and our district there is a distance between 80 to 100 werst. To bring farm equipment and machinery to our region is very difficult and their maintenance is virtually impossible. In our region, we want stores to be established for this machinery.

APPENDIX 2

MOLLA NASREDDIN, A POLITICAL AND SOCIAL WEEKLY

After the defeat of the Russian army in Manchuria in 1905 and the disturbances of the same year in Russia, a certain degree of freedom was given to the press, and a degree of liberty among the Moslem peoples of Tsarist Russia coincided with the movement of the Young Turks in Turkey and the Constitutional Revolution of 1906 in Persia. It was a time of great historical change in the region, especially in Tiflis where the exiled and mostly liberal Russian aristocracy met with the Moslem intelligentsia and with socialists of various stripes.

These events caused Jalil Mamadqulizadeh (1866-1932) to start his own journal, called *Molla Nasreddin* with his friend and colleague Omar Fayeq Nomanzadeh (1872-1940). They were supported by the philanthropist merchant Mashdi ʿAli-Asghar, who financed its publications right from the beginning. The time was indeed very opportune. According to Mamadqulizadeh's statement in the first issue (7 April 1906), the paper came into being as a result of a socio-political necessity. He further said: "*Molla Nasreddin* was the creation of its own nature and time".[1] The plan of a revolutionary future of the paper in its literary, social, and political venues was laid down in the first issue. *Molla Nasreddin* did not limit itself to the enlightenment and education of Azerbaijani society but rather took the whole colonized or so-called independent societies of the East as its domain. It aimed at showing the pitfalls of Tsarist policies toward the nations under its control, criticizing absolutism and imperialism in the Middle East, fighting against superstitious beliefs and fanaticism, and spreading learning and culture, as well as friendship, amongst various ethnic groups.

Cover of first issue of *Molla Nasreddin*
(no. 1, yr. 1, 7 April 1906)

It was also stated that the writers of the journal would use every literary and satirical form in order to achieve those ends.[2] Mamadqulizadeh was aware of the difficulties that he faced in this ambitious plan. He wrote in his Memoirs: "The despotism that had faced us like a mountain was the despotism of the king and the Sultan as well as the power and oppressiveness of those who had distorted religion".[3]

Mamadqulizadeh as chief editor was instrumental in every aspect of the journal right from the outset. He had written both in Russian and Azeri Turkish in the liberal newspapers of Tiflis before he

1. Aryanpur, *Az Saba*, II, p. 40.

2. Akhundov, p. 28.

3. Aryanpur, *Az Saba*, II, p. 42.

The Reactionary hunters of the press (no. 1, yr. 1, 7 April 1906)

published *Molla Nasreddin*. However, with creation of the journal *Molla Nasreddin* as a satirical weekly he found his own voice with a clear objective, to wit: to awaken the people of Azerbaijan and beyond to their real problems. In his 'Memoirs', Mirza Jalil writes: "At that time, we wanted to use this opportunity to explain our problems in our own language. We placed the struggle against the Tsar's government on a backburner. Our first duty was to awaken the Moslem nation, which was in deep sleep right in front of us. In the first place we asked from our dear and peerless painter-friend Schmerling with his masterful brush to draw the unfortunate sleepy eastern nation."[4] Through articles, poems and caricatures the journal and its staff of talented and outstanding poets, writers and artists challenged every major social and political issue of their time. Therefore, it is of no surprise that the first issue of the journal carried a caricature (see previous page) as well as later a poem by Saber[5] that addressed that need to awaken the people and make them think about their society and its problems.

Molla Nasreddin was a political and social weekly in Azeri Turkish, which was published from 7 April 1906 until 1917 in Tiflis (340 issues), in 1921 in Tabriz (8 issues), and from 1922 to 1931 in Baku (400 issues). From 1906 until 1912, *Molla Nasreddin* was published fairly regularly and then for two years there were long intervals because of censorship and police intervention. Between 1914

4. Mamadqulizadeh, p. 157.

5. For the text of this poem, see Appendix 3.

and 1916 as a result of war it was closed down and in 1917 a few issues were published. In 1920 Mamadqulizadeh went to Tabriz, his ancestral home, and stayed there for almost a year. This was the period of Sheikh Mohammad Khiyabani's revolution and Mamadqulizadeh had a great respect for him. Despite the suppression of Khiyabani's movement and his death, with the help of some writers and intellectuals of Tabriz he managed to publish eight issues of *Molla Nasreddin* in that city. Given his homesickness and because of an invitation from the Soviets he goes back to Baku in 1921. *Molla Nasreddin* again is published from 1922 until 1931 and a year later Mamadqulizadeh dies.

The journal was an instant success, selling half its initial print run of 1,000 on its first day. Within months it would reach a record-breaking circulation of approximately 5,000, becoming the most influential and perhaps the first publication of its kind to be read across the Moslem world, from Morocco to India. When Jalil Mamadqulizadeh went to Tabriz, eight issues of *Molla Nasreddin* were published there. According to Hamideh Khanum the first issue was in 1,000 copies and by the end of the first day 600 copies were gone. When the police came to seize the journal by the order of the governor Hamideh Khanum managed to send 400 remaining copies out of the house and gave only three copies to the police (see page TK).

Mulla Nasreddin and Ghaffar Vakil. *From Azerbaijan, 1 (1906).*

Azerbaijan look-alike cover

This eight-page weekly had a tremendous impact on the course of journalism and development of ideas not only in the Southern Caucasus but also in Iran, Turkey, and Central Asia. For example, in the constitutional revolution of Iran not only Iranian poets and writers, such as Bahar, Dehkohoda, and Jahangir Khan Sur-Israfil, played an important part, but the writings of Saber and Jalil Mamadqulizadeh (1869-1932), were not without significance. With its roots deep in Persian culture, poetry combined with journalism became an amazingly effective medium for satire and propaganda. Among the ranks of the freedom fighters combating the forces of the despotic Mohammad 'Ali Shah in the city of Tabriz, the newest compositions of the poets would be recited or printed in various journals, sustaining the fighters' morale.[2] Also among these poems were the latest works of Saber, which regularly appeared in *Molla Nasreddin*. Therefore, the paper was banned from Iran on account of its focusing on the inequalities and injustices in society (poverty, women's lack of social rights, plight of the working classes, oppression, tyranny). It was, however, often smuggled into the country inside the bales of cloth. The reactionary clerics of Tabriz, who were afraid of its anti-clerical stand, ruled that it was a deceptive paper (*awraq-e mozella*) and "worse than the sword of Shemr [the villain of the Karbala tragedy]."[6]

The immense popularity of Saber, Mamadquli-zadeh, and other contributors of *Molla Nasreddin* led to much imitation. For instance the humorous and sometimes cynical character Molla Da'i or Molla ʿAmu, which appeared everywhere in the journal as poet, and/or as the person who answered letters, advised the youth, parodied the viewpoints of the establishment and was ever present in the cartoons, was adopted by the weekly *Azerbayjan*, which began its publication in 1907 in Tabriz. *Azerbayjan* presented the figure of Ghaffar Vakil as Molla Nasreddin or Molla Da'i. On the cover of the first issue of *Azerbayjan*, Ghaffar Vakil is standing before the Molla, listening to him like a faithful disciple.

Similar characters appear in other Iranian satirical weeklies, among them *Hasharat al-Arz* (Tabriz, 1908), *Sheyda* (Istanbul, 1911), *Bohlul* (Tehran, 1908), and *Sheikh Choghondar* (Tehran, 1911). The device was taken up also by Dehkhoda in his column in *Sur-e Esrafil*, entitled "*Charand parand*," which contained some of the most telling examples of Dehkhoda's satire. Two of the pseudo-names used by Dehkhoda were reminiscent of those used by Mamadqulizadeh: "Damdamaki" (Whimsical) and "Kharmagas" (Gadfly). Some of the satirical techniques used by the former in stories such as "Democracy in Iran" are similar to those used by Dehkhoda in "Charand parand." Karbala'i Mohammed ʿAli in the former story and Azad Khan Karandi in the latter are very similar in their innocent ignorance and naiveté. Sometimes the questions raised by Saber or Mamadqulizadeh

were answered in prose or poetry in *Sur-e Esrafil* and other contemporaneous Persian periodicals. Saber's influence can be also be seen in the poems of Mohammad-Taqi Bahar and Abu'l-Qasem Lahuti. *Molla Nasreddin* created a new style and approach in journalism in Iran, particularly during the period of the Constitutional Revolution, and had a profound effect on shaping the intellectual thought and ideas of early 20th-century Azerbaijan.[7]

There were three main factors that account for the great popularity of *Molla Nasreddin*: 1. Its popular lively language; 2. The excellent satirical pieces written by is talented writers; and 3. The outstanding cartoons that evoked the spirit and themes of the poems and articles as well as social and political issues of that period.

POPULAR LANGUAGE

Right from the beginning of his career language was very important for Mamadqulizadeh. From his early short stories like "The Post-box" to his plays and longer pieces he uses colloquial Azeri. A similar language was used by most of the contributors of *Molla Nasreddin*, so much so that reading different pieces of the journal throughout its 23 years of publications, it is stylistically hard to say who the writer is since all the pieces have no real names of the writers. From the point of satire this was also helpful. Often, in his satirical works, he assumed the character of this naïve, seemingly ignorant character who is bewildered by the works of the government officials, clerics, and other abusers of power. Also, in his non-satirical works he had a very ordinary but lively language, the same language that was used by traditional comedians and theatrical groups. Also the frequent and appropriate use of well-known and saucy proverbs spoke to the imagination of the journal's readership. That this was an explicit and conscious decision is

6. Aryanpur, *Az Saba*, II, p. 45.

7. See Javadi, *Satire in Persian Literature*, chapter 6.

Azeri language not taught: "I am entrusting this boy to you and if he even in his dreams speaks a word of Azeri you have the right to kill him." (no. 20, February 1913)

clear from that fact that he choose as the name of his journal, the popular humorous figure of *Molla Nasreddin*, who traditionally admonished the rulers and the powerful and whose wise sayings were proverbial and extremely popular among the people. This amicable character was known all over the Middle East and Central Asia under the names of Molla Nasreddin and Hoca Nasreddin. Mamadqulizadeh came to be identified with him. His wife, Hamideh Khanum, relates in her *Memoirs* that illiterate women in Tabriz would come to their house to meet Molla Nasreddin. The satirical language of Saber was also very much the everyday language of the Azerbaijanis. One should remember that most of the people in the Caucasus, Iran, Turkey and other places were illiterate. Often

the journal was read to them by those who could read. It is reported that during the Constitutional Revolution, the poems of Saber were picked up by many and recited in the trenches in Tabriz. Mamadqulizadeh argues that in 1906 when he started the journal, Tiflis was one of major centers for Azerbaijani Turks. However, his readership was not only found among the Azeri speaking population of the Caucasus, but also among the Turkic speaking people of Iran, Turkey and Central Asia.

In the same article he says "we have chosen to write in our mother tongue "Ana dili". We call mother "ana" and father 'ata" whereas the Ottomans call them 'valedah" and "valed". He says that the Ottoman Turkish has become so Arabicized that if you took away some Turkish suffixes or prefixes it

would be difficult to distinguish it from Arabic. When he wanted to publish *Molla Nasreddin* in Tabriz, the governor of Azerbaijan, Mokhber al-Saltaneh said that the journal should be published in Persian. Mirza Jalil refused.

Abu'l-Fath Alavi talked with the governor and his advisors about the publication of the journal. To the suggestion that the journal should be published in Persian only Mirza Jalil replied: "I have published *Molla Nasreddin* for 15 years in (Azeri) Turkish. Like in Azerbaijan of the Caucasus in Iranian Azerbaijan also only Azerbaijanis live. Here many other people live who are literate and can speak Persian but I don't publish *Molla Nasreddin* for them, I publish it for the majority of the people. The thing is that even the Russian government permitted me to do what you are not allowing me to do. In the city of Tabriz there are four Armenian journals, but of course, there is not a single Iranian who knows Armenian. I know Armenian; so, allow me to publish the journal in Armenian." Eventually, Mokhber al-Saltaneh agreed to the publication of the journal in Azeri, provided the editorial would be in Persian. Although Mirza Jalil's friend Alavi persuaded him to accept this proposal, the editorials were never published in Persian.

TALENTED WRITERS

The exceptional success of *Molla Nasreddin* was also due to the talents of its writers. Apart from Mamadqulizadeh and Saber, other contributors included the poets `Ali Nazmi (1882-1946) and `Ali-oghlu Ghamqusar (1880-1919), the dramatist `Abdol-Rahim Haqqverdiyev (1870-1933), the famous composer and writer Uzeyr Hajibeyov (1885-1948), and the novelist Mohammed-Sa`id Ordubadi (1872-1950). There were also many other artists, poets, and writers

Frontispiece in every issue: "In Defense of of Women's Rights." The cartoon on the on this page appeared on the second page of Molla Nasreddin from its fourth year in 1909 up to the editions published in Tabriz in 1921, where it was changed to just the three characters on the left side. The cartoon on the facing page started to appear in the issues published in Baku from 1926 onwards. This was also when Soviet authorities wanted to change the journal's name to Allah-siz (godless). Mirza Jalil resisted, fought back, and was able to keep the name Molla Nasreddin.

who joined in during the paper's long history. For instance, Mo`jez of Shabestar (1874-1934), an Azerbaijani poet of some fame contributed poems when the journal was being published in Tabriz.

Mamadqulizadeh wrote under different satirical names such as *Hardam/Herdem-khiyal* (whimisical), *Dala* (gluttonous), *Serteq* (stubborn), *Qarinquli* (ever-hungry). However, he was mostly known as *Molla Nasreddin*. Mamadqulizadeh was an able playwright and short story writer. His plays like "The Dead," "My Mother's Book" and "The gathering of the mad" are interesting literary works in their own rights, but he is mostly remembered for his short stories such as "Posht qütüsi" (The post box), "Üsta Zeynal" (Ostad Zeynal), "Iranda hurriyat (Democracy in Iran), and "Saqali ¨Üşaq" (The bearded child), some of which predate *Molla Nasreddin*. He reportedly preferred his journalistic experience to his creative writings.[8]

One may divide Mirza Jalil's literary endeavors into three periods. 1. the period when he was finding his own voice and mainly produced literary works, working under Russian censorship; 2. the period in which he had found and further developed his own voice in *Molla Nasreddin* and in his plays and short stories, under a more relaxed regime of Russian censorship. During this period he in particular criticized foreign governments (Iran and Turkey in particular). 3. the muzzled period where under Soviet censorship he could increasingly less express himself and was limited by what Soviet ideology allowed and prescribed (praise the proletariat's struggle and combat religion). His earlier pre-1922 pieces about social justice were considered politically correct, but the same did not hold for his plays.

On his return from Tabriz in 1921, Mirza Jalil had high hopes for the future of Azerbaijan and his journal. However, this hope soon changed into disappointment after 1922, when it became clear that the new Bolshevik regime did not like satire. Literature and journalism had to be practiced in the service of the workers and peasants and not doing so was only displaying an unacceptable bourgeois mentality. To circumvent Soviet censorship he used the vehicle of fables to bring his points home, but this got him only so far. He was told to write about the workers and peasants and combat superstition and religion, in particular since 1925. The government of Azerbaijan even proposed that the journal change its name to *Allahsiz* or "Godless." The change in editorial focus was also evident from the emblematic

---

8. Sardari-nia, Samad, *Molla Nasreddin dar Tabriz,* Tabriz, Hadi, n.d., p.144.

The writers, *clockwise from top left:* Ali Nazmi (1878–1946), Ghamqusar (1880–1919), Memedali Sidghi Seferov (1887–1956), Mohammad Said Ordubadi (1872–1950), Mojez (1873–1934), Hagverdiyev (1870–1933)

drawing of the husband beating his wife, which had appeared in the journal since no. 1 in 1906. Now the right hand side, which up to 1925, had only shown a floral pattern now showed a flower whose petals contained anti-religious slogans.

Mirza Jalil got into trouble when after Reza Shah's accession to the throne he had written critical articles of the new regime in Iran. The government of Iran sent an official protest to the government in Moscow. The Ministry of Foreign Affairs sent a note to Baku asking the Azerbaijan government to take action. On 26 April 1926, `Ali Qarayov, the Commissar for Culture told Mirza Jalil to soften his tone in the future when writing about Reza Shah. Mirza Jalil himself wrote about this issue:

When this article arrives in Tehran His Royal Majesty will grab the collar of Moscow, but unfortunately the journal *Molla Nasreddin* has neither any connection with Moscow nor with the Soviet government. They have not created Molla Nasreddin. This journal is an independent journal and it has grown used for the last 22 years to argue with King, Emperor and Tsars.[9]

Because he did not soften his criticism of Reza Shah four months later Moscow again contacted Baku and stated that Mirza Jalil had not complied with its order and his journal's content, because the journal's content was at odds with the friendly relationship between the two governments. Surprisingly the Baku government disagreed for in September 1926, Comrade Ruhollah Akhundov in a public speech disagreed with Moscow, saying that the journal was non-partisan. Since 1906 it had criticized the feudal conditions in Iran, and he did not understand why Comrade Chicherin[10] had a problem with the journal continuing to do so, just because it upset the government of Iran. He did not find it acceptable. This was a rare support for the journal that otherwise suffered under Baku's censorship, a support which resulted in both Qarayov and Akhundov being banned in 1938 at Stalin's orders.[11]

The journal was not very much liked by the Soviet regime, despite the show of support in 1926. The Baku government did not appreciate or even like its humor. Moreover, no workers and peasant

Sharing the Iran dish (no. 45, yr. 4, 11 Nov 1909)

journalists were among its contributors, for the journal was written by a small group of like-minded literati. Therefore, it was considered to be border-line deviant, not really in line with official ideology. Moreover, the number of subscriptions was low, which Mirza Jalil ascribed to the change to the Latin alphabet in 1929. For all the above reasons, in 1932 the journal was closed down by the government. It is clear that Moscow even then still did not like the journal, because when in 1936 Ali Nazem wrote an article praising Mirza Jalil writings and that they were in harmony with Soviet ideology, this article was not included in the planned publication. Moreover one year later Ali Nazem was imprisoned, where he died in 1941. Hamideh Khanum does not write about these problems for obvious reasons, but Mirza Jalil's nervous situation, if not breakdown in 1931 may be due to the

---

9. *Molla Nasreddin* no.19, 5 May 1927.

10. Georgy Vasilyevich Chicherin was People's Commissar for Foreign Affairs in the Soviet government from March 1918 to 1930.

11. Gholam Mohammadlu, *"Molla Nasreddin" Jalil Memedqulizadanin Hayati va Khalaqiyati.* Baku 1967, p. 479.

The Cooperative sells only one size (no. 2, yr. 19, Jan 1925, Baku). *Customer:* I need boots for my wife and child; *The Coop salesmen:* All our boots are size 15, you can cut and make them for all three of you; *Customer:* Then where can we get small-sized boots? *Salesman:* From Quba Square

increasing pressure that he was put under by the Baku government.

Particularly important was the impact that the journal had on the satirical press of the time through the poetry of the celebrated Azeri satirist and poet, Saber, whose satirical poems were regularly published in the paper until his death in 1911. He has been considered "incomparable in depicting political and social problems."[12] Saber's originality of thought and form marked him as a truly great poet. The vivid realism of his poetry reflects the hardships of his own life as well as the corruption, superstition, repression, and ignorance prevalent in his society. He faced the opposition of the officials and various clerics and suffered greatly as a consequence. The same was true of Mamadqulizadeh, who, after publishing an article on the freedom for women, had to take lodging in the Christian quarter of Tiflis, away from Moslem fanatics, for the first five years of the journal contributed considerably to its fame. His biting satirical poems in praise of Sattar Khan were recited by the Constitutionalists fighting the Royalists in the bunkers of Tabriz.[13] Individual poems of Saber were also frequently translated or imitated by writers of the Persian press. His famous poem that begins with "However the nation is plundered, what do I care?" was imitated in Persian by Mirza Mehdi Khan, the editor of the newspaper *Hekmat*, and the rendition appeared in the weekly *Azerbayjan* (issue 10). Saber's influence can be also seen in his impact on poetry and journalism in Iran, particularly during the period of the Constitutional Revolution, and had a profound effect on

---

12. Dehkhoda, *Loghat-nameh*, s.v. Taherzadeh Saber.

13. Aryanpur, *Az Saba*, II, pp. 46, 57.

Oskar Ivanovich Schmerling

Joseph Rotter

shaping the intellectual thought and ideas of early upper class 20th century Azerbaijan.

The satirical works of Saber embrace a wide variety of subjects. The struggle between the reactionaries and the Constitutionalists, the social corruption in Iran, the nature of the totalitarian government of Mohammad `Ali Shah and many other aspects of the revolution are all depicted in the bitingly satirical poems of Saber. He depicted the monarch as a ruthless, hypocritical, and miserly tyrant. In one of his famous poems, Saber depicts him as a man who has put Persia up for auction, including the royal treasures, the provinces, and the country's heritage. All these poems on Mohammad `Ali Shah and on Persia were freely translated in verse by Sayyed Ashraf Gilani and published in his journal *Nasim-e Shomal* without the mention of Saber's name. Although the original terseness, beauty, and some flair of Saber's tone are lost in the process, they were a good rendition in Persian and upon publication, created a sensation in Tehran.[14]

TALENTED CARTOONISTS

The exceptional success of *Molla Nasreddin* was also due to its beautifully drawn color cartoons, which were the works of two eminent German artists in Tiflis, Oscar Schmerling (1863-1938) and Joseph Rotter, and later, those of Azim Azimzadeh (1880-1943). These cartoons were sharp satires illustrating the works of the writers of the weekly and were full of verve and caustic humor. Coming to the cartoonists and illustrators of *Molla Nasreddin* there are three main figures that are associated with it, though many more artists worked with it during its nearly twenty-one years of publication. Oskar Ivanovich Schmerling's family had come from Germany to Russia in the early years of the nineteenth century and from there to Caucasus. He was born on June 13th 1863 in Tiflis and lived most

---

14. Aryanpur, *Az Saba*, II, p. 64 ff.

Saber as the seeking Sheikh

of his life there. He learnt Russian and Georgian at school and while there he started drawing cartoons for the school bulletin and later on he worked with the Russian satiric paper "Spider". Like his friend Rotter, who also was of German origin, he had studied at the Art Academies of Petersburg (1884-89) and Munich (1891-93). In 1902 Schmerling became the director of the Art Academy of Tiflis and drew cartoons and satirical sketches for a number of newspapers and journals that were published there. From 1889 to 1890 he lived in Khankandi and later in Shusha he made stage sets for an Azeri theatrical group. In the Soviet era he was very active both academically and artistically and several of the exhibitions of his paintings were organized.

Joseph Rotter's date of birth and death are not known, but he lived most of his life in Tiflis; he was a graduate of the Munich Art School. He was of German origin, apparently from the German community of Annenburg near the Georgian border of Azerbaijan. Before *Molla Nasreddin* he had worked as a cartoonist for various Georgian journals. Along with Schmerling from 1906 until 1914 he was the main illustrator and cartoonist of *Molla Nasreddin*. One of his other works is the illustrations for Ferdowsi's Sohrab and Rustam.

Rotter[15] and Schmerling were the main illustrators of *Molla Nasreddin* and cartoons formed a

15. Rotter was also one of the illustrators of the Armenian children's journal "Hasker" edited by Stepan Lisitsyan. I. Rotter's and O. Schmerling's caricatures

very significant part (almost half) of the journal. Mamadqulizadeh for a while worked with them explaining the situation and giving ideas. He helped in creating types which were typical of Azerbaijani, Russian, Iranian or Turkish societies of that period. Even in the later period Mamadqulizadeh helped the artists to find suitable subjects. In one of the issues of *Molla Nasreddin* the famous poem of Rumi

> Yesterday, the Sheikh, lamp in hand, went all about the city, crying:
> "I am weary of beast and devil, a man is my desire!"
> They said: "He is not to be found, we too have searched."
> He answered: "He who is not to be found is my desire."[16]

Here Saber is pictured as a Sheikh with a lamp in his hand. Obviously Rotter, who drew the cartoon did not know the poem and the idea for it might have come either from Saber or Mamadqulizadeh.

Both artists were extremely skillful in depicting expressions of faces with bold lines. The cartoons were well drawn and the types so well represented that once they became established other artists followed them. This was very similar to what Saber did in his verse satire. Once it was established there was no going back to old and traditional satire. The early examples of cartoons in Iranian papers were very crude. Though in the case of Azerbaijani journals cartoons were more advanced, the works of Rotter and Schmerling were of a very superior quality.

Azim Azimzadeh

This point can also be shown in the cartoons of Sayyed Ali Behzad Mosavverzadeh, who drew cartoons for the journal *Azerbaijan* in Tabriz, and when in 1920-21 eight issues of *Molla Nasreddin* were published he illustrated them. Despite the fact the he was educated in Tiflis, Moscow, Rome and Paris his cartoons are less sophisticated than those of the two German artists and lack their refinement. The cartoons of Azim Azimzadeh (1880-1943), who in later years became one of the most important illustrators of the journal, in their early years do not have the refined and expressive quality of Rotter and Schmerling's drawings.

Azimzadeh, who is often referred to as the "Saber of Azerbaijani Art", was born in 1880 in Novkhanli, near Baku. His father was a stone-cutter and farmer and later in the oil rush he came to Baku to work. Azim went to a traditional madraseh to learn the Qur'an, but right from his childhood he liked to draw and paint. His father did not want him to continue his studies and it was through the efforts of his grandmother that he received some education. While working as an errand boy at the mill of merchant Agabala Guliyev, an industrialist of Baku, Azim came to know the Russian painter Durov, who happened to be involved in decorating Guliyev's newly built house at the time. It was through this painter that Azim began his career as an artist. He got involved in illustrating *Molla Nasreddin* from its early issues onward. During the 1920's and 1930's Azimzadeh worked with various newspapers, most significant among them was *Molla Nasreddin*. In 1914, Azimzadeh published his major work to accompany Saber's satirical volume

were included in the Armenian press of the Caucasus, see Mouradian Claire; "Caricature in the Armenian Press of the Caucasus", *Armenian Review,* Winter 1991, vol. 44, 4/176, pp. 14-22.

16. *Divan-e Shams,* Foruzanfar edition, ghazal 441. For the English translation, see *Mystical Poems of Rumi,* translated by A. J. Arberry and Hasan Javadi. Chicago 2009, p. 80.

the famous *Hop-Hop Nameh*. He not only illus-trated this book with extremely vivid and colorful cartoons, the themes of satire displayed in Saber's poetry were much to his liking and subsequently the same themes, such as harsh conditions imposed on women, religious hypocrisy, superstition, tyranny of the ruling class and many other issues find expression in his paintings. Both Schmerling and Rotter had a decided influence on him and the maturing and improvement of his work can be noticed in the later issues of the journal.

Landlord and Peasant while Molla Nasreddin observes (no. 9, yr. 2, 11 Nov 1907)

Ali Akbar Saber

'ALI AKBAR SABER, THE POET-SATIRIST OF AZERBAIJAN[1]

By Hasan Javadi

I AM A POET, THE MIRROR OF MY AGE

The advent of the press and the publication of the first Azerbaijani weekly in 1832 introduced a new era in Azerbaijani literature. Many writers who had depended upon various patrons for their living were no longer compelled to write panegyrics and play the sycophant. The writer's patron became the common people rather than kings and princes. But this transition did not come rapidly and not until the turn of the century could the poet or writer play an important role in the socio-political events of his country.[2]

Two remarkable instances of this phenomenon are the unsuccessful revolution of 1905 in Russia, which affected Azerbaijan as well, and the Iranian Constitutional revolution of 1907. In the latter not only Iranian poets and writers, such as Bahar, Dehkohoda, and Jahangir Khan Sur-Israfil, played an important part, but the writings of Saber and Jalil Mamadqulizadeh (1869-1932), the editor of the journal *Molla Nasreddin,* were not without

---

1. This essay was originally published in *Turkic Culture: Continuity and Change,* ed. Sabri M. Akural, Indiana University Turkish Studies, No. 6, 1987, pp.159-169.

2. The first newspaper was *The News of Tiflis* which appeared in Russian in 1828. A year later the same newspaper was published in Georgian, then in 1830 in Persian and in 1832 in Azeri Turkish. See Nazim Akhundov, *Azerbaijanda Dovri Matbu'at, 1832-1 920,* Baku, 1965, p. 5.

significance. With its roots deep in Persian culture, poetry combined with journalism became an amazingly effective medium for satire and propaganda. Among the ranks of the freedom fighters combatting the forces of the despotic Mohammad 'Ali Shah in the city of Tabriz, the newest compositions of the poets would be recited or printed in various journals, sustaining the fighters' morale.[3] Also among these poems were the latest works of Saber, which regularly appeared in *Molla Nasreddin*.

The life of Mirza 'Ali Akbar Saber Taherzadeh is a remarkable example of the changing role of the poet in Middle Eastern society. He firmly believed in the role of the poet as a social reformer who awakens his audience to the truth of their conditions. Employing his subtle sense of satire and pungent wit, he fought against reactionary elements and the traditionalists who opposed change. His contributions to various weeklies are yet another example of the combining of poetry and journalism, a new development in the East.

Mirza 'Ali Akbar Saber was born in May 1862, in Shamakhi in the Caucasus. He belonged to a middle class, religious family. Saber, who started writing poetry early in his school years, touchingly depicts the plight of a Moslem child in those days. His father forced him to fast during Ramazan, but his eyes were always after food. He was fortunate to find a sympathetic teacher in the poet Haji 'Azim Shirvani (1835-1888), who had recently started a so-called modern (*jadid*) school, teaching Arabic, Persian, Azeri, Russian and other subjects. Encouraged by Haji 'Azim, Saber began translating Persian poetry into Azeri verse, and, along with his own compositions, wrote them down in a notebook. Some of these early verses, such as translations from Sa'di's *Gulistan*, are to be found in the volumes of his collated poems entitled *Hop Hop-Nameh*. His

father, who was a shop keeper, deemed a few years of schooling enough and wanted Saber to work with him in the shop. During a serious clash, the father tore up the little poetry book of Saber. The poet ran away from home, writing these lines in Persian:

> I am the Abraham of the age, but my father is like Azar
> God willing, I will travel from the Babylon of Shirvan.
> Though he tore away my book of poems,
> God willing, I will restore it with my pearl-scattering talent.[4]

Saber joined a caravan, setting off to Mashhad, but his father brought him back and promised not to interfere with his career as a poet. Saber found many friends among the literary circles of Shirvan and encouraged by Sayyed 'Azim wrote numerous *ghazals* in imitation of Persian masters and more particularly Nezami. In 1885, Saber set off to travel in the Islamic world. He visited Samarkand, Bukhara, Mashhad, Sabzevar, Nishapur, Hamadan and some other cities of Iran. His travels widened his intellectual perception and later enabled him to give a vivid picture of the people in these lands. After returning home, Saber married and settled down in Shirvan.

Saber had eight daughters and one son, and in order to support his big family he had to work hard. For fifteen years he worked as a soap maker. He would humorously remark "I make soap to wash away the moral vicissitudes of my countrymen." He tried to improve his financial condition by opening a European-style school in Shamakhi, but this enterprise was not successful. Also, on account of his open criticism of the reactionary and conservative elements, Saber kept on receiving unsigned, threatening letters. According to some accounts these letters were sent by a journalist, Hashem Bey

3. Yahya Aryanpur, *Az Saba ta Nima,* Tehran, 1972, vol. II, pp. 44-46; see also Rahim Rezazadeh Malek, *Hop Hop Nameh Zaban-e Borra-ye Enqelab*, Tehran, 1978.

4. 'Ali A. Saber, *Hop Hop Nameh*, Baku, 1962, p. vi.

(1868-1916), whose poetic *nom de plume* was *bir kas (a* person). Saber answered him in a short satirical poem in the journal *Seda* (Voice), and wittily played upon the word *bir kas:*

> I am a poet, the mirror of my age;
> In me everyone sees his own face.
> As it happened yesterday, "a person" looked at
> me
> And saw in the mirror his own face.[5]

Unable to stay in Shamakhi, he left for Baku, where he was employed as a school teacher in 1910. Baku was a fairly cosmopolitan and advanced city at that time, replete with political and literary activities. There he wrote nearly all of his short satirical pieces called "Taziyanalar" (The Whips). But his stay did not last long and a liver ailment curtailed his activities. Saber went back to Shamakhi for treatment, while the weeklies *Gunesh* and *Molla Nasreddin,* with whom he had a long association, still published his poems. *Molla Nasreddin* began a publicity drive to collect funds and sent him to Tiflis for an operation. Not only the Azerbaijani Moslems, but also some Russian and Armenian contributors helped. But the poet did not consent to the operation. He returned to his native Shamakhi, where he died on September 12, 1911. In his last days, his suffering was so great that Saber was desirous of death:

> I wish to die, but death flies away from me,
> How unlucky I am to plead even with death.[6]

Russian Azerbaijan, in particular, and, to a lesser degree, Iranian Azerbaijan enjoyed a remarkable cultural revival in the beginning of the twenieth century. Of course, Azerbaijan had always been in the crosscurrents of different cultures. Its people, speaking a dialect akin to Anatolian Turkish, have looked to Persian and Ottoman literatures as models, while having a long Islamic tradition. The advent of journalism brought a new incentive to Azerbaijani literature, and many poets published their works in an ever-increasing number of weeklies. The period from 1905 to 1920, just before Azerbaijan became a Soviet Republic, may be considered the golden age of Azerbaijani journalism. Satire as a medium of social criticism and a means for the idea of reform played an important part in these periodicals. In the Caucasus a total of 405 journals and newspapers were published between 1832 and 1920 in Azeri, Turkish, Persian, Russian and a few other languages; 140 were in Turkish.[7] Of these, fifteen were satirical papers published in Tiflis from 1906 to 1917. *Molla Nasreddin* was the most influential satirical paper of all. The editor, Jalil Mamadqulizadeh, who himself was a talented satirist and short story writer, went to Tabriz in 1921 where he published eight issues of the paper. Among the well-known contributors of the journal were Sa`id Ordubadi (1872-1950), the outstanding novelist and `Abu'l-Rahim Haqverdiyov (1870-1933), the famous playwright of Azerbaijan. But the most important poet associated with the journal was Taherzadeh Saber.

The unsuccessful revolution of 1905 in Russia brought forth renewed revolutionary activities as well as the publication of a number of newspapers. Within six months of its publication *Molla Nasreddin* began to exert an important impact not only in Azerbaijan, but also in many other Islamic countries. Since close cultural and social ties existed between Iranian and Russian

---

5. *Ibid.,* p. 291. Cf. Abbas Zamanov, *Saber va Mu'aserin-e U,* tr. by Asad Behrangi, Tabriz, 1979, p. 29.

6. *Hop Hop Nameh,* p. 361.

7. Alexander Bennigsen et Chantal Lemercier-Quelquejay, *La presse et l'mouvement national chez les musulmans de Russie avant 1920,* Paris, 1964 pp. 104-134. Cf. Nazim Akhundov, *Azerbaijan Satira Jurnalari(1906-1920)* Baku, 1968, pp. 16-68.

Azerbaijanis, it was only natural to find *Molla Nasreddin* playing an important role in the Constitutional Movement of Iran and, more particularly, among the freedom fighters in Tabriz and other adjacent towns. The weekly *Azerbaijan,* which was published in Tabriz in 1907, imitated the poetry of Saber and sometimes answered him. In Tehran, the well-known journal *Sur-e Israfil* started a satirical column entitled "Charand Parand" (Charivari) by Mirza ʿAli Akbar Dehkhoda (1879-1956), whose satirical poetry and prose were influenced both by Jalil Mamadqulizadeh and Saber.[8] Sayyed Ashraf Gilani (1889-1934), an outspoken poet who ended his days in a lunatic asylum of Reza Shah, started a journal of his own called *Nasim-e Shomal* in which he either translated or adopted a great number of Saber's poems.

Saber's first poem appeared in 1903 in the journal *Sharq-e Rus* (The Russian East) in Tiflis. At that time the poet was unknown outside his native city. Three years later, and five months after its first issue, he began publishing in *Molla Nasreddin.* Within a few years Saber was well known not only in Azerbaijan, but also in Iran, Turkey and Central Asia. But on the other hand he had created many bitter enemies at home and abroad. Mohammad ʿAli Shah tried very hard to stop the smuggling of *Molla Nasreddin* into Iran, but he could not.[9] According to a contemporary of Saber, his poems helped the cause of the Iranian constitution more than an army. [10]The reactionary *ulema* of Tabriz denounced the journal as heretical and called Saber an unbeliever. At home he suffered even more. In one of his letters Saber writes: "I am sick and tired and have no patience any more. Like Joseph I am a captive among my friends... There is no one to turn

to... My life is a sad affair."[11] The campaign against him became so intense that he defended his faith in a well-known poem, addressing the people of Shirvan.

I confess that God is Great and I am a man of
  faith,
O people of Shirvan.
I am a Shiʿite, but not in the ways you desire;
I am a Sunnite, but not like the examples you
  like.
I am a Sufi, but not like the ones you describe.
I am a lover of truth, O people of Shirvan.[12]

As long as Saber was writing traditional poems, he was liked and admired by his hypocritical countrymen, but as soon as he began writing satires on social and political conditions, they could not tolerate his criticism. Saber was a great reformer and innovator in Azerbaijani literature. Unlike many of his predecessors, he did not waste his talent on writing panegyrics of various emirs or eulogies of the saints. In his biting satire and with vivid realism he depicted a society suffering from despotism, hypocrisy, sanctimony, ignorance, and male chauvinism. As an advocate of democracy, he strongly supported the Constitutional Revolution of Iran. His work appeared in many journals, *Hayat, Fiyuzat, Rahbar, Dabestan, Ulfat, Ershad, Gunesh, Sadeh, Haqiqat, Yeni Haqiqat,* and *Ma'lumat,* but most of all in *Molla Nasreddin,* with whose editor, Jalil Mamadqulizadeh, he became closely associated. Some critics assert that Saber made *Molla Nasreddin* famous all over the Middle East.[13] The fact is Jalil Mamadqulizadeh himself was a talented prose satirist, and he and Saber complemented each other in creating an exceptional satirical journal.

8. Aryanpur, *Az Saba,* II, pp. 87-95. I have discussed this point in great length in my *Satire in Persian Literature.* (Fairleigh Dickinson University Press, 1985.)

9. Ahmad Kasravi, *Tarikh Mashruteh-e Iran,* 1, p. 193.

10. Aryanpur, *Az Saba,* II, pp. 44-46.

11. ʿAli Akbar Dehkhoda, *Lughat-Nameh,* "Taherzadeh Saber".

12. *Hop Hop Nameh,* p. 359.

13. *Hop Hop Nameh,* p. xii.

Saber's most productive years were from 1905 to 1911, and in the space of these six years he became one of the outstanding poets of Azerbaijan. According to his friend and associate `Abbas Sihhat (1874-1918), himself a writer of some significance, "Saber created a revolution in Azerbaijani literature. The gap he created between old and modern poetry was comparable to a time gap of an era or a century. After that, hardly anyone dared return to the old style."[14] Apart from his originality of theme and subject, Saber's poetic language was conversational, witty and lively, and in this respect differed greatly from the formal and poetic language of his predecessors. In a vein similar to what Sihhat has evaluated as Saber's achievement, the Iranian scholar `Ali Akbar Dehkhoda in his monumental *Loghat-nameh* writes: "Saber was a great innovator in Azerbaijani literature. . . . He was a child of one night who traveled the way of one hundred years, and surpassed the thoughts and the writers of his age by centuries. He was incomparable in depicting political and social problems."[15]

Saber's departure from traditional forms is further evidenced by the charge of a contemporary critic that Saber did not write panegyric *qasidas* like his predecessors. Saber defended himself in the following poem:

> Poetry is a priceless and unique pearl.
> I will not debase it with lies.
> I write satires, my words are truthful and
>   humorous.
> To the witty I will give this sparkling sherbet of
>   mine.[16]

Believing strongly in the mission of the poet to serve his people, Saber elaborates his intention in another poem:

> I am a poet, and my duty is to write poetry,
> To write and express every good or evil that I
>   notice,
> To describe the sun as bright, the day as pale, and
>   the night as dark;
> Crooked as crooked, slanting as slanting, and
>   even as even.
> Then, o my friend, why do you frown so bitterly?
> There is no fault in the mirror, the fault is on
>   your face.[17]

The image of the mirror in which the reader sees his own face was used by Saber once before. The same image is used by Jalil Mamadqulizadeh in *Molla Nasreddin* he writes:

> O, my Moslem brothers, when you hear
> something laughable from me, and you open
> your mouth and close your eyes and laugh
> and laugh until you almost split your sides
> with laughter, and then wipe your eyes with
> the skirt of your robe, don't imagine that
> you are laughing at *Molla Nasreddin*. O, my
> Moslem brothers, if you want to know at
> whom you are laughing, take a mirror and
> look at your own blessed face![18]

Swift, in his *Battle of the Books* (1704), gives a famous definition of satire which is not unlike what was quoted above. He writes: "Satire is a sort of glass, where beholders do generally discover everybody's face but their own, which is the chief reason for that kind of reception it meets in the world, and that so very few people are offended with it."

---

14. *Hop Hop Nameh*, p. xii.

15. Dehkhoda, *Lughat-Nameh, op.cit.*, p. 101.

16. *Hop Hop Nameh*, p. 361.

17. Dehkhoda, *Lughat-Nameh, op.cit.*, p. 103.

18. *Molla Nasreddin*, No. 1, April 7, 1906.

There is a noticeable difference in the works of these three writers. Swift transmutes the harsh realities of life into a world of fantasy and make-believe, and consequently offends no one. In the works of Saber, as well as those of his colleague Mamadqulizadeh, a world of fantasy is occasionally noticeable, but the reader is struck most by the realistic and humorous depiction of pathetic or tragic aspects of society. Saber's humor is not frivolous, but deep, pungent and biting. As some literary critics have suggested, satire generally comes nearer to tragedy than to comedy. In the case of Saber's works, there is a deep sense of sadness that is not comical, but tragic. One of his pen names, that he sometimes used, epitomized this fact — "Aglian Gullen" (a weeper who laughs).

Molla Nasreddin's objectives coincided with those of Saber. As a liberal journal which bitterly attacked totalitarian rule in Turkey and Iran as well as people's superstitions. As the editor put it, the writers of the journal "opened up wounds," "showed the contradictions," and "drew back the curtains." He told the helpless people: "If you were real men, if you had a bit of courage, no one would dare deprive you of your own natural rights."[19]

Molla Nasreddin wished to awaken the backward and intimidated people of the Middle East and make them stand up for their rights; and it hoped to bring about social reform. Jalil Mamadqulizadeh wrote in his *Memoirs*: "The despotism which faced us like a mountain was the despotism of the king and the Sultan as well as the despotism of the clerics who made religion a means of their power politics."[20] It was a dark age when superstitions and bigotry, adherence to rites and rituals, and the most trivial matters, such as dressing, haircuts, the way of washing dishes and the like had taken the place of serious discussions. Saber fought against such beliefs, for he himself had suffered in a superstitious and fanatical society. According to an Oriental superstition, when someone sneezes any odd number of times, all undertakings decided on at that moment are doomed to fail. In his poem "Odd Sneeze,"[21] Saber singles out the "mighty odd sneeze" as the most important factor in the decision-making process and humorously describes its power. In another poem, the poet's wife complains to her sister about her good-for-nothing husband who is a crazy poet, wasting all his life on books. The illiterate wife is so ignorant of her husband's values that she thinks he writes all night to improve his handwriting in order eventually to become a calligrapher like the famous Mir 'Imad![22]

Frequently religious hypocrisy is the subject of Saber's poems. In "Qorban Bayrami" a wealthy Haji slaughters a sheep on the feast of Qorban. On various pretexts he distributes the meat among his own relatives and even keeps the head and skin for himself. Then he gives the most useless parts to the poor for the sake of God, saying: "May God accept this sacrifice!"[23] In the following poem Saber relates the beliefs of a fanatic Moslem who is more opposed to modern ways of life than concerned with religious morality. It is entitled "Questions and Answers":

"My friend, in what state is your glorious city today?"

"God be praised, it's the same as it was in Noah's day."

"Have you new schools for the young of your country to learn in?"

19. *Molla Nasreddin,* No. 30, August, 12, 1907.
20. Aryanpur, *Az Saba,* II, p. 42.
21. *Hop Hop Nameh*, p. 105. Cf. Azerbaijanian Poetry, ed. by Mirza Ibrahimov, Moscow, 1969, p. 226.
22. *Hop Hop Nameh*, pp. 181-184
23. *Hop Hop Nameh*, p. 267.

Go to hell! Go home! Playtime is up. Molla Amu is here, you're going to be married off. (no. 15, yr. 8, 7 May 1913)

"No, we've only Madrasehs, which stand since the year Adam was born in."

"Do the citizens in your land read newspapers every day?"

"Some literate madmen do, but I don't, I must say."

"Now tell me, my friend, are there libraries in your town?"

"Young people opened a few, but we turned them upside down."

"Are the hungry helped in your country by other men?"

"God sees their sufferings himself — Why should we help them then?"

"Do you take care of widows and women that are in need?"

"To the devil with them — can't they marry again, indeed?"

"Is the need for unity talked about in your land?"

"Yes, it is, but for eloquence's sake you must understand."

"Is the nation split into Shi'te and Sunnites still?"

"What do you mean? For such words, young man, you ought to be killed."[24]

Superstitious and ignorant women as well as chauvinistic men are the butts of Saber's satire. On the whole, however, he holds men responsible for the degraded state in which women find

_____

24. *Azerbaijanian Poetry*, p. 225. The translation is by Dorian Rottenberg. Cf. *Hop Hop Nameh*, p. 104

"Iran is for sale; everything has to go." (*Hop Hop Nameh* 1962, p. 193)

themselves. The characters he depicts are typical and true to life. In a poem entitled "Don't Let Him Come," a fifteen-year old girl is hoodwinked into marrying a seventy-year-old man, and on the wedding night she says:

O, Auntie, don't let him come!
The sight of him is hateful, don't let him come!
O, God, it's as if he is no human,
His face is not like any other man.
For love of God, he is no husband for a woman.

I was too shy to inquire when betrothed;
"He is young and nice," I was told.
This could be my husband! Heavens, what a
    thought!
O, Auntie, don't let him come!
His doings are hateful, don't let him come!

A chimney-like hat does he wear,
His eyebrows are bespeckled with white hair.
Though he seems as old as my father fair,
He is a swindler, don't let him come!
His doings are hateful, don't let him come![25]

---

25. *Hop Hop Nameh*, pp. 16-23.

Majlis attacked - Fazlollah Nuri (no. 35, yr. 2, 12 September 1907)

The men of Saber's poems proudly divorce their wives and get new ones. In the "March of the Old" [26] we find "an old man who lives like a ram." Having four wives, every year he marries and divorces three or four more. Outwardly he is very pious. He wears a beard, puts on an agate ring, and never forgets his prayers or fasting, yet he is a dirty old man who not only does not leave young women alone, but also makes passes at handsome boys. Occasionally women are satirized, too. In "Advice of an Old Witch," [27] young brides are instructed to make the best of their lives. As no faithful husband can possibly be found, a woman should spend her husband's earnings on her women friends and find happiness with them behind his back.

The satirical works of Saber embrace a wide variety of subjects, ranging from the defeat of the vainglorious Tsarist armies by Japan to scenes of social and domestic life at home. Political satire was an important part of his work. The butts of his political satire range from Emperor Wilhelm of Prussia to Mohammad 'Ali Shah of Iran and from Sultan 'Abdol Hamid of Turkey to very minor officials and ignorant Mullas.

Because Mamadqulizadeh and Saber had close ties with Iran, and more particularly, with Iranian Azerbaijan, the Iranian Constitutional Movement figured prominently in *Molla Nasreddin*. The censorship about Tsarist Russia's affairs made it difficult to publish anything on the subject, so Saber

---

26. *Hop Hop Nameh*, p. 216.
27. *Hop Hop Nameh*, pp. 33-35.

and his friends directed their satirical comments at the totalitarian governments of Turkey and Iran. For Saber "Islamiyat" and "Milliyet" are the same, and he does not favor the idea of regional nationalism, which was growing in the Middle East. For him the Turks are just part of the Islamic world; and instead of boasting of one's national glories, it is better to strive for a society of which one can be proud. In a poem entitled "Fakhrieh," he describes how all through history the Turks have wasted their energy and have not helped their brothers, which was growing in the Middle East. For him the Turks are just part of the Islamic world; and instead of boasting of one's national glories, it is better to strive for a society of which one can be proud. In a poem entitled "Fakhrieh," he describes how all through history the Turks have wasted their energy and have not helped their brothers:

> Though we are captives of the traditions of our
>   times,
> Though we are prey to the misfortunes of the
>   world,
> Yet do not think that we are hungry and starving,
> We are the same as we were in the past.
> We are Turanians, our habit is to stick to the old
>   customs.
> We are parasites on our own nation.
> We are men who like darkness since the early
>   age,
> Misfortune crops from every land, corner of
>   every rock,
> We plunder and blackmail our own brothers,
> This old habit cannot and will not leave us!
> We are parasites on our own nation. [28]

Saber believes in living harmoniously without such feuds as those which existed between the Shiites and Sunnites, or the Moslems and Armenians. His poem "To Moslem and Armenian Brothers"[29] shows his strong belief in humanism and his hatred of sectarianism. Freedom and

democracy for him are beyond all narrow considerations. He says:

> One who loves mankind, loves freedom,
> Yes, where there is freedom there is humanity.[30]

Mohammad 'Ali Shah and Sultan 'Abdul Hamid are Saber's favorite butts. They simply fail to understand why people favor democracy and oppose the divine right of kings. Saber exposes the boastful Mohammad 'Ali Shah by donning his voice:

> I am the glorious king, Iran is mine;
> Rey and Tabaristan, all are mine.
> If Iran prospers or lies in ruin, all is mine!
> What is Constitutional Law? The decree is mine!
>
> So now, my countrymen, don your coat full of
>   lice!
> Robes of honor, throne of gold, are mine!
>   Glory, splendor, dignity — all are mine.[31]

Mohammad 'Ali Shah, who never approved of his father's liberalism, was indeed one of the most corrupt and ruthless kings of the Qajar dynasty. In another poem Saber depicts him as having put everything up for auction including the royal treasures and the whole of Iran. Here are two stanzas of the poem in Dorian Rotenberg's translation:

> People won't be silent, uncle, when they hear the
>   tale;
> Bah! It doesn't matter, does it, what sneers it may
>   entail.
> Write it down on paper on a wall to nail:
> I've opened here in Rey a new tremendous sale!
>   Dirt cheap, the wares my shop displays for sale;
>   Come buy! The whole of Rey today's for sale!
> And what is more, I do not sell that article alone,

28. *Hop Hop Nameh*, p. 76

29. *Azerbaijanian Poetry*, p. 224; *Hop Hop Nameh*, pp. 331-32.

30. *Hop Hop Nameh*, p. xiii.

31. *Hop Hop Nameh*, p. 140.

But with the Jam-e Jam, Rey's subjects, Kubbad's
    throne,
Although I'm somewhat hindered, I must own,
By certain Young Iranians well-known.
But never mind them — wholesale and retail,
Come, buy, the whole of Rey today's for sale!
What shall I do with all that bric-a-brac?
So many cares it brings, it sure will break my
    back.
That "Salty Water" — not much use, alack!
I'll better sell it all before the sky looks black!
The palace of Shiraz, the heritage of Rey today's
    for sale![32]

In a poem entitled "Don't sleep for God's sake"[33]
Saber asks the Ottomans not to sleep and be duped
by clerics such as Mir Hashem Devechi and Sheikh
Fazlollah. The latter is the reactionary Mulla who
supported the king and eventually was hanged by
the Constitutionalists. Saber's anti-clerical sentiments are epitomized in another poem entitled
"What Do I Care?" in which a reactionary Mulla
expresses his views on various issues:

However the nation is plundered, what do I care?
Should she be begging from the enemy, what do
    I care?
Let me be full; I have no concern for others.
If my country, if the whole world, goes hungry,
    what do I care?

Don't make any noise, lest the sleepers wake up;
I wouldn't want the sleepers to wake up.
God help me, if even one or two are up;
Being safe, I don't care if the whole world is torn
    up.
However the nation is plundered, what do I care?
Should she be begging from the enemy, what do
    I care?

Don't remind me of the world's past;
Don't talk of the glory of the past!

For the present, bring bread and stuffed eggplant
Why foresee the future? Life hurries by!
However the nation is plundered, what do I care?
Should she be begging from the enemy, what do
    I care?

Let our countrymen keep on wandering around,
Let them sink in the whirlpool of ignorance;
Let the widow burn in poverty's fire —
Only let me know prosperity and glory!
However the nation is plundered, what do I care?
Should she be begging from the enemy, what do
    I care?

On the world's stage, every nation makes
    progress;
At every stage, every station, each one makes
    progress.
In my bed, under the blankets, if I think of
    progress,
Then perhaps in the realm of dream, I will make
    progress.
However the nation is plundered, what do I care?
Should she be begging from the enemy, what do
    I care?[34]

From the point of view of satirical technique,
Saber uses almost all the forms and techniques
employed by satirists before him. He uses a wide
range of forms and meters in his works from
qasideh to *ghazal* and from *mathnavi* to *ruba`i*.
Saber sometimes parodies a well-known poem,
or, to be more precise, he takes the first *beyt* and
writes a *nazireh* on the poem. He beautifully translated some passages of Ferdowsi's *Shah-Nameh* into
Azeri verse. In one poem, imitating the style of the
Shah-Nameh in a mock-heroic form, Saber makes
a general of Mohammad `Ali Shah, who has been
sent to fight Sattar Khan and the Constitutionalists
in Tabriz, boast of his valor. The poem turns hilar-
ious when he is defeated by Sattar Khan, and the
general tries to defend himself to the king in a letter

---

32. *Azerbaijanian Poetry*, pp. 230. Cf. *Hop Hop Nameh*,
pp. 190-191. The references to the "Young Iranians"
and "Salty Water" are to a political group opposing the
Shah and the Caspian Sea respectively.

33. *Hop Hop Nameh*, pp.138-139.

34. *Hop Hop Nameh*, pp. 1-2.

that he writes.[35] The poems adapted or imitated by Saber include those of Hafez, Sa`di, Fuzuli, Namiq Kemal, Reja'izadeh Mahmud Ekram, Hadi Bey, and `Abdollah Jevdat.

To summarize the achievements of Saber in the development of Azeri literature and in general as a poet and satirist, one should emphasize the originality of his themes, his versatility in using various poetic forms and in adopting colloquial language. By publishing in newspapers he was able to reach a much larger audience than was available to earlier poets. He also was able to exercise a remarkable influence on contemporary Azeri poetry as well as on some Iranian satirists. His influence also extended to later poets like Mirza `Ali Mo`jaz (1873-1934) and `Ali Fitrat (1890—1946).[36] As for his art as a poet and satirist, a statement by Alessio Bombaci wonderfully describes the talents of Saber: "In Saber, the anger of Juvenal, the bitter remarks of Béranger, and the infinite humanity of Nekrassov are gathered in one."[37]

---

35. *Hop Hop Nameh*, pp.167-170.

36. Nazim Akhundov, Azarbaijan Tanz Ruznamelari, Tehran, 1979, pp. 326-352.

37. Quoted in Ahmet Ceferoglu. *Azerbaicaninc mizah şairi Ali Akber Saber, Dögumunun 100 yili münasibetilye,* Turk Kulturu, Ankara, no. 3, p. 15.

TWO OF THE LAST LETTERS FROM SABER TO HIS FRIEND ABBAS SEHHAT

My Brother Sehhat

After coming for treatment to Tiflis I wrote letters to you that my condition is not very good. I am very thankful to the esteemed Mirza Jalil and Hamideh Khanum. You don't know how kind they have been to me. For some time now they have paid all my expenses and they put up with my troubles. They did not want to put me in a hotel or hospital. They took me took to their own house. I don't know how to thank them. May God almighty reward them.

Know this much; they have taken more care of me than my own family. They sent for physicians and arranged for consultations. Some of them recommended an operation. They did so because it was necessary to find out what was exactly wrong with my liver. They said: "if you consent to the operation we will do it and, if need be, we will cut off part of your liver. If it is not necessary we sew you up and treat you."

I said: "Forgive me, dear doctors, my belly is not a wallet (*port-manat*), it is not a purse that whenever you want, you open and close it. Perhaps the operation is not successful!"

What I said greatly amused the physicians and they laughed. My friends, because the physicians did not give a guarantee, they did not advise me to undergo the operation. For the time being, I am taking medicines. Doctor Qasparians is treating me.

Let us see what the Lord does. He does well in whatever he does.

I am yours truly
15 June 1912
Your friend Saber

My Brother Sehhat

I received your letter. To a certain extent my anxiety concerning my children and family was dispelled. But when I wrote you my previous letter, my health was a thousand times better. I was the cause of my own misfortune. In truth, I was so embarrassed by the incredible kindness of the esteemed Mirza Jalil and Hamideh Khanum that I wanted quickly to regain my health, but my illness became worse. There is a physician here called Qandamirov; he is the private physician of the Iranian consulate. He studied in Europe and Russia and he talks beautifully in Ottoman Turkish. I went to see him and he asked who is treating you? I said Dr. Qasparians. He said: "Qasparians is a good doctor, but he has become somewhat old." Indeed, I liked very much the way in which he said this. Because of my excessive love for the Turks I thought that the way in which this man expressed himself was my treatment!

I asked for medicines from him and he prescribed pills and syrup and said: "Every night when you are going to bed take two of these pills and from the syrup every two hours one table spoon. Before long you will be completely healed. You will put on weight and return to your home and you will praise me in the newspapers." I did not discuss this with Mirza Jalil and I got the medicines that this man had prescribed. Because I knew, if I told him, he would not agree. The physician had told me to take two pills. I only took one at night and I became so sick with diarrhea that I could not bear it any longer and I was ashamed to tell Mirza Jalil about my situation. I went to Dr. Qasparians, but I have abandoned any hope of staying alive. These are my last moments and I am writing this letter to let you know. If I get a little bit better I'll return to Shamakhi. Give my regards to Mahmud Bey. I want to write a separate letter to Mehdi Bey Hajinski, but I cannot hold the pen anymore. I entrust my family to you and you to God. I am not unhappy, because I know that you are going to publish my work. That is it, greetings.

27 June 1912, A. Saber

Kulliyat-i Hop Hop Nameh,
Tabriz, Hilal Naseri, 1941, pp. 224-5

APPENDIX 4

LETTERS FROM SCHMERLING TO JALIL MAMADQULIZADEH

Translated by Suel Hoseynzadeh

Dear old friend Jalil,

I received your letter on time, yet since I haven't had much time lately, and partially also due to my illness, I was not able to reply to your kind letter. Thank you for all the good things you brought up in your letter. Reading it, I vividly remember the good times when you and I worked together on our little cultural undertaking, being almost fanatically convinced that we were doing good for the Moslem people, and thus we were contributing to the enlightenment of the Moslem masses.

A lot has changed since then, and perhaps changed in a way you and I would have never thought of, yet the desire to work for the benefit of people of the East stayed with me: I work exclusively in non-Russian publications mostly for Georgians and to some extent for Moslems. You asked me to work for *Molla Nasreddin* and not a day goes by without me realizing that I must work for you, since the day I received your letter. Now I ask you – if you have not yet abandoned your proposal – to recruit me as one of your most devoted staff members. We can work out the mailing arrangements, so that the illustrations will make it on time. And so, if you like the idea, send in the topics, and I'll start drawing some sketches for you. If I end up coming up with any topics of my own, of course I'll send you something of mine, but for that I really need to understand the spirit of the magazine and its interests. Send at least a few issues of the magazine so I could carefully go through

them. Also do let me know what will be the weekly deadlines I'll have to meet for the timely delivery of all the illustrations; that is, on what day of the week does the magazine get published and by when does the material arrive at the lithograph press etc. That's all I need to know.

About a month ago, I briefly met with comrade Eminbeyli in Tiflis (it seems he is an editor of either a peasants' or workers' paper), who also offered me to work for him. He offered even more than that – to move to Baku altogether since I happen to have tons of work offers. Of course, moving to Baku for me is not as easy, especially since I'm not quite sure that I would be able to find a sufficient amount of work, yet, that being said, I do not refuse to work. I still have not written personally about my decision to him as well. If you know him and will happen to see him, tell him that I can work for him, but we will need to work out all the technicalities involved in advance. I will probably write him a letter as well, one of these days. It would be even better if you could tell me the address of his newspaper, and then I won't have to make any guesses.

I have been working a lot, even too much, but I've been thinking to abandon some of the publications that have been treating me in bad faith, so that I could clear up some of my time for you.

It has been already three times since Yeritsian[1] attempted publishing his "Khatabala" and every other time with the same lack of success. The magazine never worked out, and even the volumes, that were issued, were dull, not witty enough. A private and on top of that, humorless publication cannot expect success!

---

1. Ashvatzatur Yeritsian was editor of the Armenian comic weekly *Khatabala*, to which Rotter and Schmerling contributed cartoons.

How are you doing, dear Jalil? Life is not easy for you as well, judging by your letter. What can we do, we have to live, if not for ourselves, then at least for the family; and therefore, we just have to come to terms with the circumstances we have found ourselves in. After all, you never know when there will be something cheerful passing through your life as well; as I was reading about the success of your latest play, I was very happy for you – and that's a cheerful moment in your life.

How is your entire family? How big is it? How is dearest Hamideh Khanum doing? Do pass on my cordial greetings to her.

Farewell. I shake your hand firmly and wish you all the best.

Yours, still the same
Schmerling
Tribunalnaja Street 4, Apt. 4.
7-V-1925 [May 7th, 1925]

Source: Azerbaijani Institute of Manuscripts, call number: A-6, Q-232, S.V. 234

***

2.

Dear Jalil

I received the money order on Saturday, while the letter itself got here only on Monday, and I have no idea why the letter was so late. And now, I can't get to work on it, as we have the Congress of Trade Unions in session, and I have to hang around there all day long sketching portraits and scenes from the proceedings – so I'm sending in the illustrations with some delay – that being said, I am also still not sure whether I have managed to depict your topics properly.

Getting back together with the good old *"Molla Nasreddin"* makes me very pleased and I would not want to stop doing it.

It looks like you are going to Tiflis in early June, while at the same time I am planning to travel from Tiflis to Baku at first, and then further on to the Transcaspian Province. I have a job offer from Ashgabat to work with the newspaper "Turkmenistan" and a satirical magazine. I sent in my conditions almost three weeks ago, but I have not received any reply. I am thinking of taking a gamble and going there without any assurances. I am sick of Tiflis, I will seek my fortune elsewhere. I cannot afford dreaming about settling in Baku, since the apartment situation there is complicated enough, beyond the existing challenge of having to earn enough salary to provide for two households at the same time (I am leaving without my family). If I won't manage settling in Ashgabat, I will continue to Samarkand. I will be of course visiting you while traveling through Baku – then we will have the opportunity to talk much together.

In any case, I implore you to catch Eminbeyli sometime before you leave and ask him if he still needs an artist, and what salary I could possibly obtain if I ended up working for him.

Most cordial greetings to all of you.

I shake your hand firmly.

Yours,
Schmerling
25-V-1925 [May 25th, 1925]

Source: Azerbaijani Institute of Manuscripts, call number: A-6, Q-231, S.V. 235

***

3.

This letter was stuck at home for a long time (for some reason, I was sure that I had sent it already), yet I believe it is possible and desirable to send it even now.

Dear Mirza Jalil,

Today the chief editor of our "Yeni Fikir" passed on your greetings ... I remembered the good times we had together in the past, of course within the framework of our joint work on *Molla Nasreddin*. A long time has passed since, but our love for satire and humor remained unabated, although everything around us has been totally changed: you are continuing to publish the very dear to my heart *Molla Nasreddin* in Baku while I still am working in Tiflis in the same field; I work a lot, even too much, as an employee of four publications, while always remaining thankful that my fate does not leave me jobless. After all, I am already 63 years old, it would seem that I should slow down, and I dread to think of a time when I won't be able to work; I haven't saved up anything, not a penny and I can hardly count on any pension – all I've been left with is a bleak old age, but enough of that – as long I have some energy left I will continue to work.

I have often thought of you, dear Mirza Jalil, and always remembered with pleasure our time working together. And now, yet again I am working for the Moslem newspaper "Yeni Fikir." Just not quite sure for how long they will go on: we've already closed a few times since we started.

I live in the same apartment (Tribunalnaja Street 4/apt. 4, former Sudebnaja Street) but in a single room, while the other one is used as a foyer. We live in very crowded conditions since we are four people. My daughter is also a painter and I can proudly say, a very gifted one; she is now in St. Petersburg and Moscow getting acquainted with the art museums. She works as an assistant in some of their activities. My son didn't finish his studies and doesn't want to go back to school now – the times have corrupted him so much. He is now practicing photography, and whenever he will finish studying it, I am thinking of landing him a job at the editorial office of "Mush" as a photographer-correspondent. My wife meanwhile is fully occupied with the household and works all day long.

Bykhov is unemployed and cannot find anything to make a living on, he is doing horribly. Grinevskij is still here and we rarely meet nowadays, but I know, he is not doing so bad, since his wife is running a ballet school, which is going very well.

How are you? How is your dear wife doing? Give her my sincere greetings.

How are things going for *Molla Nasreddin*, which artists are working for you? I really am interested in all this, so don't be lazy and whenever you happen to have some free time – do drop me a line or two – I will be very grateful.

I shake your hand firmly, and I wish you all the best.

Yours,
O. Schmerling
15/X-1925 [October 15th, 1925]

Source: Azerbaijani Institute of Manuscripts, call number: A-6, Q-81, S.V. 233

***

4.

Dear Jalil,

I received your friendly and kind letter – and I am sending my sincere thanks for it your way. Your letter cheered me up. I have been feeling down for the last few months and so I decided to go away for some time and leave Tiflis – I'll tell you the reasons that triggered my decision, once I'll arrive in Baku. There is a big difference between settling in Ashgabat and Baku – Baku is alive, it has much Europeanness to it and most importantly, I really like Baku. And so, if Baku would welcome me, my journey to the middle of nowhere will be terminated and I will settle in Baku.

However, I am very worried about only one significant issue – and that is the housing matter. After all, it is very possible to be left on the street there! … whereas I need a bright room where it would be easy to work. I would not mind to pay for the room, "not in a Soviet way," but of course within the limits of my possibilities, given my income.

I will depart as soon as I settle my financial matters: I have to receive 1,000 rubles, which one of the editorial offices happens to owe me, and getting them under the present circumstances is not very easy – it will take some time, but I continue to be very energetic in pushing them and I hope I will be one of the first people to get paid … and as soon as it happens, I won't stay here a day longer.

Now, please be so kind and take a pen in your hand, get a postcard and send me some more details on the housing issue.

My cordial greetings to your wife.

All the best.

Yours,
Schmerling
June 1, 1927
Tiflis

Source: Azerbaijani Institute of Manuscripts
Call Number: A-6, Q-230, S.V. 236

SELECT BIBLIOGRAPHY

Nazim Akhundov, *Azərbaycan Satira Jurnalalri, 1906-1920*, Baku, 1968; repub. in Ar. script as *Ţanz ruzname-leri*, Tehran, 1979.

Ziyakhan Aliyev, "Azim Azimzade: Baku's Art School Named After Self-taught Artist," *Azerbaijan International*, Summer 1999, pp. 28-29.

Yahya Aryanpur, *Az Şaba ta Nima*, 3 vols., Tehran, 1972-95, II, pp. 40-60.

Azərbaycan Respublikasi Elmler Akademiasi, Azərbaycan Dövlət Nəşriyyati, Mulla *Nasreddin(1906-1931)*, 2 vols., Baku, 1996-2002.

Alexander Bennigsen and Chantal Lemercier-Quelquejay, *La Presse et l'mouvement national chez musulmans de russie avant 1920*, Paris 1964.

Alessio Bombaci, *La litteratura turca*; tr. Irène Melikoff as *Histoire de la Litterature Turque*, Paris, 1996.

Edward G. Browne, *The Press and Poetry of Modern Persia*, Cambridge, 1914.

Isa Habibbeyli, *Mulla Nasreddinchi kariktura ustasi*, Nakhchivan, 2002.

Turan Hajizadeh, *Jalil Memedqulizadehnin jenub seferi ve Mulla Nasreddin zhurnalinin Tabrizde neshri*, Baku, 1991.

Hasan Javadi, *Satire in Persian Literature*, Ratherford, 1985.

Idem, "I Am A Poet, The Mirror of My Age," in Sabri M. Akurai, ed., *Turkic Culture, Continuity and Change*, Bloomington, 1987.

Rahim Malilzāda, *Zaban-e borra-ye enqelab: Hop Hop*, Tabriz, 1978.

M. Azim Azimzade Nejefov, *Azerbaijan Azərbaycan Dövlət Nəşriyyat*, Baku, 1972.

Ataxan Pashayev, Mulla *Nasreddin: Döstlari, Düşmənləri*, Baku, 1982.

Nasim Qiyasbeyli, "Molla Nasreddin, The Magazine: The Laughter that Pricked the Conscience of A Nation," *Azerbaijan International*, Autumn 1996, pp. 22-23.

Hamideh Mamadqulizadeh, *Mirza Jalil haqdinexatirelərim*, Baku, 1967.

Jalil Memedqulizadeh, *Seçilmiş əsərləri*, ed. Abbas Zamanov and Hamid Memedqulizadeh, Baku, 1967.

Idem, *Mirza Jalil haqdine xatirelərim*, Baku, 1981.

Samad Sardari-niya, *Mulla Nasreddin dar Tabriz*, Tabriz, n.d.

`Ali-Akbar Taherzadeh Saber, *Hop Hop-nameh*, ed. Abbas Zamanov, Baku, 1962.; tr. Ahmad Shafa'i into Pers. verse, as *Hop hop-nameh*, Tehran, 1978.

Abbas Zamonov, *Saber i sovremenniki*, tr. Asad Behrangi as *Saber wa mo'aserin-e u*, Tabriz, 1979.

Idem, *Mulla Nasreddinchi şá'erlər*, Baku, 1986 (a collection of the poems by sixteen poets who contributed to *Mulla Nasreddin*).

Pahayev, Atakhan, "Molla Nasreddin": Dostlari, Dushmanlari, Bku, Genjlik, 1982.

Man and wife (no.15, yr. 1, 14 July 1906)

Printed in the USA
CPSIA information can be obtained
at www.ICGtesting.com
LVHW082325220923
759028LV00026B/32

9 781933 823874